ECONOMICS OF PUBLIC POLICY

FIFTH EDITION

Edwin G. Dolan

George Mason University

John C. Goodman

President
National Center for Policy Analysis

West Publishing Company

Minneapolis/St. Paul   New York   Los Angeles   San Francisco

Cover image and design: Jim Somers/Sonora Marketing & Graphics
Illustration and layout: Sonora Marketing & Graphis
Copyediting: Julie Cleveland
Cover clip art provided by the following companies: Corel Corporation, Totem Graphics,
  One Mile Up, Inc.

WEST'S COMMITMENT TO THE ENVIRONMENT

In 1906, West Publishing Company began recycling materials left over from the production of books. This began a tradition of efficient and responsible use of resources. Today, up to 95% of our legal books and 70% of our college texts and school texts are printed on recycled, acid-free stock. West also recycles nearly 22 million pounds of scrap paper annually—the equivalent of 181,717 trees. Since the 1960s, West has devised ways to capture and recycle waste inks, solvents, oils, and vapors created in the printing process. We also recycle plastics of all kinds, wood, glass, corrugated cardboard, and batteries, and have eliminated the use of Styrofoam book packaging. We at West are proud of the longevity and the scope of our commitment to the environment.

Production, Prepress, Printing and Binding by West Publishing Company.

 TEXT IS PRINTED ON 10% POST CONSUMER RECYCLED PAPER    PRINTED WITH SOY INK™

Contents

Preface

The traditional learning triad for the principles of economics course is textbook, professor, and student. The textbook is filled with abstract principles. The student struggles to learn them. The professor stands in the middle, shoveling abstractions out of the text into the students' heads the way a stoker shovels coal into a boiler. Unfortunately, the coal is so hard that sometimes the fire goes out for lack of air.

Real world applications must be added to the mix in order to ensure combustion. Textbooks, and professors, if they do their job conscientiously, do their best to bring in applications. But there are limits to what they can do in this area. In textbooks and lectures, real world applications are necessarily brief. Scarce pages and class time must be parsimoniously allocated between theory and applications, with theory often winning.

That's where this book comes in. It adds the needed fourth element in the form of a set of in-depth applications of basic theory. Each application puts to work the abstractions that are covered in every textbook and every professor's lectures. What is more, it does so in depth. It goes beyond the usual one-page application of a graph or concept to explore several dimensions of each issue: Why do policies so often have unintended consequences? How does economics interact with politics in determining the policies we get? And how can policies be evaluated in terms of the normative standards of efficiency, equality, and liberty?

This new edition of *The Economics of Public Policy* is published at a time of change in economic policy. The preceding edition came out at the end of a period where an equilibrium of sorts had been reached between the reforming zeal of the "Reagan

Revolution" of the early 1980s and the contrasting political objectives of a Congress controlled for decades by Democrats. Since that time, the political equation has changed, twice. First there was a brief experiment in one-party government, with the White House and Congress both controlled by Democrats. This period saw several ambitious legislative initiatives, some successful (like the thrust toward free trade in the NAFTA and GAAT treaties), some failures (like the Clinton administration health care reforms). Then, starting in 1995, the configuration that dominated the 1980s was reversed, with a Democratic president facing a Republican House and Senate. That brought on a new spate of legislative initiatives, including new calls for deregulation, a reexamination of immigration policy, and new thinking about the environment.

Any Ph.D. economist can read the newspaper and see the theoretical and empirical issues that underly the policy disputes going on in Washington and in state capitals. Beginning students need to have the relationship between economic theory and the headlines spelled out more carefully. This book does just that.

The Economics of Public Policy is written so that it can be used beginning the first week of class. Chapter 1 sets out the framework of analysis in simple, nontechnical language. It can be read together with the introductory chapter in any textbook. Chapter 2, which uses the concepts of opportunity cost and the production-possibility frontier to explore the policy issue of global warming can also be assigned early in the semester.

The next group of four chapters are built around the concepts of supply and demand. Chapters 3 and 4, entirely new for this edition, apply them to the debate over health care policy—a debate that by no means ended with the defeat of the Clinton administration's specific legislative proposals of 1994. The next two chapters continue the supply-and-demand theme, adding the notion of elasticity. Both are expanded versions of topics covered in the fourth edition.

Chapters 7, 8, and 9 cover topics that are high on the agenda of the new Republican congress: regulation and privatization. Chapter 7 looks at safety regulation, featuring the views of Stephen Breyer, an expert in this area who is the most recent appointee to the Supreme Court. Chapter 8 covers privatization and is expanded to include a section on privatization of education. Chapter 9 discusses the market for air travel, a case that deregulationists like to portray as a success story.

The next two chapters cover issues that are not new, but that are not likely to go away, either. One is that of equal pay for comparable worth. This was once billed as "the women's issue of the 1980s" but that decade left it far from resolved. The other is Social Security which not only must play a central role in the battle over balancing the federal budget, but also increasingly pits a younger against an older generation.

The final two chapters of the book, both of which are new to this edition, cover topics with an international emphasis. Chapter 12 discusses the impact of immigration on the economy and looks at possible policy changes. Chapter 13 looks at an aspect of the Russian economy in its transition to the market economy—the breakdown of the rule of law—that has abundant implications for the American economy as well.

For your convenience, an Instructor's Manual to accompany this book is available from West Educational Publishing. Each chapter of the IM includes comments on how to use the chapter in your course, a list of key terms with definitions, a narrative chapter outline, answers to discussion questions, and multiple choice questions with answers. The manual also includes a summary table of key concepts and textbook linkages to help you plan your course.

We are grateful for all the help we have received in preparing this edition of *The Economics of Public Policy*. Input from students, colleagues, and users of previous editions has been incorporated at many points. We particularly want to thank the very able staff of West Educational Publishing for bringing this book out with a quality and timeliness that will maximize its usefulness to professors and students.

Edwin G. Dolan
John C. Goodman

Thinking About Public Issues and Policies

Every day we hear about public issues. Some of these issues are called crises: a health care crisis, a drug crisis, or an immigration crisis. Others are problems that could become crises. We hear about problems of the school system or of global climate change and wonder if things are getting worse. Other issues are simply constant irritations without ever becoming crises: unsafe products, confusing air fares.

All of these issues raise questions of public policy. Should the government play a bigger role in health care? Should more resources be devoted to fighting the drug menace? Should workers in the United States be protected from the competition of immigrants? Typically, the list of proposals for dealing with any given crisis is a long one, and people often turn to economists for help in deciding what course of action should be taken. But what kind of help can economists give?

Economists can, of course, offer their personal opinions as to the best course of action. "Nationalize health insurance," one might say. "Close the borders to immigrants," another might chime in. Offering opinions such as these is as much the right of an economist as of any other citizen. But offering opinions is not really economists' professional specialty. Their real specialty is providing a certain way of thinking about public issues and policies—a way of thinking that can help others form their own opinions about the proper course of action.

That is where this book comes in. We haven't written it just to give you our opinions. Instead, we have written it to help you understand the economist's way of thinking by showing that way of thinking in action, applied to some of today's major issues of public policy. In doing so, we will organize our discussion of each issue according to three aspects of the economist's way of thinking: tracing the effects of policies, evaluating policies, and explaining policies.

Tracing the economic effects of public policy

Learning what questions to ask is a large part of understanding the way economists think about issues and policies. Probably the most important question, and often the most difficult to answer, is, What are the effects of a certain policy? This question is difficult to answer because public policies usually have a network of direct and indirect effects, some intended, others unintended. One of the most characteristic aspects of the economic way of thinking about public policy is an insistence on tracing the unintended, often hidden, consequences of public policies. The task is a challenging one because people react to public policies on two levels: the level of maximizing and the level of entrepreneurship.

Maximizing At the first level, people react to changes in public policy through a process that economists call *maximizing*. Maximizing simply means doing the best you can to achieve your goals, given the constraints that circumstances place on you. Economists see consumers as attempting to achieve maximum satisfaction of their wants, given their limited budgets and the prices of the things they buy. They see business firms as attempting to maximize profits, given the constraints imposed by technology, consumer demand, and the prices of the productive inputs they use. Changes in public policy—taxes, regulations, subsidies—can also change the constraints that consumers and firms face, and, in the new circumstances, they may make different choices. Economics offers a set of tools to help us understand the ways in which changes in policies affect people's choices.

Consider a real-world example. In 1981, faced by a rising tide of automobile imports, the U.S. government reached an agreement with Japan under which shipments of Japanese cars to the United States would be limited to 1.68 million units per year. It was expected that this import quota would drive up the retail prices of Japanese cars. The higher prices would represent a change in the constraints faced by U.S. consumers: To buy a Japanese car, they would now have to forgo the purchase of a greater quantity of other goods. The intended consequence of the policy was that consumers would buy fewer Japanese and more American cars, thus creating more jobs for U.S. autoworkers.

The hope that the quotas would protect jobs in the U.S. auto industry seemed reasonable enough as far as it went. However, those who favored the quotas as a means of protecting jobs for U.S. workers failed to consider an important unintended consequence of the quotas. Before the quotas were imposed, the threat of Japanese competition was one of the important constraints limiting the price that U.S. firms could profitably charge for their cars. The quotas changed this constraint. As a result, U.S. automakers raised their prices by several hundred dollars per car. The price rise boosted their profits, but faced by higher prices of both American and Japanese cars, consumers cut back their purchases of new cars altogether. U.S. autoworkers gained far fewer jobs than they had hoped—none at all by some estimates. And this is not to mention the jobs lost by U.S. workers employed in transporting, selling, and servicing Japanese imports.

The conclusion: In tracing the consequences of a policy change, the first step is to consider how the policy will affect the circumstances that consumers and businesses face, and how they will change their decisions to maximize their satisfaction or profits under the new conditions.

Entrepreneurship But considering how people react to changes in constraints is just the first level of analysis. People do not always accept constraints passively, shrugging their shoulders and making marginal adjustments as new policies are put into effect. Instead, people are always looking for ways to break through constraints by inventing new techniques, developing new products, devising new methods of organization, and experimenting with new ways to achieve their goals. Economists refer to this aspect of economic life as *entrepreneurship*.

When most people hear the term entrepreneurship, they think of the founders of new firms—Henry Ford founding the Ford Motor Company, Mary Kay Ash starting Mary Kay Cosmetics, Steven Jobs making the first Apple computers in his garage. These are, of course, important examples of entrepreneurship. But people act as entrepreneurs in less spectacular ways all the time. A supermarket produce manager who comes up with a new way of displaying vegetables is an entrepreneur. So is a salesperson who figures out a new way to get customers to try her product. And, in an important sense, consumers are entrepreneurs too when they experiment with new products, new ways of shopping, and new ways of satisfying their wants.

The case of auto import quotas shows why entrepreneurship must be taken into account when tracing the effects of a change in policy. Since their first entry into the U.S. market, the Japanese auto firms had specialized in production of small, low-priced cars. Profit margins on those cars were modest, but many of them could be sold, so Toyota, Nissan, and the rest did well in this segment of the market. When the quotas were imposed, the Japanese firms faced a new constraint: 1.68 million cars per year, no more. The economics of profit maximization suggests that other things being equal, the Japanese would react by simply raising the prices of their small cars until the U.S. market would absorb just the allowed 1.68 million units.

That, at any rate, was how the backers of the quota policy expected the Japanese to react. The prices of Japanese small cars did indeed rise. But there was an important entrepreneurial element in the Japanese reaction as well. Rather than simply selling the same small cars at higher prices, the Japanese firms rapidly began introducing larger, more powerful, more luxurious models such as the Acura, Lexus, and Infiniti lines. The Japanese move into the upscale market segment left room at the low end of the market for other entrepreneurs in South Korea, Taiwan, and even Brazil to enter the U.S. market for the first time. In the end, then, the U.S. automakers were left facing a more complex competitive situation than that before the quotas were introduced.

The conclusion: In tracing the unintended consequences of a change in policy, one must consider both how firms and households will react to the changed constraints of new policy as maximizers, and also the efforts they will make as entrepreneurs to break through those constraints.

Evaluating economic policy

After we have examined the effects of a policy, we are in a position to ask a second important question: Is the policy good or bad? Should we institute the policy, or, if it is already in force, should we keep it? Should we instead reject the policy, or should we abolish it if now in force?

The evaluation of economic policy is often called **normative economics,** but this term is misleading in an important sense. What we call normative economics is not really a branch of economics at all; it would be more accurately described as the application of ethics or political philosophy to economic issues. The economist's special tools of the trade, so useful in tracing the effects of a policy, cannot tell us whether that policy is good or bad.

But this fact does not mean that we have to grapple with these questions bare-handed. To determine whether a policy is good or bad, we need not rely on whims, hunches, or reflexes. Instead, in this book we will examine each policy in the light of three established normative standards: efficiency, equality, and liberty. As we will see, not everyone agrees on the relative importance of these three standards. However, whatever priority one accords to them, the three standards at least give us a framework within which to think and express ourselves clearly. Let's look briefly at each of these standards in turn.

Efficiency Our first standard is one that occupies a prominent place in the thinking of many economists—economic efficiency. In the most general sense, the word **efficiency** means acting in a way that best achieves goals given the circumstances, or, what amounts to much the same thing, acting in a way that achieves given goals with a minimum of expense, waste, and effort. Whether you are repairing a car, baking a cake, or processing customers' deposits as a bank teller, there are usually a number of ways to perform the task. The efficient way is the one that minimizes time, effort, and money. The concept of efficiency also applies to the choice of how to spend your income. Efficiency in this case means buying those items that give you the most satisfaction or happiness for your limited budget.

The notion of efficiency can be brought to bear on any activity—college courses, a career, or leisure activities. In each case, the efficient choice is the one that results in the largest benefit, given the cost, or the one that results in the smallest cost, given the benefit that is sought.

Most of us have some idea of what efficiency means when applied to our personal lives. We may even have some idea of what it means for a business firm to be efficient. But economists go beyond this: They not only apply the concept of efficiency to individuals and to business firms—they also ask about the efficiency of economic policies. What we mean by an efficient policy is a set of rules, regulations, laws, and property rights that help people maximize the benefits that can be obtained from given resources or minimize the costs of obtaining given goals.

As an example of how the notion of efficiency can be applied in the area of public policy, consider the enforcement of contracts. The policy of maintaining a system of courts in which contracts can be enforced is one that lies at the heart of a market economy. If a person fails to keep a promise agreed to in a contract, courts of law stand ready to enforce the contract or to award damages to the injured party. Imagine what would happen if there were no contract law or no system of enforcement. You would spend an enormous amount of time and energy investigating the character and reputation of the people with whom you wanted to make agreements. Most sellers would insist on cash. There would be less lending, fewer long-term agreements, and many goods and services we now enjoy would not be produced at all. The situation is not entirely imaginary: In a later chapter, we will see that absence of a well-functioning system of contract enforcement greatly hampers development of the Russian economy today. By comparison, a reasonably effective system of contract enforcement makes the U.S. economy much more efficient than it would be otherwise.

Almost every public policy involves a cost. Whether we are paving a road, building a bridge, constructing a dam, or enforcing contracts, the benefits are not free. A policy or a change in policy is judged to be efficient if the benefits exceed the costs. It is judged to be inefficient if the costs exceed the benefits. But, applied in this way, the standard of efficiency does not require that the people who benefit bear the costs. Typically, some individuals will be better off because of a policy; others will be worse off. Efficiency requires only that we look at the sum of the benefits and the sum of the costs.

In comparing the costs and benefits of a policy to see if it is efficient, economists often find it useful to ask this question: Can the people who like a policy potentially compensate the people who do not like it and still be better off than they would have been without the policy? If compensation is possible, the benefits of the policy are said to be greater than the costs of the policy.

Consider, for example, a policy of prohibiting all smoking in restaurants. Let's say that Ed, a typical nonsmoker, would be willing to pay $10 more than the cost of his meal to enjoy his food in a smoke-free environment. John, a typical smoker, would be willing to pay up to $8 for the pleasure of enhancing the taste of fine food and drink with that of fine tobacco. Given these preferences, Ed could pay John $9 in return for a promise not to smoke during dinner, and both would be better off than if John smoked.

Suppose instead that the city where Ed and John live adopts a policy that no smoking is allowed in restaurants. This policy makes John worse off and Ed better off, unlike the private agreement that made both of them a little better off. But in the reasoning used by most economists, the antismoking ban is efficient because Ed's gain, as measured by the compensation he would have been willing to pay, is greater than John's loss, as measured by the compensation he would have been willing to accept, even though in the case of the smoking ban, no compensation is actually paid.

Equality Efficiency is an impersonal standard; it weighs the costs and benefits of a public policy without regard for whom they fall upon. Is Ed more worthy than John? Is John someone toward whom we ought to feel special compassion and for whom we ought to make special efforts to shape policy? The efficiency standard does not ask such questions, let alone answer them.

But, in the eyes of many economists, as well as noneconomists, such personal questions are important. Many people consider them to be particularly important when it comes to the issues of wealth, poverty, and economic inequality. They see policies that promote equality as good and those that promote inequality as bad, quite apart from the issue of whether the policy is efficient.

For example, federal, state, and local levels of government routinely tax the wealthy and spend part of the proceeds on programs intended to benefit the poor. Because administering the taxes and the benefit programs involves administrative costs, the dollar burden of the taxes exceeds the dollar value of the benefits received by those whom the program helps. Nonetheless, many people see such transfer programs as good because they promote equality.

To take another example, suppose that a benefit-cost analysis shows that building a freeway through a central city neighborhood will cut commuting costs for suburbanites by more than enough to cover the costs of land acquisition and construction. Many people might nonetheless object to a project that destroys neighborhoods where many poor people live so that rich lawyers and stockbrokers can whiz by in their BMWs.

Just as economists have developed ways of measuring costs and benefits, they have developed ways of measuring the degree of inequality. This allows them, in principle, to say whether a policy creates more equality, even if it affects millions of people in different ways. There are some sticky problems, however. Suppose one family has two children. Another has no children. To achieve equality, should the first family have twice the income of the second? Or suppose that one person works eighty hours a week while another only works forty. Does equality mean that both workers should receive the same monetary income? Or should the extra leisure time enjoyed by the second worker count as a form of noncash income?

When they think about creating more equality, most people are typically thinking about raising the incomes of those in poverty. And, true enough, most policies that help the poor tend to create more equality, and most policies that hurt the poor tend to create more inequality. But not always. Consider a policy that takes a little income from the poor, a lot of income from the rich, and transfers all of this income to middle-class citizens. Such a policy could actually increase overall equality while hurting those at the bottom of the income ladder—and we will see actual examples of such programs in later chapters.

Liberty Our third standard of liberty is like the standard of equality—a personal one. Those who follow this standard care about who benefits from and who bears the costs of a policy, not just how large the benefits and costs are. The importance of liberty comes from a long tradition in Western political thought. In particular, liberty, as understood in the United States, is shaped by the views of the English philosopher John Locke and the later contributions of Thomas Jefferson and other founding fathers. Simply put, the standard holds that there is a broad area within which each individual has a right to act in accordance with private choice, free from force, threat, or coercion by others. People who take this point of view are usually referred to as *classical liberals* or *libertarians.*

Most of us are familiar with such fundamental civil liberties as freedom of the press and freedom of religion. But economic liberties are included here too: the right to own property, the right to produce goods and services, and the right to engage in voluntary exchange with others. As applied to the evaluation of public policy, this standard says that any policy is bad if it violates a person's civil and economic liberties. For example, forcing a landowner to donate land for a public park, without compensation, would be considered a violation of the landowner's economic rights, even if the project might be efficient and might benefit the poor. Requiring a private company to keep open a money-losing plant to save the workers' jobs would violate the owners' right to put their resources to the most profitable use. A law that prohibited smoking not only in public but also in private places would violate a person's right to choose goods and services.

What about taxation and governmental ownership of public facilities such as schools and highways? Some advocates of liberty take the position that all taxes are violations of liberty and that all goods and services (even the police and courts) should be provided by private firms. Some interesting books advocating this point of view have been written, but the view of economic liberties used in this book is a more moderate and traditional one, according to which a certain limited range of actions by government need not unduly infringe on liberties.

The relationship of the standards The three standards of efficiency, equality, and liberty are not the only ones that could be used to evaluate public policy. We will not, for example, be concerned here with the standard of whether public policy accords with religious doctrine as revealed in the Bible, the Koran, or other works, despite the fact that such a standard is of great importance to many people. But although some standards are left out of consideration, the three we focus on will provide a wide scope for discussion.

We suspect that many of our readers will not fully agree with any one of the standards we have listed. That creates no problem when a policy is judged to be good by all three standards. Enforcement of contracts, for example, promotes economic efficiency, is consistent with liberty, and protects the rights of the poor against abuse by the rich and powerful. Many other policies are consistent with all three standards.

But many policies are not. That's where value trade-offs come in. For example, a progressive income tax, which imposes high rates on high-income families and low or zero rates for the poor, pursues the goal of equality at the expense of efficiency. There are other kinds of trade-offs as well. For example, laws requiring affirmative action in employment, according to their backers, are said to help equality by providing wider opportunities to members of minority groups. However, opponents say they violate employers' freedom to choose whom they want to employ.

The purpose of this book is not to tell you how these value trade-offs should be resolved. It is, instead, to help you think clearly about the issues and trade-offs. As you read the book, then, be honest with yourself. Don't just make knee-jerk decisions about what policies you like and then search for a way to rationalize them. Instead, decide first what fundamental values you accept, and then see what these imply about public policy. You may be surprised.

Explaining public policy

In addition to tracing the effects of public policies and evaluating those policies, this book will tackle a third job—trying to explain why we have certain policies rather than others.

On first consideration, it might seem that in discussing the goals that policies serve, we have already explained why we have these policies. Thus, it might be said that we have policies limiting mergers among large firms because promoting competition among many firms is thought to promote the goal of efficiency. Similarly, we might explain governmental programs that provide food and shelter for the poor in terms of the goal of equality. However, for a number of reasons, economists tend to think that it is not enough to explain economic policies simply by listing the goals that they serve (or are intended to serve).

First, to say that we have a certain policy because it serves a certain goal does not explain why we do not have a different policy that would serve the same goal. For example, why is it that we construct subsidized public housing for the poor rather than giving the poor cash grants that would allow them to rent housing at market rates? On the face of it, both would equally well serve the goal of equality.

Second, explanations couched in terms of goals are not adequate when goals conflict. They do not, for example, explain how the conflicting goals of efficiency and equality are reconciled in formulating tax policy.

Third, explanations couched in terms of such broad social goals as efficiency, equality, and liberty fail to explain why we have many policies that appear to conflict with all three of these goals. Consider the case of quotas on sugar imports into the United States, for example. These quotas have the effect of raising the price of sugar in the United States to a level more than double its world price. The quotas are inefficient in that they encourage production of sugar in the United States, where costs are relatively high and environmental conditions relatively unfavorable compared with costs and environmental conditions in neighboring Caribbean countries. They are inequitable, in that the greatest benefits go to wealthy farmers whose incomes are higher than those of the average consumers who bear the policy's costs. And the complex rules that govern sugar imports limit farmers' freedom to decide for themselves which crops to grow, and candy makers' freedom to decide from whom to buy sweeteners.

Public choice theory To explain policies in terms of the goals they serve confuses the issue of what policies we ought to have with the issue of what policies our political system actually gives rise to. Instead, the branch of economics known as *public choice theory* takes an approach that focuses not on the broad social goals of efficiency, equality, and liberty but rather on the political system as a set of institutions through which people act in pursuit of their own private goals, which may or may not be consistent with the broader standards.

Consider, for example, why relatively small special-interest groups often obtain favors from government at the expense of the great majority of consumers and taxpayers. The sugar import quotas just mentioned are a case in point. By raising sugar prices, they benefit the relatively small number of U.S. sugar growers at the expense of the much larger number of people who consume sugar. How is it that in a democratic country a minority is able to exploit a majority in this fashion?

Public choice theorists have an explanation—one that considers the costs and benefits of political action in a democracy. Political action of any kind—voting, writing to one's representative in Washington, hiring a lobbyist—is costly. If a policy strongly benefits or harms a person, it will be worthwhile to act despite the costs. If a policy has only a small effect on a person, it may not seem worthwhile to act; that person will save his or her political energies for another cause. The result is that a relatively small interest group, each of whose members is strongly affected by a policy, is likely to be much more vocal and politically active than a large interest group, each of whose members is only slightly affected. The case of sugar growers (each strongly affected by import quotas) versus candy eaters (each affected only to the extent of a few dollars) illustrates this principle. Thus, policy is shaped to serve the interest of the one group rather than the other.

Rent seeking Autoworkers' and manufacturers' lobbying for import quotas is just a single example of the widespread tendency of people to invest time and resources in attempts to influence the process of policy making. The efforts of business firms, households, labor unions, and others to influence economic policy in ways favorable to them are known to economists as *rent seeking*.

The term rent seeking is an odd one to noneconomists, who tend to think of rent as the sum one pays each month for one's apartment. To economists, however, the term *rent* has a much broader meaning: the difference between what one receives from the sale of a good or service, and what could have been earned by devoting the same time or resources to the next best use. The profits of a business firm are one example of a rent in this economic sense: The difference between what Wally Amos earns from his Famous Amos cookie business and what he could earn instead from, say, teaching school or investing in municipal bonds is a "rent." But business profits are not the only kind of rents. The difference between the $20 an hour that a union electrician earns and the $10 (say) that a nonunion job would pay is also a rent. The difference between the high pay that substitute football players briefly earned during the 1987 NFL strike and what they earned in their regular jobs as (say) high school coaches is still another example of a rent.

Given this concept of rent, rent seeking can be understood as the activity of seeking policy changes that increase one's rents. Rent seeking takes many forms. In this book, we will look at many examples of rent seeking that affect policies ranging from medical care to garbage collection to immigration.

So much for generalities. Having announced our intention to trace the economic effects of public policies, evaluate those policies, and explain where they come from, it is time to move on to specific cases. We will begin with an issue familiar to everyone who follows the daily news—the effects of human economic activity on the global climate.

Questions for thought and discussion

1. You are scheduled to fix dinner tonight for six people with whom you share a rented house, but because you had to study for an econ exam, you didn't have time to go shopping. You open the refrigerator and see that there are certain things there that could be eaten—three pork chops, five eggs, half a can of tuna, some onions, and so on. Various dry ingredients are on the shelf—salt, flour, spices, and so on. Describe how you could approach the problem of fixing dinner on the level of *maximization*. On the level of *entrepreneurship*.

2. Try to make a list of policies that you think pursue one normative standard at the expense of another—equality at the expense of efficiency, efficiency at the expense of liberty, liberty at the expense of equality, and so on. List as many different types of trade-off as you can. Compare your lists with those of other students. Do you agree on the type of trade-off involved in each policy? After you have finished this book, look back at your list again. Have you changed your opinion about any of the trade-offs?

3. At the time this book was being revised, professional baseball players were on strike. The main issue centered on a change in the contract mechanism according to which the total revenues received by baseball teams would be divided between players and owners. Can this be considered an example of rent seeking? If you are

familiar with the baseball situation, discuss various proposed solutions. Did any actions by either side in the strike attempt to get the government involved? Could those actions, too, be considered a form of rent seeking?

Selected references

Friedman, Milton. *Capitalism and Freedom*. Chicago: University of Chicago Press, 1962. *One of the best short statements of the classical liberal viewpoint ever written.*

Hazlitt, Henry. *Economics in One Lesson*. New York: Harper & Brothers, 1946. *The "lesson" of this classic (which has been reprinted many times) is that economists should pay attention to the hidden and unintended consequences of policy as well as to the overt, intended consequences.*

Johnson, David. *Public Choice*. Mountain View, Cal.: Mayfield Publishers, 1991. *A good general introduction to public choice theory.*

Rothbard, Murray. *For a New Liberty*. San Francisco: Fox & Wilkes, 1993. *Presents a radical version of the libertarian view that economic problems of all kinds are best solved without the aid of government. Other books by the same author, also representing this view, are* Man, Economy, and State, *and* Power and Market.

Key Terms

Maximizing. Doing the best one can to achieve one's goals, given the constraints imposed by circumstances.

Entrepreneurship. The process of looking for ways to break through constraints by inventing new techniques, developing new products, devising new methods of organization, and experimenting with new ways of achieving goals.

Normative Economics. Ethical or philosophical evaluation of an economic situation of policy as good or bad.

Efficiency. Acting in a way that best achieves goals given the circumstances of that achieves given goals with a minimum of expense, waste, and effort.

Classical liberal (libertarian). One who shares the views of such political thinkers as John Locke and Thomas Jefferson, to the effect that there is a broad area within which each individual has a right to act in accordance with private choice, free from force, threat, or coercion by others.

Public choice theory. A branch of economics that focuses on the political system as a set of institutions through which people act in pursuit of their own private goals.

Rent seeking. The efforts of business firms, households, labor unions, and others to influence economic policy in ways that favor their own economic interests.

Rent. The difference between what one receives from the sale of a good or service, what could have been earned by devoting the same time or resources to the next best use.

2

Global Climate Change: The Economics of Opportunity Cost

In the year 870, a Norwegian Viking named Ingolf Arnarson, fleeing a murder charge, moved with his family to Iceland, which up to then had been inhabited only by a few Irish monks. Other Vikings followed, and in the short span of 60 years, Iceland was fully settled: a thriving country of 30,000 inhabitants with its own democratic parliament, the *Althing*.

Iceland of the tenth century, like any frontier, was full of rough characters. One was Erik the Red, who, like Arnarson, had fled to Iceland from Norway because of a killing. Even Iceland could not hold Erik. He quarreled with his new neighbors and was banished. Rather than returning to Norway to take his chances with the king's justice, he sailed west with a flotilla of 25 ships and established a colony on the southwest coast of Greenland. By the eleventh century, the Greenland colony numbered some 3,000 people and had a parliament of its own. A cathedral from this period, more than 100 feet long, stands to this day.

Not long after Erik's first settlement, Bjarni Herjolfsson, a merchant bound for the new Greenland colony, was blown off course and sighted land still farther to the west. Later Leif Erikson, son of Erik the Red, bought Bjarni's ship and set out to investigate. He landed somewhere on the Atlantic coast of Canada, in a place he called Vinland because of the wild grapes he found there. Encouraged by Leif's report of a land where the pastures were frost-free all winter long, his brother-in-law, Thorfinn Karlsefni, attempted to found a colony there. Thorfinn's expedition wintered over, and at least one Viking child was born in the colony.

Supply lines were long, however, and the natives were hostile. The surviving members of the expedition returned to Greenland.

Thorfinn Karlsefni's failed attempt to colonize North America came at the height of the Viking age. The Greenland colony began to decline by the end of the next century, and the last Europeans left or died out by the fifteenth century. The Icelanders hung on, but they lost their independence and their homegrown democracy.

Where exactly was the Vinland colony? Why did the Viking expansion lose its earlier vigor? Although many details remain unclear, scientists agree on one contributing factor: The Iceland, Greenland, and Vinland colonies were established during a period of pronounced global warming. As shown in Figure 2-1, by the fourteenth century the climate turned sharply colder, and the world was gripped by the Little Ice Age. This cold period lasted until the seventeenth century. Since that time, global temperatures have steadily risen again and are today about the same as in the days of Erik the Red.

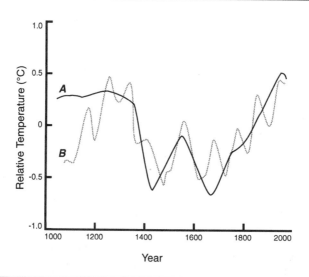

Figure 2-1 Surface Temperatures During the Past 1,000 Years

But although the global warming of the tenth century brought freedom and prosperity to the Vikings, today's rising temperature trend sparks warnings of disaster. Although further warming might bring a wine industry to Iceland, it might also flood millions of farmers from their homes in low-lying Bangladesh. What is more, although humans of a thousand years ago could neither blame themselves for the world's climate nor hope to change it, today, human activity is believed by many scientists to be a key factor in climate change. That makes today's global warming an issue for economic policy as well as for climatology.

What is known and not known about global climate change

Scientists do not know all that they would like to know about the world's climate. They do not know, for example, just what caused the Little Ice Age, or the even greater climate swings of prehistoric times. However, they do understand the basic mechanism that keeps the world warm.

That mechanism is the greenhouse effect. Certain gasses in the atmosphere, including carbon dioxide, methane, nitrous oxide, and chlorofluorocarbons (CFCs), are relatively transparent to sunlight on its way to the earth's surface but limit the amount of heat that is radiated back into space, in much the way a layer of glass does for a greenhouse. Without the greenhouse effect, the earth's surface would average a chilly 0° F.

A second fact not subject to dispute is that the concentrations of greenhouse gasses have risen measurably as the result of human activity. Since the beginning of the Industrial Revolution, the level of carbon dioxide in the atmosphere has increased by about 50 percent, chiefly as the result of burning coal and other fossil fuels. The amount of methane in the atmosphere has more than doubled over the period, with livestock production, rice paddies, and other agricultural practices as the chief sources. CFCs, used in air-conditioning and other industrial applications, are a relatively recent arrival. They increased rapidly in decades following World War II, but their use is now being phased out.[1]

Linking these two undisputed facts—the existence of the greenhouse effect and increasing concentrations of greenhouse gasses—creates a *prima facie* case that human activity is causing global climate change. At this point, however, the scientific evidence gets a bit muddier.

One problem is that observed temperature changes over the past 100 years do not track changes in greenhouse gasses very closely. Most of the half-degree increase in global temperature over this period occurred in the period 1900-1940. Over the next 30 years, global temperatures declined somewhat, before resuming their upward trend in the 1970s and 1980s. However, the rate of emission of greenhouse gasses increased steadily over the entire 100-year period.[2] Clearly, many factors in addition to greenhouse gasses influence the earth's climate.

---

[1] CFCs are being phased out not because of their role in the greenhouse effect, but because they are implicated in a different environmental problem: depletion of the atmospheric ozone layer. Depletion of the ozone layer poses a potential threat of increase in harmful ultraviolet radiation reaching the earth's surface. A partial mitigation of the threat of global warming can thus be regaded as a beneficial secondary effect of attempts to deal with ozone depletion.

A second problem is that local climates are not affected uniformly when the mean global temperature changes. If every morning and every night at every point on earth the temperature were a degree warmer or colder than normal, almost no one would notice. But climate does not work that way. Slight changes in mean temperatures can affect the patterns of ocean currents and atmospheric circulation in ways that produce much more dramatic seasonal and local changes. Look again at Figure 2-1. There we see that the Little Ice Age was associated with less than a one-degree change in the mean global temperature. Yet, from historical sources, we know that its effects on Northern Europe were dramatic and substantial.

Unfortunately, even the most elaborate models of climate change currently in use are not very good at predicting these details. For example, will warmer air over the poles melt polar ice thus causing ocean levels to rise? Or will warmer, and hence more humid, air in these regions increase snowfall, so that ice accumulates and the oceans drop? Some studies predict one effect, some the other. Similarly, we don't know if global warming will dry out the American corn belt or allow corn to be grown in Siberia; we don't know whether it will raise, for example, daytime summer temperatures and cause a greater energy demand for air-conditioning, or raise winter nighttime temperatures and reduce energy demand for heating.

The situation is further complicated because if global temperatures were to rise by one to four degrees Fahrenheit over the next century, as some models predict, that would take us outside the range of global temperature observed in historical times. We know that people found satisfactory ways to adjust to the Little Ice Age and the subsequent recovery. But we don't really know what the next couple degrees of warming would bring. The impact might be trivial (shorter ski seasons and longer beach seasons), or it may be catastrophic in some unforeseen way.

We can make no contribution here to resolving these scientific uncertainties, but we cannot simply ignore them either. Consequently, we take a two-step approach. First, in the next two sections of the chapter, we will ask what policies might be chosen, assuming that global warming is really a matter of concern. Then, in the second section, we will discuss how policy choices are affected by our uncertainty regarding what is happening to the world's climate.

---

2 Here we take historical records of temperatures at the earth's surface at face value. Some observers think this record exaggerates the actual temperature increase because many points of measurement are near growing cities. Satellite measurements of the earth's temperatures show no warming trend over the past 15 years, in contrast to surface measurements.

If the sky really is falling, what should we do about it?

We can begin our economic analysis by noting that people do not produce greenhouse gasses just for fun. Rather, greenhouse gasses are by-products of industrial and agricultural activities that have many benefits. The burning of coal, a major source of carbon dioxide, fuels the American industrial Midwest. Rice paddies plowed by farmers with water buffalo produce vast quantities of methane, but they also feed millions in Asia. In short, the problem of global warming illustrates the principle that every economic activity involves **opportunity costs.** This term is used by economists to refer to explain how the cost of obtaining one benefit is a foregone opportunity to obtain another benefit instead. In the case at hand, the opportunity cost of generating electricity or growing rice is an atmosphere with more greenhouse gasses. Conversely, the opportunity cost of slowing greenhouse gas emissions is less electricity and less rice.

The opportunity costs with which environmental policy is concerned can be illustrated with the aid of a graph known as a **production possibility frontier.** Figure 2-2 shows such a graph, the horizontal axis representing environmental quality, the vertical axis representing other goods and services.

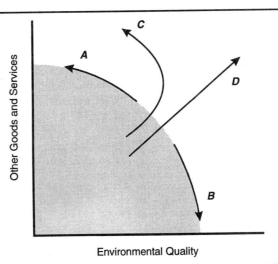

Figure 2-2 Production-Possibility Frontier

The frontier can be thought of as representing a menu of alternatives facing society. Point A on the frontier represents a higher material living standard with a lower-quality environment by comparison represented by Point B. Environmental policy debates are often depicted as a sort of tug-of-war between environmentalists and industrialists, each side trying to pull the economy one way or another along the frontier.

Note that the production possibility frontier is not a straight line. This indicates that as one moves toward either of the goals indicated on the axes, the opportunity cost of further movement in that direction increases. For example, several technologies are available for reducing the amount of carbon dioxide emitted by electric power plants, some relatively cheap, others relatively more expensive. Design of coal-fired boilers can be optimized to reduce coal burned per kilowatt-hour of electricity; this might even reduce electricity costs, but only within the limits of engineering knowledge. Boilers can be fueled with natural gas rather than coal, since gas contains less carbon per Btu of energy value. However, gas is costlier than coal. Thermal plants can be replaced by wind or solar generators. They emit no greenhouse gasses, but their capital costs are high. If we were worried enough about global warming, we could resume construction of nuclear power plants. These, too, emit no greenhouse gasses, although they have opportunity costs in the form of other environmental threats.

By using the cheapest of these techniques first, and then more and more expensive techniques, the economy could be pushed down and to the right along the production possibility frontier toward a cleaner environment, as shown by Arrow B in Figure 2-2. Each step would entail a higher opportunity cost per additional ton of carbon dioxide eliminated.

Movements along the production possibility frontier, then, illustrate the concept of opportunity cost as applied to the issue of global warming. However, not all policy issues involve movements along the frontier. Considerations of economic growth and efficiency add other dimensions to the problem at hand.

Economic growth and the environment The production possibility frontier sets a limit to the range of environmental amenities and other goods that the economy can produce with given population, natural resources, capital, and technology. Once the limit is reached, more of one good can be obtained only at the opportunity cost of reduced enjoyment of another. Over time, however, technological change, investment in new capital equipment, and growth in size and skill of the labor force permit the economy to break out of old limits. It can then move beyond its original production possibility frontier.

With economic growth, the economy faces a new set of choices: What direction will be taken as the economy expands beyond the old frontier? Two possibilities are illustrated in Figure 2-2. Along the path marked by Arrow C, growth of material output is accompanied by a reduction in environmental quality. This is the path along which the economies of many countries have moved in the past. Thus, a rising material standard of living was accompanied by the extinction of many species of birds and animals in the United States, chemical and nuclear pollution in the former Soviet Union, and deforestation and flooding in many Third World countries.

The figure makes it clear, however, that there is no logical reason for growth of material standards of living to be accompanied by deterioration of the environment. If, as the economy expands, greater investments are made in pollution control, both environmental quality and material living standards can improve, as shown by Arrow D. In fact, some aspects of environmental quality have improved even as the economy has grown. An example is investment in better water supplies and sewage treatment. This investment has largely eliminated the risk of water-borne infectious disease in the United States, which was a major environmental problem in this country less than a century ago and is still a serious problem throughout much of the world. More recently, investment in pollution control has begun to improve air quality in many U.S. cities.

Economic growth, then, does not automatically mean further deterioration of the environment, as some environmentalists appear to believe. The relationship between economic growth and environmental quality depends on the choices that people make, and the policies that guide those choices. We turn to these choices and policies next.

Choosing an environmental optimum If we had a choice between following Path C or Path D in Figure 2-2, which would be better? We could restate this question as follows: As we get richer, would we like to spend part of our additional wealth on improving the quality of our environment (Path D)? Or would we prefer to make the world a dirtier, less healthy place in order to accumulate cars, stereos, and steaks at an even faster rate? The answer depends on whether environmental quality is what economists call an inferior good or, instead, a normal good. An *inferior good* is a good people want less of as they get richer. Examples are bus rides (rich people drive their own cars), shoe repair (rich people just buy new shoes), and hot dogs (rich people eat steak). A *normal good* is good clothing, housing space, and entertainment goods that people buy more of as their incomes rise.

There is strong evidence that environmental quality, in general, is a normal good. One indicator is that in most cities, the suburbs where wealthy people live are on the side of town upwind from local pollution sources, although property is cheaper on the other side of town, downwind from the pollution. If environmental quality were an inferior good, wealthy people would not systematically bid up property prices to avoid pollution. They would instead move to more polluted neighborhoods and have more money left over to buy other goods. Another indicator is that the richest countries tend to have better environmental quality than less wealthy countries. Evidently, their citizens are willing and able to devote part of their growing wealth to cleaning up their air and water.[3]

---

3 Reported by G.M. Grossman and A.B. Krueger, "Environmental Impacts of a North American Free Trade

But if people want a cleaner environment as their incomes rise, why do they not always get what they want? The answer is that the quality of their environment is affected not only by the decisions that they themselves make, but also by those that other people make. For example, people in Minetown might build a coal-fired power plant to supply themselves with cheap electricity and allow the smoke to blow across the river to Forestville where it kills the trees. Then people in Oil City, still farther upwind, might build a dirty refinery that would pollute Minetown, and so on. Unless the victims have some mechanism for protecting their property from pollution, or unless some government policy intervenes, everyone ends up with a worse environment than anybody really wants.

Fighting global warming with a carbon tax   The situation where everyone pollutes everyone else's backyard, with everyone ending up worse off as a result, arises because market prices of energy and other goods do not reflect their true opportunity costs. For example, when coal is burned to produce electricity, we forgo not only the opportunity to use the coal for another purpose (say, as a raw material for producing chemicals) but also the opportunity to breath slightly cleaner air and live on a slightly cooler planet. What is needed is some way of ensuring that the market prices of electricity and other goods reflect all aspects of opportunity cost, including environmental ones. Many different means of doing this have been proposed. Here we consider only the approach most widely discussed in the case of global warming: a tax on emissions of carbon into the atmosphere.[4]

Such a tax would fall most heavily on carbon-intensive activities like burning coal to generate electricity. Less carbon-intensive fuels like natural gas would be taxed more lightly. Carbon-free technologies, like solar and wind power, would not be taxed at all. People would thus have an incentive to switch from dirtier to cleaner technologies, and emissions of greenhouse gasses would slow.

How large a tax would be needed? Given the enormous uncertainties involved, no precise answer can be given. Nonetheless, some estimates made by economist William Nordhaus of Yale University provide a rough idea of the magnitude of tax that might be needed to achieve various objectives.[5] Nordhaus notes that one objective would be to bring the price of carbon-based fuels up to the level of their true opportunity costs, including costs in the form of environmental harm. This objective, he calculates, would require a tax of about $10 per ton of carbon. Such a tax would allow some future increase in carbon emissions, to the extent that the

---

Agreement," Discussion Paper No. 158, Discussion Papers on Economics, Woodrow Wilson School, Princeton University, November 1991. The relationship holds for countries with moderate incomes and higher; in the range for $0 to $1,000 per capita income, air quality deteriorates as income rises.

4 One might also want to impose a tax on methane, nitrous oxides, or other greenhouse gasses. Antipollution taxes on CFCs have already been implemented. For a discussion of other approaches to controlling externalities, see Dolan and Lindsey in the list of references at the end of this chapter.

5 See the paper by Nordhaus in the Symposium on Global Climate Change cited at the end of this chapter.

benefits outweighed the costs. Stabilizing carbon emissions at their current levels, a stronger objective favored by some environmentalists, would require a much higher tax, about $100 per ton. The real pessimists point out that, even if carbon emissions were stabilized, global warming would continue for some time. To be safe from disaster, they think we should cut back emission levels enough to stop global warming now. That would require a higher tax still, perhaps $200 per ton.

Stated in practical terms, a $100-per-ton carbon tax would raise consumer gasoline, electricity, and natural gas prices in the United States by about 30 percent. The burden of such a tax could instead be stated as a percentage of **gross domestic product (GDP)**, the most commonly used measure of the nation's total output of goods and services. Nordhaus estimates that the loss of output from a $100-per-ton tax would be about 1.4 percent of GDP. Other economists think the cost might be closer to 4 percent of GDP. Such a tax would roughly double the economic burden of current environmental protection efforts for the United States.

These numbers, however, may be misleading unless we take into account the way other markets and government policies would adjust to policies aimed at slowing global warming. We turn to some of these considerations in the next section.

An evaluation of a carbon tax

As we will do in the case of each issue in this book, we turn now to an evaluation of a carbon tax in terms of our criteria of efficiency, equality, and liberty. In this section, as in the preceding one, we will continue to assume, for the sake of discussion, that global warming as a result of greenhouse gas emissions is a real threat.

Efficiency Markets work most efficiently when market prices reflect opportunity costs. The logic of a carbon tax is to raise the price of carbon-intense energy sources, which would otherwise be too low, to a level that reflects their true opportunity costs. Thus, in theory, a carbon tax (or a tax on any other good that gives rise to pollution) holds out the possibility of making the economy operate more efficiently.

However, not just any tax will have the desired result. For example, a carbon tax could be set so high that prices of carbon-using technologies will be raised above their opportunity costs. Coal, oil, and other fossil fuels could become so expensive that people will undertake wasteful steps to avoid their use. Capital that could be used to build schools and housing will be diverted to building windmills. Research funds that could help develop life-saving medicines will be diverted to work on better solar panels, and so on. In short, people could end up living on a planet that is ever so slightly cooler, but at the cost of significantly worse schooling, housing, or medical care.

This is a point where opinions of environmentalists with economic training tend to differ from those of environmentalists with a background in natural sciences. The natural scientists often focus on some easily understood technical goal, such as no increase in carbon emissions or no further rise in global temperatures. Economists tend to focus on striking a balance between the benefits of moderating global warming and the costs of doing so. The study by Nordhaus, cited earlier, is typical in this regard. Nordhaus is not among those who consider the global warming issue to be a product of bad science or unfounded emotionalism. He sees it as a potentially serious problem. Nonetheless, he thinks a carbon tax of about $10 per ton, rising in the next century to about $20, would correctly balance the costs and benefits. He sees higher taxes to achieve more radical goals as inefficient.

Of course, Nordhaus could be wrong. His calculations could understate the harm from global warming. On the other hand, they could also overstate it, so that even a $10 tax would be inefficiently high. We will return to uncertainties of this kind in the next section. Here we simply make the point that whatever the efficient level of tax, too high a tax could do more harm than good. If the efficient tax rate is $100, a $200 tax might be just as bad as no tax at all, and so on.

The preceding discussion applies to any tax used to bring market prices into line with opportunity costs, say, a fee imposed on wilderness hikers to compensate for their tendency to trample rare flowers and frighten endangered wildlife. A carbon tax, however, differs from many other proposed environmental taxes in that it would raise a huge amount of revenue. For example, a $100-per-ton carbon tax could raise $200 billion per year in the United States, as much as employer contributions for Social Security and half as much as the personal income tax. What should be done with all this revenue? Many economists think that it could be "recycled" in ways that would be beneficial for economic efficiency, for example, by cutting other burdensome taxes or reducing the deficit. We will return to the tax-recycling issue in the last section of this chapter.

On balance, then, a carbon tax is neither necessarily good nor necessarily bad for efficiency. A tax at just the right level could enhance efficiency, and proper recycling would make this more likely. Too high a tax or one not properly recycled could be harmful to efficiency.

Equality Equality is not the primary motivation of those who favor a carbon tax. Their biggest concern is a global disaster that could drown or fry the world's rich and poor together. Nonetheless, discussions of global warming policy often include some attention to the issue of equality. Two points in particular are worth making.

One point concerns the relative effects on rich and poor within rich countries. As mentioned earlier, circumstantial evidence suggests that environmental quality is a normal good. That means that relatively wealthy people are more likely to be willing to sacrifice other benefits for a better environment than relatively poor people. For this reason, some advocates of the poor are suspicious of anything that looks like a slow growth agenda on the part of environmentalists. As Margaret Bush Wilson, then head of the NAACP, once said, "A limited-growth policy tends to freeze people to whatever rung of the ladder they happen to be on. That's OK if you're a highly educated 28-year-old making $50,000 a year as a presidential adviser. It's utter disaster if you're unskilled, out of work, and living in a ghetto."

Another point concerns the international effects of an attack on global warming. Some observers think that Third World countries are more vulnerable to the potential harm of global warming than developed countries. They are more dependent on agriculture. Many of them are located near sea level, where they are in danger of flooding, or near the equator, where it is already too hot. In general, their ecosystems are more fragile. Developing countries might thus receive a disproportionate share of the benefits of efforts to slow global warming if this reasoning is valid.

On the other hand, the inhabitants of developing countries are likely to be less willing and less able to pay the costs of global warming. Many of them are just beginning to reach a stage where they can enjoy some of the things developed nations have had for decades—modern transportation systems, air-conditioned hospitals, high-paid industrial jobs, and so on. They view radical attempts to slow growth or raise energy costs in the way late-comers to a party would view an attempt, by guests who arrived early and have already drunk their fill, to take away the punch bowl.

On balance, even the most ardent proponents of doing something about global warming tend to be uneasy about the equality issue. Very often they suggest linking policies like a carbon tax to efforts to recycle taxes internationally through subsidies from rich countries to poor ones.

Liberty The liberties most directly related to global warming are the rights of resource owners, land owners, and corporate stockholders to conduct their businesses free of government regulation. The classical liberal tradition that underlies a market economy holds that anyone who produces something useful has an inherent right to sell it to someone who needs it at a price to which both parties voluntarily agree. Government attempts to tax or regulate such voluntary, mutually beneficial transactions are not just inefficient—they violate basic human rights.

However, libertarians emphasize that this point of view holds only when all parties directly affected by a transaction voluntarily agree to it. One-sided "exchanges"—if you give me your purse, I will agree not to whack you over the head—are not within the rules of the game. Often pollution can be viewed as just such a nonvoluntary transaction. I'll build a steel mill and sell some cheap steel at a profit, and if you don't like the smoke, too bad.

Protecting the rights of victims of pollution, then, is consistent with the standard of liberty. It is a matter of debate whether taxes are the best way of doing so, but they are one possible way. Looked at in this way, a carbon tax would not necessarily be all bad from the point of view of liberty. But it would not necessarily be all good, either. Libertarians are suspicious of proposals that would impose taxes out of proportion to measurable economic harms. They are also suspicious of recycling proposals that are disguised attempts of low-income groups at home or abroad to get something for nothing under a smokescreen of environmental correctness. On balance, it would be fair to say that the standard of liberty provides support at most only for relatively moderate steps to combat global warming.

What should we do if we don't know what will happen?

Now that we have examined what might be done to avert global warming if we were certain of the nature of the threat, we return to the problem of uncertainty. Recall that the uncertainties are both scientific (Is warming really caused by human activity? Will it bring warmer days or warmer nights?) and economic (Will warming cause more hurricane damage or faster crop growth? Less heating demand or greater air-conditioning demand?)

There is nothing unique about the fact that we must decide what, if anything, to do about global warming in the face of great uncertainty. People make decisions in the face of uncertainty all the time. Among the strategies used in other situations of choice under uncertainty are the following:

- *Wait and see.* When misfortune may occur but is not certain to, we often follow such common sense rules as "Wait and see," or "If it ain't broke, don't fix it." For example, although a TV picture tube may fail as the set gets old, no one ever replaces the tube before it fails. It might never fail, and the cost of replacing a failed tube is no greater than the cost of replacing one that has not failed yet.

- *Minimize the expected loss.* A more sophisticated decision-making rule is to minimize the **expected value** of loss from some uncertain but harmful event (that is, the size of the loss multiplied by the probability that it will occur).[6] For example, a bank knows that more borrowers default on car loans than on home loans. To protect itself, it charges a higher interest rate on car loans so that the expected value of the profit, taking defaults into account, is the same as for both types of loans.

- *Minimize the maximum loss.* When the worst possible case is a catastrophic loss, we sometimes take precautions that do not minimize the expected value of loss. For example, people buy fire insurance for their homes even though,

---

6 As an illustration of the concept of expected value, suppose a farmer knows that on average, one cow in 10 will become ill each year (a 10 percent probability), and that the vet bill for tending a sick cow is $50. The farmer will then include the *expected value* of illness, which is $5 per cow per year ($50 x 0.10), when drawing up a budget of expenses for maintaining a herd of any given size.

because of administrative costs, the premiums charged for such insurance are higher than the average amount paid out in claims.

Which of these strategies makes the best sense in dealing with the uncertain threat of global warming? It turns out that none fits perfectly, and, as a result, each strategy has some advocates.

A good case can be made for the philosophy, "If it ain't broke, don't fix it." It is possible that global warming may turn out not to be a threat after all. Even if there does turn out to be a real threat, it will be a gradual one—not something that happens all at once, like Noah's flood. There will be time enough to deal with global warming when it is better understood.

However, the analogy with replacing the TV picture tube is imperfect in one respect that undermines the "wait and see" strategy. In the case of global warming, the costs of fixing the problem may be greater if we wait. The advantage of starting early to combat global warming arises from the fact that the costs are much lower if control measures are phased in slowly, no faster than the rate at which existing industrial equipment wears out. For example, a study by the Energy Modeling Forum at Stanford University estimated the costs of lowering U.S. carbon emissions to 20 percent below their 1990 levels by various dates. Achieving this goal over a 20-year period would require a $350-per-ton carbon tax, whereas achieving it over a 60-year period would require a tax of just $200 per ton.[7] Estimates like these probably understate the advantages of a slow phase-in because they assume existing technology. The longer the phase-in period, the more time there is to develop new, more efficient low-carbon technology.

Mainstream economists tend to favor mimimization of the expected value of loss. This is a tried and true method for pricing bank loans, deciding how many spare parts a trucking company should keep in its shop, or estimating how much a dairy farmer will have to spend on veterinary bills in a given year. However, it cannot really be implemented when the size and probability of loss cannot be calculated.

We have already mentioned some of the difficulties in calculating the size of loss from global warming. The difficulty of calculating the probability is even greater. Nordhaus cites a survey of experts, who were asked how likely they thought it was that a 6° warming by 2090 would cause a catastrophic loss equal to 25 percent or more of GDP. The median estimated probability was 3 percent. However, such a result is not a true measure of probability. It is better understood as a measure of the average degree of ignorance. Furthermore, the median figure masks a broad range of disagreement. The most pessimistic quarter of those surveyed (who were mostly natural scientists rather than economists) estimated the probability of catastrophe at 40 percent.

---

7 See the paper by John P. Weyant in the Symposium on Global Climate Change cited at the end of the chapter.

Not surprisingly, those whose preferred strategy is to do something now to minimize the possibility of maximum loss base their case on the fears of these pessimists. To them, a business-as-usual policy amounts to "playing dice with the universe." They see this as not just imprudent in an economic sense, but as morally wrong.

Nonetheless, this point of view is not the dominant one in discussions of global warming. Perhaps the reason is that there are too many contending voices urging us to spend vast sums to avoid poorly understood dangers, ranging from carcinogenic food additives to radiation from electric power lines to collision with an asteroid. The politically realistic policies are relatively moderate ones. We turn to political aspects of global warming policy in our last section.

The political economy of global warming policy

As yet, few countries have undertaken policies specifically aimed at reducing the threat of global warming. The issue was discussed at a 1992 United Nations Conference on Environment and Development, but no action was taken there. We can, however, get some idea of some of the political aspects of the problem by looking at some other areas of environmental policy. When we do so, two issues emerge: The need for international cooperation, and the impact of rent seeking.

The need for international cooperation. The emission of greenhouse gasses is a problem of global scale. Over time, carbon dioxide produced in Ohio and methane produced by African cattle herds all mixes together in the atmosphere that blankets the earth. It follows that any effective action must also take place on an international scale. Without international cooperation, each country might be tempted to enjoy the benefits of other countries' cleanup efforts without sharing the costs.

Optimists on the prospects for international cooperation draw encouragement from the 1987 Montreal Protocol. This agreement, signed by 93 nations, adopted a timetable for phasing out production of CFCs. To build consensus for the agreement, advanced industrial countries made concessions that cushioned the impact on less developed countries. The latter were given longer periods to phase out CFC use and were promised financial help in doing so. Since 1987, CFC emissions have actually fallen more rapidly than the protocol requires.

However, several factors made CFCs easier to control than greenhouse gas emissions. First, CFC production is of relatively trivial economic importance by comparison with activities producing carbon dioxide and methane. Second, developing countries are not important producers of CFCs, so that they needed to be compensated only in their roles as users. Third, the scientific basis for believing that CFCs pose a significant risk via their effects on the ozone layer, although far from absolute certainty, is somewhat stronger than that underlying the fear of global warming.

Other international attempts to control externalities are somewhat less encouraging. The United States and Canada negotiated for years before achieving a limited agreement on controlling sulfur dioxide emissions, linked to acid rain. The 1985 Helsinki Protocol, which attempted to do the same for Europe, has still not been signed by 13 nations, including the United Kingdom and Poland, both major sources of acid-rain-related pollutants. The economic stakes in the case of sulfur dioxide emissions (which result primarily from burning high-sulfur coal) are much higher than for CFCs, and there is the additional problem that some relatively poor countries are significant emission sources.

On the whole, prospects for success of global negotiations to control industrial emissions of carbon dioxide together with agricultural emissions of methane, not to mention related problems such as deforestation, seem slim for the foreseeable future.

Rent seeking In Chapter 1, we introduced the concept of rent seeking. This term refers to attempts to use political processes for private economic gain, for example, by obtaining a subsidy, a restriction on competitors, or a price higher than what the market would allow. Environmental policy, like any other area of economic policy, offers opportunities for rent seeking.

Attempts of some countries to gain advantages at the expense of others in international negotiations can be seen as a form of rent seeking. For example, suppose Third World countries refuse to lend their support to a treaty to control CFCs without promises of financial aid from developed countries. To some extent, they might simply be asking for compensation for policies that would otherwise be costly to them. But they also might use their voting power in an international environmental forum to blackmail developed countries into giving them aid they would not otherwise get.

Rent seeking affects environmental policy on the national level, too. A notorious example concerns amendments made to the U.S. Clean Air Act in 1970 and 1977.[8] These amendments were aimed at controlling acid rain by limiting sulfur dioxide emissions. The main source of such emissions in the United States is combustion of high-sulfur coal produced in Appalachia and burned in the Midwest.

At the time of the amendments, environmentalists did not have enough strength in Congress to impose strong acid rain controls on their own. They needed allies. They found those allies in Midwestern members of Congress who wanted to protect industries in their "rust belt" districts from the competition of new industry in the rapidly growing sunbelt of the South and West, and also to protect the jobs of union miners who produced high-sulfur coal. These legislators were willing to vote for sulfur dioxide controls on two conditions. One was that emission

---

8 The story of rent seeking and the Clean Air Act is told in Robert W. Crandall, "An Acid Test for Congress," *Regulation*, September/December 1984: pp.21-28.

standards imposed on new Sunbelt sources be stricter than those imposed retroactively on existing rust belt sources. The other was that pollution sources should be required to use a technology known as "scrubbing." Scrubbing removes sulfur from smokestack gasses after a high-sulfur fuel has been burned. It is much more expensive than burning coal that has low sulfur content to begin with. However, high-sulfur coal is mined underground by unionized miners in Appalachia, whereas low-sulfur coal comes primarily from less labor-intensive open pit mining operations in the West. In sum, the Clean Air Act amendments were designed to protect the rents of rust belt industries and union miners as much or more than to protect the environment. These economically senseless and environmentally ineffective provisions of the Clean Air Act remained in force until 1993, when they were partially modified by yet another round of amendments.

Is there hope for a rational solution? There is a danger that negotiations over global-warming policy could become dominated by a coalition of profits of doom and industrial special interests. However, that is not the only possible outcome. One can at least imagine conditions under which environmentalists could make common cause with advocates of efficiency, equality, and liberty to achieve a world that would be both cleaner and more prosperous.

One way of doing so is to attack global warming selectively through policies that are desirable for their own sake. Happily, some such policies are already being implemented. For example, until the 1980s, a web of regulations and price controls artificially restricted the use of relatively clean natural gas in the United States. These policies have now been largely dismantled, freeing natural gas to compete more widely with oil, coal, and other high-carbon fuels. The CFC controls discussed earlier are another example. Although damage to the ozone layer is the big worry related to CFCs, they are also a significant greenhouse gas. It is also encouraging that relatively efficient methods were chosen to control CFCs, including a system of gradually rising taxes. Finally, economic reforms in Eastern Europe and the former Soviet Union, highly desirable for their own sake, will have the side effect of slowing global warming. Prior to reforms, these centralized economies used energy as much as five times more wastefully than Western countries. Markets will force them to be more efficient, and incidentally, cleaner.

Another possible coalition could be built in the area of tax policy. We mentioned earlier that a carbon tax could potentially raise a colossal amount of revenue, which would be available for recycling. Any tax, including a carbon tax, has the potential to distort incentives in way that reduces efficiency or work effort. These distortions, in turn, tend to raise the true economic burden on taxpayers above the amount of revenue received by government. However, there are a number of other taxes already on the books that may cause even greater distortions than would a carbon tax. For example, payroll taxes, such as those used to support Social Security, raise the cost of hiring workers and therefore increase unemployment. Capital gains taxes on the profits from selling corporate stocks and other investments penalize saving and entrepreneurship, thus leading to slower economic growth. In principle, a carbon tax could be recycled in a way that reduced total distortions if it replaced taxes that are even more burdensome.

Suppose, for example, that liberal Democrats in Congress, responsive to environmental lobbying groups, got together with conservative Republicans, whose supporters would like to ditch the capital gains tax. Throw in support from small business interests, who would be eager to hire more workers if payroll taxes were cut, and the result could be a winning coalition: a cleaner, cooler, world; more capital to support modernization of industry; and more jobs at the local hardware store.

Perhaps the worst fears of the pessimists will not come to pass after all.

Questions for thought and discussion

1. Some forms of pollution arise from the actions of consumers rather than those of producers. Smoking tobacco is a case in point. Recently, many laws have been enacted to limit smoking. Consider regulations that would prohibit smoking in (a) a public library, (b) privately owned restaurants and bars, and (c) any indoor space, including private homes. In your opinion, would such laws be consistent with the standard of efficiency? Equality? Liberty? Discuss.

2. A growing tree takes carbon out of the atmosphere and turns it into wood. Burning a tree releases carbon into the atmosphere. On balance, the forested area of the United States has been increasing in recent decades, while that of many developing countries, such as Brazil, has been decreasing. How do you think the issue of deforestation should be treated in international negotiations to combat global warming? Should countries where deforestation is taking place be threatened with penalties if they don't stop? Should they be offered incentives to stop? Discuss.

3. Instead of imposing a carbon tax, some economists have suggested that to control carbon dioxide emissions, each country should be given a fixed number of "carbon permits." Each permit would allow emission of one ton of carbon in the form of carbon (or the equivalent amount of another greenhouse gas). The total number of permits would be limited to a number judged to be safe for the environment. If such a system were implemented, how do you think the U.S. government should distribute its carbon permits? Should it give them away in proportion to existing emissions? Auction them to the highest bidder? Should international trading in carbon permits be permitted? If so, who might be the buyers, and who the sellers? Discuss.

Selected references

Dolan, Edwin G. and David E. Lindsey. *Economics,* 7th ed. Ft. Worth, Tx: Dryden Press, 1994. *Ch. 32 compares taxes with others economic techniques for controlling pollution.*

Firor, John, et al. "The Greenhouse Effect." *Contemporary Policy Issues, July 1990, pp. 3-42. The three articles in this symposium discuss both scientific and economic aspects of the greenhouse effect, focusing on efforts to control carbon dioxide emissions.*

Magnusson, Magnus and Hermann Pálsson, eds. *The Vinland Sagas: The Norse Discovery of America.* London: Penguin, 1965. *A collection of writings that tells the story of the Viking voyages to American in the medieval Icelanders' own words, with a detailed introduction by the translators.*

Michaels, Patrick J. *Global Warming: Science or Myth?* Washington, D.C.: Cato Institute, 1992. *A skeptical look at the scientific basis of the global warming issue by a University of Virginia climatologist.*

Schmalensee, Richard, et al. "Symposium on Global Climate Change." *Journal of Economic Perspectives,* Fall 1993, pp. 3-86. *In addition to an introduction by Schmalensee, this symposium also contains articles by William D. Nordhaus, John P. Weyant, and others. Together they provide a good survey of the economics of global climate change.*

Key terms

Opportunity costs. The costs of obtaining one benefit stated in terms of the foregone opportunity to obtain another benefit instead.

Production-possibility frontier. A graph showing the various combinations of two goods that can be obtained on the basis of available resources and technology; obtainable combinations are represented by points on or below the frontier.

Inferior good. A good that people want less of as their incomes increase.

Normal good. A good that people want more of as their incomes increase.

Gross domestic product (GDP). The most commonly used measure of the nation's total annual output of goods and services.

Expected value. The value of a loss (or gain) multiplied by the probability that it will occur.

3

Economics of Health Care (I):
Patient Power

In 1993, a misfortune befell Reitha and Kenneth Lakeberg, a young Chicago couple. They learned that Reitha was pregnant with conjoined babies—so-called Siamese twins. Their doctors advised an abortion as the most humane solution to the problem, but the parents were unwilling. The twins were born sharing a heart and other internal organs.

At one time, conjoined twins, if they lived, were doomed to a life of discomfort and seclusion, or worse, that of sideshow freaks. Today, many can be separated and live normally. Even where internal organs are shared, it is sometimes possible to save one twin by sacrificing the other. The case of Amy and Angela Lakeberg was so extreme, however, that the doctors at Loyola University Hospital in Chicago saw no hope at all. The odds against saving even one of the girls were, as one doctor put it, like those of "walking into a bowling alley and bowling three 300 games."

The Lakebergs did not like this answer. They went doctor shopping, and found a team in Philadelphia that would give the risky operation a try. Amy was sacrificed to give Angela a chance at life—but that chance proved too slim. After eleven months clinging to life in an intensive care unit, fed by tubes and breathing with a respirator, Angela died.

The bill for these medical heroics came to $1.3 million. Two hospitals, three state health care programs, and the federal Medicare program are still arguing over who will eventually bear this cost, but it is certain that the bill will not be paid by the Lakebergs. As is the case with 95 percent of all hospital expenses in the United

States, the Lakebergs knew they would be spending someone else's money when they made the risky, emotionally wrenching choice to try to save Angela's life.

The Lakeberg case made national headlines at a time when the American health care system itself was perceived to be in crisis. By 1993, health care expenditures in the United States had reached 14 percent of GDP—far more than in other industrialized countries. Yet 39 million people were without health insurance, and American life expectancy and infant mortality statistics were not as good as those of many other industrialized countries. Not surprisingly, many people saw spending $1.3 million in a long-shot attempt to save the life of a single infant as a case of priorities gone haywire.

This chapter and the next will look at some key aspects of the health care crisis. In this chapter, we will look at conditions that determine the demand for health care. We will try to understand why health care spending has grown so much, and whether consumers of health care are really getting what they want for all the money that is spent. We will also examine one proposal, which goes by the name patient power, that could restore the consumer to a position of influence in the market for health care.[1] Then, in Chapter 4, we will turn to the market for health insurance.

The demise of consumer sovereignty in the market for health care services

Since 1960, the share of GDP spent on health care services in the United States has more than doubled. Because GDP itself has grown, the increase in health care spending per person is even more dramatic. In *real* terms (that is, adjusted for inflation), health care spending per person today is more than three times what it was in 1960.

But the fact that spending on health care has grown does not by itself mean that there is a crisis. Consumers today also spend more on travel and consumer electronics than they did in 1960. Relative to their incomes, they spend less on food and clothing. Yet we do not have a travel crisis or a consumer electronics crisis. In those other markets, we take it for granted that a change in spending patterns reflects consumers' own choices in response to rising incomes and the appearance of new goods on the market. These are markets where consumer sovereignty prevails: If people want to travel more, they do. If they want to trade in their record players for CD players, fine. If they do these things by cutting back (relatively speaking) on food and clothing, well, that's their choice.

How do we know that, given rising real incomes and new, more effective treatments for disease and injury, consumers have not freely chosen to spend more?

---

1 *Patient Power* is the title of a book by John C. Goodman and Gerald L. Musgrave on which this chapter draws extensively.

We can provide at least a tentative answer by using the economists favorite tool, the theory of supply and demand, to analyze the various factors that lie behind observed changes in health care expenditure.

Supply and demand for health care Figure 3-1 sets the stage for our analysis. In the usual manner, the vertical axis of the figure represents the price of health care services and the horizontal axis the quantity supplied per year. For present purposes, the price that interests us is the price that consumers pay for health care relative to other goods and services, adjusting for any changes in the general cost of living. The figure assumes a long enough time horizon for changes in the quantity of health services supplied to respond to changes in price, that is, for additional doctors to enter and complete medical school, for new hospitals to be built, and so on. Because the resources needed to increase health care services can, given time, be drawn away from other sectors of the economy without sharply bidding up their prices, we have drawn the supply curve with a moderate positive slope.

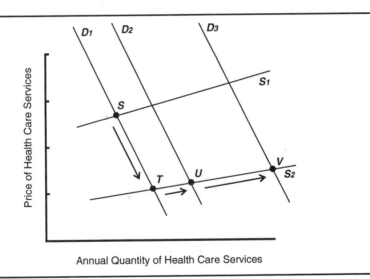

Figure 3-1

Demand for health care is also shown as responsive to price. Other things being equal, people will buy more health care if its price decreases and less if its price increases. The demand curve for health care thus has a negative slope, like the demand curve for other goods, although we have drawn the demand curve with a steeper slope than the supply curve.

For the sake of discussion, we will assume that supply curve S_1 and demand curve D_1 represent market conditions as of the 1950s. The corresponding equilibrium is point S. Starting from that point, we can analyze a change in the quantity of a good purchased in terms of movements along the good's demand curve (changes in quantity demanded) and shifts in the demand curve (changes in demand).

Movements along the demand curve Movements along a demand curve reflect consumer reactions to changes in the price of the good in question under conditions where the supply curve shifts while the demand curve remains in place. If we were to take at face value data put out by the U.S. Department of Commerce, our inclination would be to look for a movement up and to the left along the demand curve D_1. These official data indicate that the prices of health care services have doubled relative to other prices since the 1960s. (While the average prices of all goods and services have increased by a factor of four, the measured price of health care services has grown by a factor of eight.)

However, the apparent doubling of health care prices cannot be taken at face value. There are two major problems. One is that the official data measure the cost of inputs into health care—such as days in the hospital—but not the cost of treating disease. Because they fail to take into account changes in the quality of medical care, they overstate the price increase, although it is hard to know exactly by how much. Joseph Newhouse, a professor of health care policy and management at Harvard, flatly states that the measurement problems in the medical care price index are so severe that no inferences can be drawn from it.[2] We cannot, in other words, tell whether price changes have pushed the market upward or downward along the demand curve.

A second problem with the official price data is that they do not reflect what consumers actually pay for health care services. A large part of the costs of health care are paid for by "third parties"—insurance companies and government programs like Medicare and Medicaid. The real price of health care services to consumers, then, depends crucially on the **copayment rate**, that is, the percentage of the cost of services paid out of pocket. Taking changes in the copayment rate into account, the price of health care services has fallen significantly over the past 40 years. Forty years ago, consumers paid two-thirds of their own health care costs. Today, they pay only a little more than a fifth. In terms of our diagram, a reduction in the copayment rate shifts the supply curve for health care downward, as viewed from the consumer's perspective. That is, with a lower copayment rate, the consumer can purchase a given quantity of medical care for a smaller out-of-pocket outlay.

As the copayment rate decreases, other things being equal, consumers move down and to the right along their demand curve. The impact on the quantity of health care demanded is substantial. One study found that people who have a copayment rate of zero—so-called *first dollar coverage*—are 25 percent more likely

---

2 See Joseph P. Newhouse, "Medical Care Costs: How Much Welfare Loss?," *Journal of Economic Perspectives* (Summer 1992): 10.

to see a physician and 33 percent more likely to enter a hospital than people who pay 95 percent out of pocket, up to a limit of $2,500. Another study suggests that a reduction in the average copayment rate from 67 percent in the 1950s to 21 percent today would cause an increase of about 50 percent in real health care spending.[3] In terms of Figure 3-1, the change in copayment rate, taken by itself, would have moved the health care market from the initial equilibrium at Point S to a new equilibrium at Point T.

Shifts in the demand curve In fact, however, changes in the average copayment rate for heath care did not occur in isolation. Other factors were also at work that would have caused the demand for health care services to increase even if there had been no changes in the percentage of cost borne by consumers. In terms of Figure 3-1, these factors can be represented as rightward shifts in the demand curve.

One factor causing the demand curve to shift is a change in the age structure of the U.S. population. Since the 1950s, the share of the population over 65 has grown while the share of those under 19 has fallen. Among the elderly, the number of very old—85 years and up—has risen as well. These demographic changes can account for an increase in demand of about 15 percent.

Rising real incomes are a second factor causing the demand curve to shift. Between 1960 and 1990, real per capital GDP in the United States increased by about 80 percent. It has been estimated that each 10 percent increase in real income will increase health care spending by 2 to 4 percent, other things being equal, so this factor would have been expected to increase expenditures by between 16 and 32 percent over the period under consideration.

Taking changes in age and income both into account would explain an increase in demand of something in the neighborhood of 50 percent, shown in Figure 3-1 by a shift from D_1 to D_2. This would imply a movement in market equilibrium to Point U.

All of the changes considered up to this point—a falling copayment rate, a changing age structure, and rising incomes—would together account roughly for a doubling of real per capita health care expenditures. In fact, we know that real per capita health care spending more than tripled between 1960 and 1990, rising from about $500 to about $1,700 by 1990. This suggests that the demand curve in fact shifted even farther to the right, to a position like D_3 in Figure 3-1. To understand this extra shift, we need to turn from such factors as price, income, and demographics, which affect demand in every market, to some considerations of special importance to the market for health care.

Information, agency, and demand In many situations—buying clothes, ordering food in a restaurant, or filling a car with gasoline—consumers rely on their own

---

3 The book by Goodman and Musgrave and the article by Newhouse cited previously both discuss studies of demand for health care services.

judgment. But in other cases, not every consumer is able to make a fully informed choice. Buying a house, corporate stocks, or even airline tickets fit this pattern, as does buying health care services. In such cases, consumers frequently rely on an agent to help them make a decision.

The term *agent* in this context refers to a person who acts on behalf of another person, known as the *principal*. In some cases, the agency relationship is a formal one, as when a home buyer hires a real estate agent. In other cases, the relationship is less formal, as when a person shopping for a new stereo system consults a knowledgeable retail salesperson. When making health care decisions, the physician performs the role of agent for the patient (who is the principal), making a diagnosis and offering expert advice on alternative courses of treatment.

A problem that arises in every situation of agency is how to ensure that the agent really acts in the best interests of the principal. Among the mechanisms used to deal with this problem in a market economy are the following:

- *Legal and ethical restraints.* Many professions have codes of ethics, often backed up by law, that require the agent to act in the principal's interest. For example, a real estate agent who concealed a known defect in a house would violate both ethical and legal standards.

- *Economic incentives.* Often the contract between the principal and the agent contains incentives that help align their interests. For example, a person who employs a real estate agent to sell a house benefits from the fact that the agent will get a larger commission by selling the house for a higher price. This particular incentive might work against the interest of a buyer, however.

- *Competition.* Another very strong incentive for agents to serve their principals honestly is competition among agents. For example, if you think your stockbroker is "churning" your account—making unnecessary sales and purchases to generate additional commissions—you can switch to a different broker.

If these mechanisms work perfectly, consumers, relying on the advice of agents, will purchase just the quantity of each good that they would buy if they themselves had complete information. In such a case, the presence of the agent in the market does not disturb the principle of consumer sovereignty. But if the protective mechanisms do not work perfectly, consumers may be persuaded to buy more or less than they really want. For example, car dealers, on whom some people rely for advice in purchasing a car, may try to talk their customers into purchasing expensive rustproofing and upholstery protection that, in the opinion of many independent consumer advisers, is not worth the price charged. To take a different kind of example, a racially motivated real estate agent might make up imagined defects to steer a well-to-do African-American couple away from an expensive home in an all-white neighborhood to a cheaper home elsewhere.

In economic terms, we can say that agents have the power to shift consumers' demand curves by imparting a bias to information provided. The advice of an agent biased toward selling more than the consumer really wants would shift the demand curve to the right, whereas the advice of an agent biased toward selling less would shift it to the left.

Are doctors biased or unbiased agents in providing advice to their patients? Let's consider one by one the various mechanisms on which patients could depend to ensure that their doctors serve their interests evenhandedly.

First, it is clear that legal and ethical restraints operate rather strongly in the market for health care. Every doctor learns a code of ethics in the first year of medical school. A central principle, dating from ancient times, is that the doctor has a duty not to harm, but to help. In modern times, this norm is reinforced by the legal doctrine of malpractice liability. A doctor who prescribes a treatment knowing that it will harm the patient, or who fails to take precautions known to be helpful, can be sued for damages by the injured patient or by his or her survivors.

The economic function of these legal and ethical restraints is to make the doctor a reliable agent of the patient. In practice, however, they restrain only departures from unbiased agency that exceed some practical threshold. Day after day every doctor is confronted with situations in which a certain test, medication, or procedure might be helpful and will almost certainly do no harm, but in which omission of the procedure also cannot be reliably predicted to be harmful. Within this ethically and legally safe middle ground, economic incentives strongly influence doctors' behavior.

These economic incentives, in turn, depend on how the doctor is paid. From World War II through the 1980s, three features dominated the health care payment system. One, which we have already mentioned, is the spread of third-party payments. By the 1980s, the bulk of medical costs were being paid not by patients, but by their insurance companies or government agencies. The second feature was the fee-for-service principle. Instead of paying doctors a fixed amount for treating a given condition requiring care, most insurance plans paid a specific fee for each service rendered—each office visit, test, surgical procedure, and so on. Under this approach, the doctor performs whatever treatments are thought to be medically necessary, sends the bill to the third-party payer, and waits for a check to arrive. The third feature was retrospective payment, a procedure for setting the fees for each service rendered. Retrospective payment meant reimbursing hospitals for actual costs incurred in rendering a treatment rather than on the basis of a market price for that treatment. If doctors or hospitals practiced medicine in a way that increased the costs of treatment above their competitors' costs, they were still fully reimbursed.

Limited only by the duty to do no harm, a doctor working on the basis of third-party payments, a fee-for-service billing structure, and retrospective payment to cover full costs of treatment will tend to bias the advice given to the patient in the direction of more, rather than less, service. In borderline cases to test or not to test, to prescribe a brand name or generic drug, to discharge from the hospital a day sooner or a day later, the doctor's economic interest is in more treatment. If a third party pays, the patient is harmed neither medically nor financially.

Hospital administrators faced the same set of incentives. Why not buy the latest magnetic resonance imaging scanner or life support system if Blue Cross or Medicare is there to pay for it? Why push patients out the door sooner, if beds might then remain empty?

Down the road from the hospital, the medical research laboratory also got a message from the cost-plus system. The message said, "Anything you can think up, we will buy, regardless of cost, if it in any way even slightly improves treatment." So an even more expensive positron emission scanner is invented to supplement the magnetic resonance scanner. Hospitals buy it, doctors send their patients to be scanned, and third parties shovel out the money.

But wait—what about competition? In other markets, competition provides a key discipline for agents. Doesn't a car dealer have the same incentive to sell a turbo charger or four-valve-per-cylinder engine to every customer as a doctor has to sell high-tech medical services? Yes, but: Even though car buyers may be as ignorant of automotive engines as of the workings of their gall bladders, they shop around among competing dealers until they get advice that makes sense to them. And once they decide what they want they can compare the prices offered by various dealers. In the market for health care services, such competition barely exists. First of all, most patients aren't spending their own money, so why bother to comparison shop? And second, if they did want to shop around, they would come up against a nearly complete information barrier. Most doctors and most hospitals simply will not quote prices in advance of treatment. Even after treatment, many of them issue bills that the average consumer cannot understand.[4]

The combination of incentives just described lie at the center of most economic diagnoses of the crisis in the U.S. health care system. It is these features of the system that appear to have given the critical extra push rightward to the health care demand curve. The result is a system in which consumer sovereignty is defeated. Many patients get more treatment than they really want or need, while others are priced out of the market altogether.

---

4 Cosmetic surgery provides an interesting exception. Because most insurance policies and government programs won't pay for a nose job or a tummy tuck, these procedures lie outside the third-party, fee-for-service, retrospective payment system. As a result, it is easier for consumers to negotiate a fixed price in advance and shop around among competing providers.

What can be done to control health care demand?

If uncontrolled demand is a big part of the problem with the American health care system, what can be done to control demand? This is one of the central issues in today's health care debate. Two general kinds of solutions have been proposed. One of them relies on government regulation, or in some cases, regulation by private health care bureaucracies. We will call this the regulatory approach. The other approach is patient power, which relies on restoring consumer sovereignty.

The regulatory approach to health care reform The regulatory approach to controlling health care demand relies on rules and regulations to change the behavior of health care providers without directly involving health care consumers. A leading example of this approach is the replacement of retrospective reimbursement by a prospective reimbursement system for Medicare patients.

Under this system, introduced in 1983, the Medicare bureaucracy introduced a number of "diagnosis related groups" (DRGs), on the basis of which doctors and hospitals are paid for treating a given condition. Consider coronary bypass surgery as an example. Under the fee-for-service, retrospective payment system, a patient was admitted to the hospital and Medicare was billed for each day's stay, each test, and each bandage. Under the prospective payment system, a standard amount is paid for the DRG covering this treatment. The standard is based on the national average cost of treating the given condition. If the hospital in question treats the given patient at a cost less than the average, it earns a profit. If treatment costs more than the average, the hospital suffers a loss. In the years since 1983, other payers, including some large employers and large insurance companies, have introduced various prospective payment mechanisms of their own.

Prospective payment is just one kind of bureaucratic regulation. In other countries, where government-run health systems provide universal coverage with low or zero copayments, a variety of means are used to control demand. Canada's national health system, for example, controls spending in part by providing hospitals with fixed budgets. The hospitals then have to decide how to allocate limited resources. One way they do so is to limit modern medical technology to just a few hospitals. For example, the city of Seattle, Washington, with fewer than half a million people, has more CAT scanners than the entire province of British Columbia, with a population of 3 million. The province of Newfoundland has only one CAT scanner, while the province of Prince Edward Island has none. Another allocation technique is rationing by waiting. In 1993, patients in Alberta waited six months for elective bypass surgery. Patients in British Columbia waited an average of nearly five months for orthopedic surgery and three months for hernia repair.[5]

5 Cynthia Ramsay and Michael Walker, "Waiting Your Turn: Hospital Waiting Lists in Canada," 4th ed., Frazer Forum Critical Issues Bulletin (Vancouver, B.C.: Frazer Institute, 1994)

ɔuntries use age as a criterion for rationing medical care. In Great
1970s, for example, a third of kidney dialysis centers refused to treat
r 55, half refused to treat patients over 65, and those over 75 rarely
eatment. Without dialysis, kidney failure is quickly fatal. Organ
transpla.. ʒ, hip replacements, and other procedures are still rationed by age in
Britain, although kidney dialysis and transplants are more easily available than in the
past.

The health care reform proposals submitted to Congress in 1994 by the Clinton
administration made wide use of bureaucratic controls, which it referred to as
"managed care." These included price controls, controls on technology, budget
caps, and many layers of review of medical decisions. The aim was to limit the
number of services doctors could deliver.

Figure 3-2 shows how all these methods work to regulate the demand for
health care. There, D_1 represents the demand curve of a patient under the care
of a doctor who acts as an unbiased agent, that is, one with no economic incentive
to undertreat or overtreat. Point W shows the amount of care chosen by a patient
receiving unbiased advice and paying 100 percent of the cost of treatment. This is
the point of consumer sovereignty. Earlier we saw that a third-party payment
system that cuts the copayment rate below 100 percent will shift the supply curve
(as perceived by patients) downward. Patients are thereby induced to move down
along the demand curve to a point like X, where more than the optimal amount of
treatment is provided. If a fee-for-service, retrospective reimbursement system
gives the doctor/agent a bias toward overtreatment, the demand curve will be
shifted to D_2. In that case, the patent ends up at Point Y, even further from the
optimum.

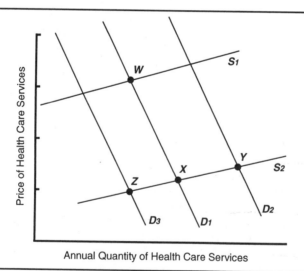

Annual Quantity of Health Care Services

Figure 3-2

The aim of bureaucratic regulation is to introduce an opposite bias on the part of heath care providers, one that will shift the demand curve leftward to D3. Because patients still face a low copayment rate, they will choose Point Z. This lies well below Point W, but because the demand curve is shifted leftward, it lies to the left of Points Y and X.

In short, the regulatory strategy amounts to offsetting one bias with another: The consumer, influenced by a low copayment rate, perceives health care as very inexpensive, and wants lots of it. But the provider, under the pressure of a prospective payment system or a budget cap, tries to provide the least amount of care consistent with legal and ethical restraints. In principle, if just the right degree of bureaucratic pressure is provided, total spending could be the same as under consumer sovereignty. However, regulators are unlikely to be able to apply just the right degree of pressure. And, as we will see shortly, even if regulation did somehow achieve the optimal total expenditure of health care, that does not mean that each patient receives the optimal amount of care.

Patient power The alternative to bureaucratic rationing of health care is to restore consumer sovereignty. The most widely discussed plan for doing so is that popularized by John C. Goodman and Gerald L. Musgrave in their book Patient Power. Their plan would give people the option of participating in a new kind of health care payment system having the following features:

- Third-party payments would be limited to major medical expenses (in most cases those in excess of $3,000 per patient).

- The copayment rate for most routine services would be 100 percent; that is, these expenses would be paid out of pocket.

- Tax incentives would encourage families to establish medical savings accounts (MSAs) that would be earmarked for routine medical expenses.

The reality that makes the patient power approach attractive is the fact that health insurance is a very inefficient way to pay for small medical bills. Let's look at how insurance works. In addition to a copayment clause that specifies the patient's share of health care bills (usually up to a certain limit), most health insurance policies have a **deductible clause** that specifies a limit below which the patient must pay everything. This limit may be $250, $500, $1,000, $2,500, $3,000 or even higher. The lower the deductible, the more expensive the policy.

In a city with average health care costs, a family must pay an extra $1,605 to lower the deductible from $3,000 to $250. For a typical policy with a 20 percent copayment rate, that $1,605 buys at most just $2,200 of added coverage (80 percent of the difference between $3,000 and $250), even if one member of the family incurs all of the expense. Moreover, the deductible and copayment rates on many policies apply to each member of the family, whereas high-deductible policies often include an "umbrella" provision, meaning that the deductible limit needs to be met only once per year for the entire family. Accordingly, even if the family is certain to incur at least $3,000 of medical expenses each year, the low-deductible policy barely pays for itself. But only one person in ten has a medical bill of more than $3,000 in any given year. If expenses in a given year fall more than $600 below the $3,000 level, or if four members of a family have $750 in expenses each, the family doesn't get its money's worth out of the low-deductible policy.

But if low-deductible insurance is such a bad deal, why are such policies so common? There are two reasons. One is that employers are allowed to pay for employee's health insurance with before-tax dollars. When Social Security taxes, federal income taxes, and state income taxes are combined, it costs the employer only about half as much to pay for insurance with before-tax dollars as it would cost many employees to pay for it with after-tax dollars. The other reason people prefer low-deductible insurance is that many families don't have enough money in the bank to cover even $3,000 in medical expenses without a severe strain on their budget. To get along comfortably with a high-deductible policy, they need more savings.

This is where tax-advantaged medical savings accounts come in. The idea would be to let each family, or the employers of family members, contribute up to a certain amount each year to an MSA from before-tax income. The money in the MSA would be subject to rules somewhat like those for Individual Retirement Accounts. Like IRAs, they would be managed by a bank or other financial institution of the family's choice. The funds could be withdrawn only to pay medical bills, and perhaps also for other extraordinary expenses. On reaching retirement age, funds could be used to purchase long-term nursing home care, if needed, and perhaps to meet other retirement needs. If a person died with funds left in an MSA, the funds would go to his or her estate just like other assets.

Here is how it would work: As soon as the program is implemented, the Jones family, or the employer of a family member, trades in the family's $250-deductible heath insurance policy for a $3,000-deductible policy. The $1,605 premium savings is put in an MSA. Even if the family has the bad luck to have $3,000 in medical bills the first year, the MSA covers all but $595 of the added cost. But nine times out of ten, that won't happen. After a year or two, the MSA account builds up to the point where it might make sense to buy insurance with an even higher deductible, say $5,000 or $10,000, for an even greater premium savings. The family has medical security and saves money, too.

But the savings in health insurance premiums are only the beginning of the story, according to Goodman and Musgrave. More importantly, their scheme would restore a large measure of market discipline to the relationship between patients and health care providers:

- Patients, who would be spending their own money, would only buy services for which the benefits exceeded the costs. They would weigh the advantages of outpatient treatment against a hospital stay, or the benefits of a visit to a doctor for a minor complaint against a visit to the drugstore to buy a nonprescription medication. (They would not be foolishly tempted to skimp on medical care to buy a new car, because MSA funds could be used only for health care purposes.)

- Doctors would no longer have the excuse that "someone else will pay" to ease their ethical pangs when prescribing unnecessary tests or treatments. They would be more likely to help their patients evaluate alternatives in a balanced way, knowing that the patient will seek out another doctor if they do not.

- Hospitals would be forced to price their services and compete the way other businesses do. Patients would find it worthwhile to ask in advance for an estimate of costs, and hospitals that did not comply would lose patients to those who did.

- Competition would also be stimulated between fee-for-service health care providers and health maintenance organizations (HMOs), which charge a set yearly fee for a broad range of services. Patients could evaluate the relative benefits and costs of each form of medical care and choose accordingly.

Medical savings accounts do not address every health care problem. They would only indirectly affect the way major medical problems are solved. They would not guarantee universal coverage without supplementary programs to deal with the uninsurable chronically ill or those too poor to contribute to an MSA. And they represent only a partial solution to the problem of long-term care for the aged. But MSAs would in any event not be compulsory. People could continue to participate in other kinds of plans if they did not find the new option to be attractive. But the economics of MSAs would be persuasive for millions of people. Patient power is a very real, market-based alternative to regulation as a response to America's health care crisis.

Patient power vs. regulation: an evaluation

We have now explained the reasons for uncontrolled growth of health care spending in the United States and outlined two proposed remedies: bureaucratic regulation and patient power. We turn now to a comparative evaluation of these alternatives in terms of our standards of efficiency, equality, and liberty.

Efficiency An efficient market is one in which each good or service is provided up to the point where the benefit to consumers of one more unit is just offset by the cost of one more unit. For the health care market to operate efficiently, both consumers and doctors must face proper incentives to balance benefits and costs.

As we have seen, the third-party-payer, fee-for-service system does not meet this standard. It encourages wasteful overtreatment of patients and overinvestment in research and technology.

The built-in inefficiency of this system is made even worse by the huge tax benefits it gets under current law. Anyone who wants to opt out of the system by setting up a one-family medical saving account faces a severe tax disadvantage—well over two-to-one for many families.

Both patient power and regulation aim to reduce the excess spending. In principle, as we have shown, just the right degree of regulatory pressure could result in the same level of total spending as a market-based system. However, that does not mean that both systems would be equally efficient.   An efficient system must not only achieve a certain amount of total spending but must also have the flexibility to balance relative costs and benefits within the total for various patients and treatment strategies. Experience with bureaucratic controls in the United States and abroad casts doubt on their ability to operate efficiently in this regard.

One problem is the constant temptation of government officials to provide politically popular benefits while hiding the costs. Medicare's prospective payments system provides an example. In concept, it is supposed to improve cost-control incentives by compensating hospitals at a level reflecting the actual average cost of treating each medical condition. In practice, budgetary pressures have caused Medicare reimbursement levels to drop below the true average cost of treatment. To break even, hospitals have to overcharge patients who have private insurance. That makes the private insurance system operate even less efficiently and prices even more families out of the market altogether. Soon the cure becomes as bad as the disease.

Another example of the priority of politics over economic considerations was the attempt, under the Clinton administration health care proposal, to finance universal coverage by requiring employers to pay 80 percent of the cost of insurance for all employees. The political motivation for this "employer mandate" was the hope of providing something people want—universal coverage—without raising taxes. This aspect of the Clinton proposal met with a skeptical response, however, because most people understood the government mandate to be just another form of tax, like the taxes paid by employers to support a Canadian- or British-style national health system. Such a mandate would have the same distorting effects on the labor market as any other payroll taxes, for example, those now used to finance Social Security and Medicare. By raising the cost to employers of hiring workers, a requirement that all employers purchase health insurance would pose the same threat to jobs, especially the jobs of low-paid workers.

Still another kind of inefficiency that affects many government-run health care systems is a tendency to overspend on minor complaints while rationing care for life-threatening conditions. Earlier we mentioned that it is harder for a British citizen to get expensive high-tech treatments or elective surgery than for an American to get those treatments. Yet the British national health care system spends lavishly on conditions that are not life-threatening. The health care service provides free eye examinations and glasses, free telephone attachments for the hard of hearing, and tens of millions of dollars annually for cough medicines, antacids, tranquilizers, and sleeping pills. Enough ambulance rides are provided to transport half the British population each year, far more proportionately than in the United States. That is fine for those who want free taxi service, but there is an opportunity cost: British ambulances are not equipped to American standards with the life-saving equipment needed for a true emergency.

The same tendency is seen in other countries with national health services. It has an easy explanation in terms of public choice theory. Only four people out of a hundred each year have really major medical needs (for the United States, $10,000 or more). That is not many votes compared with the millions who are nearsighted or need cough medicine.

On balance, then, there is no reason to think that bureaucratic regulation can make the health care system operate with the efficiency of a market system, even if it could achieve the same overall level of spending.

Equality The current U.S. health care system gets low marks by the standard of equality. Many poor, inner city residents have no contact with the health care system except through the overburdened emergency rooms of public and charitable hospitals. Among the working population, low-wage workers often receive "bare bones" health care benefits or none at all, while high-paid managerial and unionized workers get lavish first-dollar coverage. The tax advantage given to employer-paid health care is far more valuable to people in high tax brackets than to those lower on the economic scale. And studies show that when it comes to organ transplants, whites get more than their share compared to African-Americans, and wealthy people of all races get more than their share compared with poor people.

What is less well known is that bureaucratic control of health care in other countries also falls short of the mark in terms of equality. Consider the Canadian system. Canada is much more racially and culturally homogeneous than the United States, but its small minorities do not fare well. A study of Inuits and Crees in Quebec showed much higher infant mortality and shorter life expectancy than for other Canadians, in part because of less availability of health care services. Northern Ontario's aboriginal people were found to be similarly underserved. New Zealand, another country with comprehensive national health care, has a more significant minority population, the Maoris. They, too, have lower life expectancy and higher infant mortality than the general population, with only 20 percent of the difference explainable in terms of socioeconomic factors. Deaths from coronary diseases are higher, but the availability of cardiac surgery is lower in comparison to their numbers.[6]

---

6 See Goodman and Musgrave, "Twenty Myths About National Health Insurance," National Center for Policy Analysis Report No. 166, Dec. 1991.

Urban-rural inequalities in health care services can also be compared across countries. One British study found that the number of kidney patients receiving dialysis or transplants was 25 percent higher in London than in rural Yorkshire, and nearly twice as high as in the West Midlands. In Ontario, Canada, rural counties have only one-fourth the number of physicians per inhabitant as the provincial average. Overall, British Columbia has some of the best health care services-but even there, urban residents receive 37 percent more physician services and 55 percent more specialist services than rural residents.[7]

In short, bureaucratic regulation of the health care system is no guarantor of equality. Experience with such systems shows that politically influential groups-the relatively wealthy, members of dominant ethnic groups, and residents of major cities-come out ahead at the expense of the poor, ethnic minorities, and rural residents.

Next, we need to ask how patient power fares according to the standard of equality. In its simplest form, because it is a market-based system, it is neutral with regard to ethnic and geographical factors, and more capable of delivering health care services to those with money to save and spend than to those without. Even in its simplest form, it might provide more equality than today's hybrid of fee-for-service and bureaucratic elements. However, as Goodman and Musgrave point out, the patient power concept is flexible enough to build in additional equalizing tendencies without destroying its basic features. For example:

- In place of a simple tax deduction for contributions to MSAs, a refundable tax credit could be used. That would make an MSA just as attractive for families in low tax brackets as for their wealthy neighbors.

- The present Medicaid system that is supposed to provide health care for the very poor costs the government billions without doing its job very well. The same money could be used to subsidize medical savings accounts and catastrophic insurance coverage for people who have no incomes from which to make contributions of their own.

- Even with MSAs in place, a small percentage of the population would lack catastrophic health coverage because of uninsurable chronic diseases. A safety net program to subsidize catastrophic coverage for these individuals would not prevent the patient power system from doing its job for the two-thirds of health care costs that come to less than $5,000 per patient.

---

7 *Ibid.*

Liberty The standard under which patient power wins hands down is that of liberty. It does not force anyone to do anything. It represents an effort to remove existing barriers to a rational health care system, not a utopian scheme to build an ideal new system from the ground up.

Consider some of the options that are available under patient power:

- Individuals may buy high-deductible insurance policies and invest what they thereby save in tax-advantaged MSAs, but they do not have to do so. They can go right on buying low-deductible policies if they prefer.

- Employers may terminate health care benefits and use the savings to pay higher wages. Unlike today's system, employees will suffer no tax disadvantage by taking that money and buying health care on their own. But if workers and employers agree to do so, the employer (or a labor union) may act as the workers' agent, using its bargaining power to negotiate a better deal with hospitals or insurance companies.

- People may decide to pay for routine care out of their MSAs. But, if they prefer, they may, just as they can today, enroll in a health maintenance organization that provides those services for a fixed annual fee. The rules for tax deductions and tax credits would be written to make the system neutral with regard to the choice between MSAs and HMOs.

Admittedly, all this freedom of choice bothers some people. For example, First Lady Hillary Rodham Clinton has spoken out against MSAs because people might sometimes forego a visit to the doctor today in order to built up their MSA balance for the future, and many well-informed, rational consumers might want to do exactly that. A more rational balance between treatment of minor and major ailments is one potential source of increased efficiency. It is also possible that some foolish health care consumers would neglect a cut until it got infected or neglect a lump in their breast until it became inoperable. But people do such foolish things today. They also smoke, drink too much, and eat too much fatty food.

Wherever there are foolish people, there are others who think themselves wise enough to manage their neighbors' lives down to the last detail. To them, it is equally urgent to impose one set of regulations to keep some people from spending too much on health care, and another set of regulations to keep them from spending too little. "Too much" and "too little" always means what the all-wise regulator wants, not what the consumer wants. So if you like one-size-fits-all health care, patient power is not the system for you.

Questions for thought and discussion

1. College students often lack good information about what they ought to study in a course in economics. (Questionnaires given on the first day of class often show that students think economics is "about how to make money" or "about the stock market.") As in other courses, they rely on their professor as an agent to tell them what is important for them to learn. Do you think the incentive structure of a typical university provides professors with good incentives to be honest, unbiased agents in this respect? Might there be circumstances under which they would get lazy and teach too little, or get carried away, and try to cram too much into the course? Do you think the situation would be improved by introducing a fee-for-service system of compensation under which professors were paid extra for each book and each homework problem that they assigned to their students? Discuss, with comparisons to health care.

2. One reason health insurance is so expensive in the United States today is that many states have "mandated benefit" laws that specify what a policy must cover. Lobbyists from every branch of health care and related professions all want their specialties covered. Many states insist on coverage for *in vitro* fertilization, alcoholism, and drug abuse. Minnesota covers hairpieces, California covers marriage counseling, and Massachusetts covers deposits to sperm banks. In these states, insurance companies are forbidden to offer, and consumers forbidden to buy, "bare bones" coverage without these extras. How do you think these nonessential health care services should be handled under a patient power system? Should people be allowed to use MSA accounts to pay for some of them? Any of them? What definition of "health care" would you apply?

3. Long before the Angela Lakeburg case, the case of a five-year-old boy named Donjie McNair made headlines. Donjie needed a $140,000 liver transplant, and his parents had no insurance. Finally, the state of Illinois agreed to pay, but it was too late—Donjie was by that time too weak to undergo the operation, and he died. Jerome Kraut, a Chicago pediatrician who cared for Donjie, was quoted as saying "little sick kids should get whatever's necessary, no matter what it costs."

   a. In a world of scarcity, is it really possible to provide medical care for children "no matter what it costs?" Which system do you think would come closer—today's system, patient power, or bureaucratic regulation?

   b. In your opinion, should "little sick kids" get a higher priority than big sick adults? Than old sick grandparents? On what economic or ethical standards do you base your opinion? Which system would treat various age groups most equitably in your view—today's system, patient power, or bureaucratic regulation?

Selected references

Goodman, John C. and Gerald L. Musgrave. *Patient Power: The Free-Enterprise Alternative to Clinton's Health Care Plan.* Washington, D.C.: Cato Institution, 1994. *A concise exposition of the market-based health care system discussed in this chapter. A longer version was published in 1992 under the title,* Patient Power: Solving America's Health Care Crisis.

Newhouse, Joseph P. "Medical Care Costs: How Much Welfare Loss?" *Journal of Economic Perspectives,* Summer 1992, pp. 3-22. *Analyzes the costs of rising health care costs in the United States. Two related papers appear in the same issue of this journal.*

President's Council of Economic Advisers. *Economic Report of the President.* Washington, D.C.: Government Printing Office, annually. *The 1993 edition outlines the health care policy views of the outgoing Bush administration. The 1994 edition sets out the Clinton administration's ideas.*

Weisbrod, Burton A. "The Health Care Quadrilemma." *Journal of Economic Literature,* June 1991, pp. 523-552. *This discussion places special emphasis on the interaction of the health care payment system and the incentives for research and investment in new medical technology.*

Key terms

Real. A term used to denote an economic measure that has been adjusted to take into account the effects of inflation.

Copayment rate. Under the terms of an insurance policy, the percentage of a given loss that the policyholder must pay out of pocket.

Agent. A person who acts on behalf of another, known as the principal.

Principal. A person on whose behalf another person, known as an agent, acts.

Deductible clause. A clause in an insurance policy that specifies a limit below which the policyholder must pay the entire cost of a loss.

4

Economics of Health Care (II): The Insurance Mess

Thirty-nine million Americans without health insurance at any one time! Fifty-eight million Americans without health insurance at some time during the year! How many times has that fact been repeated in Congressional debate, in presidential press conferences, on talk shows and on editorial pages. These numbers convey a stunning image of inequity: super-high-tech, gee-whiz care for some, nothing at all for others, and in the world's richest country, at that. Small wonder President Clinton made universal coverage the centerpiece of his proposal for health care reform in 1994. He declared a willingness to compromise on any detail of reform legislation so long as it guaranteed universal coverage.

To be sure, this figure, like many statistics, contains an element of overstatement. It is an exaggeration to think that the 58 million, who constitute a fifth of the entire population, are simply locked out of the health care system by cruel economic necessity. For example:[1]

- Sixty percent of the uninsured are under 30 years old, in the healthiest group of the population. Many of these choose not to purchase insurance because it is cheaper for them to cover medical costs out of pocket.

---

1 See John C. Goodman and Gerald L. Musgrave, *Patient Power*, (Washington, D.C.: Cato Institute, 1993), Ch. 4; and National Center for Policy Analysis, "The Myth of Universal Coverage," *Brief Analysis 103*, May 11, 1994.

- Although many poor people lack insurance, not all the uninsured are poor. More than half live in families with a full-time working adult member. Nine million of the uninsured live in families with annual incomes over $30,000, more than twice the poverty level.

- Lack of insurance is not a long-term problem for most people. Half of the 58 million who are uninsured for at least one month during the year are uninsured for six months or less, three-fourths for 12 months or less, and less than a fifth for two years or more.

- Uninsured people are not deprived of medical care altogether. Once hospitalized, they receive virtually the same care as the insured. Total health care received by the average uninsured person is 64 percent of that received by insured persons.

- Data on those lacking health insurance should be seen in context of other insurance and health care systems. For example, although most states require automobile liability insurance, 14 percent of drivers lack such insurance. In Hawaii, where an employer-based, mandated insurance system is in effect, from 6 to 11 percent of the population is uninsured. Even in the Canadian province of British Columbia, 2 to 5 percent of the population lacks health insurance.

Still, even if uninsured Americans are not left to bleed to death in the street because they don't have a Blue Cross-Blue Shield card to show the ambulance driver, it would be wrong to think that all is well. In fact, the U.S. health insurance system is a mess. It suffers from historical quirks that set it apart from other kinds of insurance. It is heavily distorted by government regulation. In many cases, it does not deserve the name of insurance at all.

Thus, even though many of the uninsured are voluntarily outside the health insurance system today, they might well join it if it worked better. This chapter will look at the health insurance mess and examine a variety of ideas on what to do about it. The first section of the chapter will review some principles of insurance in general. Next, we will see how health insurance differs from other forms of insurance. The last section of the chapter will evaluate possible reforms.

How insurance works

To understand the strengths and weaknesses of the U.S. health insurance system, we first need to know a little about how insurance in general works. Most families carry several kinds of insurance: automobile insurance to cover theft, collision damage, and liability; homeowners insurance to cover fire, storm damage, and burglary; life insurance; disability insurance; and perhaps other kinds of coverage as well. All of these share some general principles of operation.

Risk pooling Most kinds of insurance cover risks that cause a potentially severe loss but have a low probability of occurring. Home fire insurance is a good example. Suppose that the loss from destruction of your house by fire would be $100,000, but that there is just one chance in 1,000 that such a fire will occur in a given year. The expected value of loss is just $100 per year ($100,000 ÷ 1,000). However, behind this small expected value stands the reality that the uninsured loss of your home would be a catastrophe that would be more than 1,000 times more painful than the loss of $100.

Fortunately, the risk of fire is one that can be managed by *risk pooling*. Reduced to its simplest form, it works this way. You and 999 of your neighbors make an agreement. Each year each of you will pay $100 into a common fund. Anyone whose house burns down then has the right to take $100,000 out of the fund to rebuild. On the average, there will be enough money in the fund to compensate the victims of fire.

Of course, there are many technicalities. The fund would need a reserve in case, by bad luck, two or more houses burned down in one year. There would be administrative expenses to cover, so everyone would have to put in a little more than $100 per year to pay those. Inspectors might have to be hired to deal with possible fraud, and so forth. For all these reasons, people don't usually insure through simple neighborhood associations like that we have described. They hire an insurance company to administer the plan, just as they hire a banker to invest their savings. But in one way or another, the idea of risk pooling lies behind all insurance.

Insurable risks Not all risks are easily managed by insurance, however. Experience has shown that certain characteristics are required to make a risk insurable. An *insurable risk* is one that fits, or comes close to fitting, the following characteristics:

- The loss should be *fortuitous*. A fortuitous loss is one that is accidental, unforeseen, and unexpected. Losses caused purposely by the insured party are usually not insurable.

- *Many similar units* should be exposed to the risk. Home fire insurance and automobile theft insurance are examples. Unique risks are harder to insure.

- The probability and magnitude of loss should be *measurable*. For example, the likelihood that a certain model of car will be stolen can be calculated from police records and the dollar amount of loss calculated from standard listings of used car prices.

- The loss should strike *at random*. Risk pooling requires that only a few units suffer the loss each year. Catastrophic risks—those that strike most or all units in a pool at once—are usually not insurable. For example, war risks are generally considered uninsurable.

- *The probability of loss should be small*. If the loss is certain, the concept of risk pooling makes no sense. When the loss is very likely (although not certain), the premium, when administrative costs are included, may exceed the amount of loss.

These five characteristics are matters of degree. Few risks fit them perfectly. In some cases, special techniques can be used to insure risks that violate one or another of these characteristics.[2] But if too many of the conditions for insurability do not hold, private companies will not cover a risk. The risk of unemployment is a good example. Private unemployment insurance is not sold, partly because the risk is not fortuitous (people's choice of occupations and behavior on the job affect their likelihood of unemployment) and partly because unemployment losses strike many people at once during a national recession.

Moral hazard When losses are not entirely fortuitous, but depend to some extent on the behavior of the insured person, a situation of **moral hazard** is said to exist—a situation in which the insured, knowing that a loss will be covered, takes fewer precautions to avoid loss.

Extreme cases of moral hazard involve outright fraud. For example, the owner of a building, unable to find a buyer, may obtain insurance and then burn the building down. Or the owner of a valuable painting may insure it and then arrange for it to be "stolen" by a partner. Moral hazard is by no means limited to such cases, however. In less extreme cases, the insured person is simply somewhat less careful than would be the case if the loss were not covered. The owner of an expensive car may leave it parked in an unsafe neighborhood. A homeowner may forget to

---

2 For example, the famous insurance association Lloyds of London is often able to cover unique risks, like the risk of an actor not being able to finish the filming of a movie. By insuring many risks, each of which is unique, and spreading the risk among many investors, Lloyds engages in a special sort of risk pooling. Another technique is reinsurance. It would be hard for a locally based company to sell hurricane insurance, because all houses in town might be damaged in a single storm. However, reinsurance allows the risk to be shared with other companies operating in other areas.

change the batteries in the basement smoke detector, or leave costly jewelry around the house instead of keeping it in a safe deposit box.

Insurance companies have a number of ways of limiting moral hazard. One method is to require certain precautions, or give a discount if those precautions are taken. (For example, a restaurant may be required to have a sprinkler system or a homeowner may get a discount for installing a burglar alarm.) Another method is to require the policy holder to share part of the loss. As discussed in Chapter 3, this can be done with a deductible clause that requires the insured party to pay the first several hundred dollars before insurance coverage takes over. It can also be done with a coinsurance clause that requires the policy holder to pay a share (say, 20 percent) of the cost of the loss. Finally, insurers employ investigators to look carefully into the circumstances of any suspicious loss to discover fraud or violation of the policy agreement.

In many cases, losses that are not purely fortuitous can be insured despite moral hazard. However, the costs of guarding against carelessness and fraud raises the premium, making the policy less attractive economically.

Adverse selection   For a loss to be insurable, it must be measurable. This is necessary in order to classify losses into similar groups and calculate an appropriate premium—a process known as **underwriting**. For example, automobile insurance companies charge different premiums by age and gender, because their underwriters know, from experience, that young drivers are at a greater risk of accident than more experienced drivers, and that young men have more accidents, on average, than young women.

An insurance plan that offers the same coverage and premium to groups with different degrees of risk encounters a problem called **adverse selection**. This term refers to the tendency of people most likely to suffer a loss to be most likely to seek insurance.

For example, suppose the Fair Play Insurance Corp. decides to do away with separate auto insurance rates for young men and young women. It knows that young men suffer an average loss of $2,000 per year and young women an average loss of $1,000 per year. Expecting to insure equal numbers of young men and women, it offers a unisex policy at a premium of $1,500 (plus a little extra for administrative expenses profit). Its competitors charge young men $2,000 and young women $1,000.

Much to the company's surprise, it will find that few if any young women buy the unisex policy. However, droves of young men leave their former insurers in order to switch to Fair Play. As a result, Fair Play experiences losses averaging $2,000 per policy—$500 more than the premium charged. To stay in business, it must raise its premium. If it does not return to the industry practice of separate rates for young men and young women, it will end up insuring only high-risk drivers. This is adverse selection in action.

Skillful underwriting can often control adverse selection, provided that the insurer can calculate each group's risk accurately. The problem becomes much harder to control in a situation of *information asymmetry*—one where the insured person can more accurately estimate the degree of risk than the insurer. For example, suppose Fair Play Insurance Corp. decided to offer grade insurance for college students. A covered student who got an "F" in economics would be eligible to claim $1,000 to cover the cost of taking the course over.

The company's underwriters could try to estimate the various probabilities of different groups passing the economics course. For example, it might find that math and engineering majors are more likely to pass than students who have not yet declared a major. The premium could be varied accordingly. Still, individual students are subjectively much more able than the company to judge their danger of failing. Weak students would buy the insurance and strong ones would not. This would push the premium higher and higher until the policy was attractive to no one.

Moral hazard, adverse selection, and information asymmetry often interact in troublesome ways. The case of automobile insurance for young men is an example. The reason they have more losses, on average, than young women, is because some young men drive carelessly. This is a problem of moral hazard. However, it is hard for insurance companies to know in advance which young men will drive carefully and which carelessly, even though the individuals themselves may know how often they exceed the speed limit or drive after drinking. This is a problem of information asymmetry. Thus, although some young men drive just as safely as the average young woman, the company can't tell who they are. Any attempt by insurance companies to offer them special safe-driver discounts leaves the company open to the problem of adverse selection.

Having provided this overview, we turn to the special problem of health insurance. Health insurance shares many problems with fire, theft, or accident insurance, but it also has some special problems of its own. In the next section, we will look at what is different about health insurance as well as what it has in common with other varieties.

Why health insurance is different

The origins of the American health care system. Few sectors of the economy have been transformed more completely in the past 100 years than the health care system.[3] In the nineteenth century, hospitals were rare. They were charitable institutions where the poor were sent to be treated—and often to die. In a world without effective antiseptics, let alone antibiotics, it was safer to be treated at home.

---

3 For a short history of the American health care system, see Stuart M. Butler and Edmund F. Haislmaier, eds., *A National Health System for America* (Washington, D.C.: Heritage Foundation, 1989), Ch. 1. That account, in turn, draws on Paul Starr, *The Social Transformation of American Medicine* (New York: Basic Books, 1982).

Health care for most people meant a visit from the doctor. They paid the doctor out of pocket, just as they would pay to have a dress made or horse shod.

In the last quarter of the nineteenth century and the first quarter of the twentieth, a revolution took place. Between 1873 and 1923, the number of hospitals in the United States grew from 149 to 6,830. Hospitals were transformed from warehouses for the dying into "medical workshops" where all manner of diseases were treated-and increasingly often, cured.

By the 1930s, the country had as many hospital beds per capita as it does today. The health care payment system had hardly changed, however. Between 80 and 90 percent of health care costs continued to be paid out of pocket, and much of the rest was provided by private charities. Insurance plans were a rarity.

The Great Depression hit the newly built hospital system hard. Doctors, like many other professionals, had to tighten their belts when their patients couldn't pay. Hospitals, which had high fixed costs, were hit even harder. In 1929, the Baylor University Hospital hit upon a new idea. It introduced a plan for 1,500 schoolteachers, under which each teacher would pay a fee of $6 per year, and in return, would be guaranteed up to 21 days of hospital care. The plan made health care costs more predictable for the teachers and gave the hospital a steady flow of cash. Everyone liked it. It was followed by other similar plans that grew into the not-for-profit Blue Cross system.

After the Depression came World War II. During the war, strict wage and price controls were used to combat inflation. With millions of men in the military, labor shortages were widespread. To compete for skilled labor, employers found a loophole: They couldn't raise wages, but they could offer added fringe benefits. One of the most popular was employer-paid health insurance. When the Internal Revenue Service ruled employer-paid health insurance to be tax deductible, the new concept got the advantage it needed to survive in the postwar economy.

By the 1950s, the distinctive features of the U.S. health care payments system were all in place:

- The system was strongly oriented toward providing a steady flow of income to hospitals and other health care providers.

- It often provided first-dollar coverage for small medical expenses while leaving catastrophic and long-term needs uncovered.

- It was provided primarily through employers.

Some of the perverse incentives inherent in this system were discussed in Chapter 3. We can now get a further understanding of its problems by comparing it to other forms of insurance.

Insurance that is not insurance We begin by noting that many of the losses covered by conventional health insurance do not fit the characteristics of insurable risks. In particular:

- Health insurance is not limited to purely fortuitous risks. Self-inflicted injuries are covered. Illnesses due to imprudent behavior-overeating, smoking, unsafe sex-are usually covered. Both patient and doctor often have considerable discretion in whether and how to treat.

- It is not limited to random losses suffered by only a few policyholders each year. A high percentage of policyholders make claims each year and few of them never use their insurance.

- It is not limited to risks with a small probability of loss. Even small, routine services are covered. Increasingly, services like eyeglasses and dental care are covered, which many people take full advantage of every year.

There are two possible explanations of this situation. One is that health insurers or regulators have found a way to make water run uphill. The other is that so-called "health" insurance is not insurance at all.

Both explanations are partly correct. In some cases, regulations and tax rules make it profitable or compulsory to cover risks that would normally not be uninsurable. At the same time, much health coverage is not insurance in the normal sense, but rather, a system for prepayment of nonrandom, nonfortuitous health care expenses.

To understand the difference between true insurance and a prepayment plan, let's return to the familiar automotive example. Most car owners, unless their vehicle is a real clunker, buy collision insurance. Although there are some problems of moral hazard and adverse selection, a collision is basically a fortuitous, random event. With careful underwriting, automobile collision insurance is profitable for the companies that offer it and provides security to policyholders.

Automobile insurance policies do not, however, cover the risk of mechanical failure or preventative maintenance. One reason is that the problems of adverse selection and moral hazard are more severe than in the case of collisions. Another is that many repairs are nearly certain occurrences—a timing belt at 40,000 miles, an alternator at 60,000 miles, and so on.

Nevertheless, it is possible to buy prepaid automobile maintenance services. A basic mechanical warranty is included with every new car. Extended service agreements that cover all costs for five years or 50,000 miles are sold as an extra with both new and used cars. These maintenance agreements are not insurance. The provider enters into them with the certainty that the services will actually be used. There is still some element of risk pooling for the customer. For example, the owner is protected against the bad luck that a new timing belt will be needed at 20,000 rather than 40,000 miles. But still, over the life of the agreement, the amount paid for service will not be very different whether an extended service plan or out-of-pocket payments are used.

In the health care field, one alternative to conventional insurance, the health maintenance organization (HMO), closely resembles an automotive extended service agreement. An HMO is a group of providers of hospital and physician services who agree to supply all needed care in return for a fixed annual fee. An HMO is sometimes described as a hospital married to an insurance company, but prepaid medical care is a better description.

In sum, health insurance includes a strong element of prepayment for routine, predictable, nonfortuitous health care. However, both conventional plans and HMOs do include an element of true insurance to the extent that they cover relatively rare, random, and catastrophic conditions as well: major cancer, kidney failure, and so on.

Prepaid health care and fee-for-service medicine don't mix For reasons discussed in Chapter 3, prepaid, first-dollar health care coverage for routine services, combined with retrospective, fee-for-service reimbursement, makes poor economic sense. The combination provides patient, doctor, and hospital alike with incentives to provide any and all possible services constrained only by the maxim, "do no harm." It lies behind much of the growth of health care expenditures in the United States during the post-World War II decades.

In retrospect, we can see that this inherently defective system came into being and survived primarily because government regulations and tax laws artificially favored it over market-oriented alternatives. In Chapter 3 we explained why medical savings accounts (MSAs) are an economically more attractive alternative for small and moderate health care expenses. All they need to become widespread is to level the playing field in terms of tax advantages.

In addition, it is worth adding a further comment on HMOs. They offer an economically reasonable alternative, attractive to many people, just as automotive extended service agreements are attractive to some, but not all, car buyers. A full discussion of the economics of HMOs is beyond the scope of this chapter. They are not the perfect solution to all problems of health care economics, but they would probably earn a place, in competition with alternatives, in a market-oriented health care system.

But if this is true, why are HMOs not already the dominant form of health care? When paid for by employers, they do, after all, enjoy the same tax advantages as conventional insurance, and they offer superior incentives for cost containment. Part of the answer turns out to be that up to 1973, state laws restricting "corporate practice of medicine" made it difficult to form HMOs. In 1973, Congress passed the Health Maintenance Organization Act that preempted state laws in this area. Over the next 15 years, enrollment in HMOs grew from 3 million to 28 million people, and is still growing.

Reforming insurance for catastrophic medical risks

In the previous section, we concluded that insurance does not work well as a way to pay for small, routine health care expenses. However, this does not get us very far in answering the question, Why do so many people not have any health care coverage? Discussions of the uninsured usually focus not on routine care, but on coverage of acute, catastrophic medical needs.

It is possible to separate the two kinds of coverage. Most insurers offer special catastrophic coverage with high deductibles ($2,500, $5,000, or even $10,000), but also with low copayment requirements (or none), high lifetime maximum coverage, and relatively few exclusions. The risks covered by these policies more closely fit the criteria of insurability than do small, routine expenses. Because they are free of some of the perverse incentives inherent in low-deductible policies, they cost much less. A $10,000 deductible policy can cost only a third as much as a $250 deductible policy. Why is it, then, that so many people lack even catastrophic coverage? The answers vary for different groups.

People with low income or few assets One reason some people lack health insurance is that they are poor. Of the 39 million uninsured Americans, about an estimated 13 to 15 million live in households with less than $10,000 annual family income. They cannot afford decent housing or clothing and in some cases do not even get enough to eat. This group also includes people who have difficulty managing their lives in a general sense—alcoholics and drug addicts, habitual criminals, and the noninstitutionalized mentally ill. Providing health care coverage for these people is part of antipoverty policy as a whole. No matter what kind of health care system we had, some poor people would be left outside it unless subsidized by public agencies or private charity.

In addition to the very poor, another ten million or so of the uninsured have family incomes in the $10,000-$20,000 range. In many cases they cannot afford coverage of the kind offered by today's health insurance system. However, if insurers were encouraged to offer slimmed-down policies that focused on essential health needs, and at the same time tax credits were used to equalize tax advantages, many of the near-poor might be able to participate in the market for health care.

Still another group of the uninsured—it is hard to say how many—consist of healthy, young people with jobs and reasonable incomes but with few assets. They face a somewhat different calculus that may lead them to choose not to purchase health insurance. First, they do not find it attractive to join high-priced insurance pools that, because of adverse selection, are filled with people less healthy than they are. And second, they know that the health care system is not likely to deprive them of care altogether if they become acutely ill.

If such a person does become seriously ill, there are ways to obtain care. One, not always but often possible, is to join an employer-sponsored group after becoming ill, perhaps by changing jobs or perhaps through coverage of another family member. Another recourse is to show up at the emergency room of a public or charitable hospital and throw one's self on the mercy of the attending physicians. Well-publicized horror stories notwithstanding, such cases are rarely thrown out to die on the sidewalk. For a person who has substantial assets, say a home or large cash savings, this is not an attractive strategy. The hospital will take them to court and attach their property to pay their bill. But if the person is young, lives in an apartment, and has few savings, the financial risk is small.

Health care reform should aim to draw as many as possible of this group into a market-based system. Unfortunately, as we will see shortly, some current and proposed regulations have the opposite effect.

Unemployed, self-employed, and small-business employees Another group of uninsured people consists of people who are temporarily unemployed, self-employed, or employed by small businesses. They end up without insurance largely because of the system's bias toward employer-paid coverage.

In part, as we said before, the problem is one of taxation. An employer paying for health benefits with pretax dollars is often able to buy coverage at less than half the cost of buying the same benefits with after-tax dollars. Making privately purchased health insurance, HMO membership, and/or MSA contributions tax deductible would help alleviate this problem. Making them subject to a tax credit would help even more. The reason is that a tax credit would have the same dollar value to a high-income, self-employed professional, a person temporarily unemployed between two well-paying jobs, and a person holding a steady low-wage job with a small employer.

Taxes are not the only issue, however. Other factors also favor employment-based plans. To begin with, the employees of a large corporation are likely to be at least as healthy as the average for their communities. Because they do not include people with severe health problems that prevent them from working, they in fact tend to be healthier than average. The fact that it is not easy to join such a corporation just to get the health benefits (you also have to be able to do your job) makes employer-based groups at least partially free of the problem of adverse selection. Moreover, the employees of a large corporation are a large enough group to offer extensive risk pooling, which makes such groups less costly to cover. And finally, a large firm may have the bargaining power needed to drive a particularly good bargain with an insurer, hospital, or HMO. All of these factors help control the cost of employer-provided plans.

Small business plans do not share these advantages. Unlike large corporations, where risks are spread among many employees so that losses vary little from year to year, the cost of medical care for employees of a small business can be strongly affected by just one major illness or injury. To guard themselves against adverse selection, insurers often recalculate the premium to be charged each year on the basis of the past year's experience. This turns the policy into a "get sick now, pay later" plan that is often not economically attractive and cannot really be considered true insurance.

One possible solution to this problem is "guaranteed renewable" insurance. Such a policy does not allow cancellation or a prohibitive premium increase after an illness begins. Some individual plans already have these provisions. If such policies were available to small businesses as well, it would become more feasible for them to provide insurance to their employees. Another approach favored by some reformers is to make it easier for several small businesses to join together to bargain for health insurance coverage, thus gaining some of the advantages that large employers already enjoy.

The chronically ill A final group who lack insurance coverage are people with expensive, long-term, chronic illnesses. Examples are genetic disorders, multiple sclerosis, diabetes, chronic kidney disease, and AIDS. These conditions pose problems of insurability under the best of circumstances, and the current system tends to make matters worse.

Chronic illnesses become uninsurable when the point is reached where the need for expensive treatment becomes a certainty. People who are HIV positive but have not yet developed the symptoms of AIDS are a good example. Putting together a group of such people provides very little by way of risk pooling, since all of them will require expensive treatment sooner or later, unless, perhaps, they die in an auto accident before they become ill. If an insurance company did offer a policy for HIV positives, the premium would be so high that the policy would become just another prepayment mechanism.[4]

Several points need to be made about coverage for the chronically ill. First, it has become popular in some circles to blame their problems on the alleged greed of insurers who heartlessly insist on enrolling only healthy people. But greed and heartlessness have nothing to do with it. Adverse selection makes it literally impossible for a private insurer in a competitive market to offer low rates to the chronically ill.

Remember Fair Play Insurance, which tried to offer automotive coverage at the same rate to young men and women. Suppose Fair Play now decides to offer an individual health policy without requiring an HIV test, while its competitors do require tests. Soon everyone who is HIV positive will buy from Fair Play. If Fair Play then raises its premium to reflect the increase in claims, it will drive away all its healthy customers. If it keeps its rates low to retain its healthy customers, it will receive less revenue from premiums than it pays out in claims, and it will be driven out of business.

Moreover, even if almost all companies try to be good guys and cover the chronically ill, just one company can force all the rest to abandon the practice.

---

4 In this section, we focus on high probability of loss as the reason for uninsurability. It is worth noting in passing that some serious chronic illnesses also involve a high degree of moral hazard. Those associated with substance abuse are one kind of example. AIDS also falls into this category to the extent that many victims contract the disease as the result of high-risk behavior.

Imagine that tomorrow, a researcher discovers a test, which, administered at age 15, can definitely predict multiple sclerosis. If one company starts using the test, it can offer those who test negative a somewhat lower rate. That company will progressively attract more and more MS negatives. As the percentage of MS positives in the pools insured by other companies grows, they will have to raise their rates to break even. Eventually, this process of adverse selection makes the rate differential so great that companies are forced to test in order to survive.

The only way of insuring against catastrophic chronic illnesses is to enter into a guaranteed renewable contract with an insurance company before the risk becomes known. Once the policy is in force, the company cannot cancel it. However, this strategy does not always work.

First, the disease may be developed in childhood or it may be possible to test for it in childhood, even if the disease itself develops only later. Advances in genetic testing are putting more and more conditions in this category each year. Thus, by the time a person becomes an adult and seeks insurance on his or her own for the first time, it may already be too late.

Second, insurance companies are less enthusiastic than they once were about offering guaranteed renewable policies, in some cases because of regulatory restrictions. Because guaranteed renewable polices are expensive or hard to find, some people, especially when they are young, will buy coverage that is not guaranteed renewable. They will then find their coverage canceled or their premiums raised to the sky as soon as they become ill.

Third, employer-based insurance hampers the guaranteed-renewable strategy. In some cases, people who have developed a chronic illness get locked into a job that they would like to change because they know they could never be covered again after leaving their current employer. These are the lucky ones. The unlucky ones become too sick to work, or get laid off in a recession, or are working for a small business with inadequate coverage at the moment they develop the chronic illness. They then get shut out of the insurance system altogether.

No purely market-based reform can overcome all the insurance problems of the chronically ill—although some, such as separating insurance from employment, could help. Most discussions of health care for the chronically ill focus on some role for the government as an "insurer of last resort." Twenty-eight states already have plans that make coverage available to the chronically ill at rates that, although higher than those paid by healthy people, are still affordable. These plans lose money because they pay out more in claims than they take in as premiums. The losses are not enormous, however. According to one estimate, extending such plans nationwide would cost only about $300 million—less than one-tenth of one percent of total national health care costs.

Community rating proposals Many people are angered by insurance companies' practice of rejecting sick people and writing policies only for the healthy. This seems to them the opposite of what is needed. When they are told that insurance companies are forced by competition and adverse selection to act this way, their response is to regulate competition out of existence. If all companies were forced to sell policies to the sick and the healthy alike, they reason, no company would have a competitive advantage over another. The cost of caring for the chronically ill would be spread among the healthy policyholders of all companies, with a resulting increase in fairness and accessibility of coverage.

Reforms of this type are called community rating because they require the same rate to be charged to everyone in a given community, regardless of age or health. There is an element of logic in favor of community rating: If the idea of insurance is to pool risks, then the larger the pool, the better risks are spread. To put it another way, today's insurance protects people against the risk of being struck by a specific, fortuitous illness, but it does not fully protect them against the risk of falling into a high-risk group, such as diabetics or HIV positives. Community rating aims to cure this perceived defect of the system.

Unfortunately, like many well-intentioned proposals, community rating is subject to the law of unintended consequences. Experience shows that the scheme does not eliminate adverse selection, but only causes it to emerge in a new form.

A 1993 community rating law adopted by New York State illustrates the problem. Before the reform took effect, a 25-year-old male in Albany could buy an individual policy from Mutual of Omaha for $64.45 a month.[5] A 55-year-old male paid $141.79 for the same policy. After the reform, the price became $107.33 for both customers. If no residents of the state had changed their behavior in response to these price changes, community rating would have accomplished exactly what it set out to do.

However, people did change their behavior, and in exactly the way the law of demand would predict. Young, healthy people became less likely to purchase insurance, because the premium now far exceeded their expected health care costs. Older people and people with chronic illnesses became more likely to purchase insurance, which was now a great bargain. As a result, the average age of insured people rose by 3.5 years in the first year the plan was in effect. People over 50 jumped from 20 percent of enrollment to 26 percent. The total number of insured in the state dropped by 1.2 percent, with the decrease concentrated among individual policyholders. Their enrollment dropped by 12.4 percent. In all, 500,000 people with individual and small group coverage canceled their policies, reducing the total number of insured from 2.8 to 2.3 million.[6]

Because of these changes, the average size of claim jumped dramatically. For Mutual of Omaha, it increased from $3,800 to $7,900. (Nationwide, the company's claims increased by an average of just $400 that year.) In response, insurance

---

5 See Leslie Scism, "New York Finds Fewer People Have Health Insurance a Year After Reform," *The Wall Street Journal*, May 27, 1994, p. A2.

6 Marke E. Litow and Drew S. Davidoff, *The Impact of Guaranteed Issue and Community Rating in the State of New York*, (New York: Millman and Robertson, 1994).

companies were forced to raise rates. In 1994, the rate for a 55-year-old male in Albany went up to $145.19—$4 per month higher than before community rating was enacted.

The tendency of young, healthy people to drop out of insurance pools is not the only effect of community rating. Over a longer period of time, such a policy encourages large corporations to opt for self-insurance for their employees rather than buy coverage from an insurance company. A company that self-insures simply pays its employees' health costs directly. For a firm with many employees, the degree of risk pooling within the firm is enough to make this practical. Because corporate employees are somewhat healthier than the average population, any increase in corporate self-insurance adds to the tendency of community rating to load insurance pools with high-risk policyholders.

In short, while driving adverse selection out at the door, community rating lets it back in through the window. The New York State experience shows the full force of the law of unintended consequences: The actual (as opposed to intended) result of community rating is to reduce (not increase) the number of insured persons and to increase (not reduce) the premium for older policyholders of average health. There is still a gain for the minority of chronically ill who could not get insurance at all before. But compared to subsidized risk pools for the chronically ill, community rating as a grossly inefficient way to benefit this group.

Mandated benefits Mandated benefits are another popular type of health care reform. As noted in Chapter 3, such laws, which now exist in nearly every state, force companies to include certain treatments or conditions in their minimum package of coverage. Chiropractic care and treatment of AIDS, alcoholism, and drug abuse are mandated in many states. The services of acupuncture therapists, naturopaths (practitioners of herbal medicine), marriage counselors, and laboratories for *in vitro* fertilization are mandated in some states.

Two sets of forces lie behind these laws. One is pressure from well-intentioned reformers who like mandated benefits for the same reason they like community rating. They see policies that exclude conditions like AIDS and alcoholism as just another way that greedy insurance companies make profits on the backs of the healthy while refusing to serve those truly in need. By mandating coverage, the reformers, once again, hope to broaden the risk pool and spread the cost of treating these conditions more fairly.

The other force behind mandated benefits is rent seeking on the part of health care providers. Obviously chiropractors, naturopaths, and sperm banks want to get in on the mandated benefits gravy train. So what if most people would never buy these exotic health care services if they had to spend their own money? Give them someone else's money to spend! Before mandated benefits, these specialties had to price their services competitively to attract any customers at all away from conventional medicine. Now they can charge as much or more as conventional doctors and still attract clients. The only losers are those who doubt the need or efficacy of such treatments—too bad for them!

Not surprisingly, mandated benefit laws, like community rating, fall victim to the law of unintended consequences. To see why, we need to understand why insurance companies tend to exclude coverage of the listed conditions and treatments in the first place.

Recall that the first requirement for insurability is that the insured risk be fortuitous. To the extent a claim is the result of a choice made by the policyholder, there is a problem of moral hazard. If information asymmetry is also present—that is, if policyholders know better than insurers how likely they are to engage in risky behavior—moral hazard will be compounded by adverse selection. Alcoholism, drug abuse, artificial fertilization, and cases of AIDS originating in risky behavior all fit this pattern. They are simply not insurable risks in the ordinary sense. Services of chiropractors, acupuncture specialists, and naturopaths are uninsurable for a closely related reason. Many people seek treatment from these specialists not for acute, life-threatening conditions, but rather, for less clearly defined conditions of chronic discomfort. Unlike a broken leg or a breast tumor, these conditions are less clearly fortuitous. In some cases, it is even difficult for insurers to know whether the condition is real or exists only in the policyholder's imagination.

Coverage for abortion, as would have been required under the Clinton administration health reform proposal, is an especially clear example of the flaws of mandated benefits. There are two problems here. First, the need for an abortion usually does not arise fortuitously. Sexually inactive people, people who want children, and people who do not want children but use effective birth control are all at very low risk of needing an abortion. Second, a great many people are morally opposed to abortion. Even if they do engage in behaviors that risk unwanted pregnancy, they will not turn to abortion as the solution. Yet it is hard for insurance company underwriters to deal with the different degree of risks faced by different individuals because of information asymmetry. People who engage in sexual relations without contraception or the desire for children are likely to lie about the fact to their insurers, who, they know, cannot police their policyholders' bedrooms. Nor can policyholders reliably be expected to report their religious or moral convictions regarding abortion. What would keep a freedom-of-choice advocate from pretending to be a right-to-lifer if doing so would cut her insurance premium? In short, the risk of needing an abortion is simply not insurable.

Losses characterized by moral hazard and information asymmetry are inherently expensive to insure. Therefore, mandating their coverage drives up premiums. The result is an adverse selection cycle exactly like that resulting from community rating. As the cost of policies rise, young, healthy people—especially those who do not drink excessively, use drugs, or engage in high-risk sexual behavior—drop out of insurance pools. Corporations choose self-insurance, which is not subject to mandated benefits. The final result is decreased insurance coverage for young people, people with low incomes, and employees of small businesses.

Health insurance reform: An evaluation

We have now seen how insurance works in general and how health insurance differs from other kinds. We have also mentioned a number of proposed reforms of health insurance policy. To complete the chapter, we will evaluate a number of these reforms in terms of the standards of efficiency, equality, and liberty.

Efficiency In a competitive market context, insurance is inherently beneficial to efficiency. It is most obviously so in the case of a pure mutual insurance pool, where risks are voluntarily shared among a number people similarly exposed. But the same is true for a policy bought from a commercial insurance company. For such a company, the premium charged must be higher than the total of claims plus administrative expenses to allow for a profit. For the insured party, however, even though in statistical terms the expected value of benefits received is smaller than the premium paid, the policy is still attractive because a small risk of catastrophic loss is converted into a small annual payment whose value is known with certainty.[7]

However, insurance is efficiency-enhancing only where insurable risks are concerned. In fact, careful thought shows that the concepts of insurability and efficiency are virtually identical. In a literal sense, no risk is uninsurable. We, Dolan and Goodman, Inc., could, for example, sell you lunch insurance to protect against the risk that you would get hungry in the middle of the day.[8] You could take your lunch insurance card, go into any restaurant in town, eat whatever you wanted, and send us the bill. There would be some premium—a high one, of course—that would be adequate to cover our cost of offering the policy plus a profit.

The reason lunch insurance doesn't make sense is that if the premium were high enough to give us a profit, it would be more than you would want to pay. This would be true in part because of the huge moral hazard involved—you would have an incentive to eat much larger and more costly lunches than if you were spending your own money. And in part, the premium would be high because our costs of administering the policy would be greater than your administrative costs of paying for your own lunch. If we cut the premium low enough to make it a good deal for you, it would be a bad deal for us.

---

7 One might think that not-for-profit mutual insurance associations would always be able to offer a better deal than for-profit, commercial insurance companies. It could be reasoned that the latter have to cover the cost of claims, plus administrative costs, plus a profit, whereas the former share any profits among members of the association. However, the difference is less than meets the eye. All insurance plans need capital to operate, in the form of a reserve fund. In a commercial company, profits compensate the owners for the opportunity cost of capital they contribute. In a not-for-profit mutual association, members have to contribute the capital themselves. The opportunity cost of doing so offsets the gain from not including a profit margin in the premium. Therefore, in practice, not-for-profit mutual and commercial insurers compete more or less on equal terms.

8 See Gerald L. Musgrave, Leight Tripoli, and Fu Ling Yu, "Lunch Insurance," *Regulation*, Fall 1992, pp. 16-24.

In short, it is efficient to insure insurable risks. But where moral hazard, adverse selection, and high administrative costs make it impossible to set a mutually beneficial premium, the risk in question is uninsurable and coverage would be inefficient.

It follows that reforms that remove barriers to covering insurable risks will be efficiency-enhancing. Reforms that equalize tax treatment of individual and employer-purchased insurance are one example. Another is any reform that lets policyholders and insurers choose more freely what risks to cover, for example, to decide whether or not to cover the cost of an abortion. The removal of regulatory barriers that inhibit companies from offering guaranteed-renewable insurance are still another example.

On the other hand, attempts to force people into insurance contracts that they would not voluntarily enter into are likely to be detrimental to efficiency. Compulsory community rating and mandated benefits fall into this category. Because many people will abandon insurance altogether rather than buy it on unattractive terms, such regulations are not only inefficient, but often fail to achieve their own goals of broadening coverage.

Equality The equality standard plays an especially strong role in health care policy. The reason is that many people consider health care to be a *merit good*—one that everyone merits a minimum fair share of regardless of ability to pay. Even many people who have no enthusiasm for equalizing incomes in general think that health care is a special case. Outside the United States, most other developed countries have national health policies designed with this goal in mind.

Economists cannot provide a purely technical answer to the question of how much equality in health care is good. What they can do, however, is to analyze the consequences, both intended and unintended, of various plans that try to achieve equality.

As we showed earlier in the chapter, community rating is an example of a policy that scores poorly by the standard of equality. Although it does equalize insurance rates within the pool of insured people, it drives many people, especially young people, people with low incomes, and employees of small businesses, out of the pool altogether. It thus creates a system of medical haves and have-nots. If affordable coverage for the uninsurable chronically ill is desired for reasons of equality, subsidized risk pools targeted at those individuals is a more efficient and effective solution than community rating.

The objections to mandated benefits are very similar. In the name of equalizing access to certain treatments, they drive many people out of the insurance pool. From the point of view of equality, mandated benefit laws are especially perverse when they prevent insurers from offering affordable, "plain vanilla" coverage to low-income workers and employees of small businesses. It is as if the law tried to mandate transportation equality by forcing auto dealers to sell nothing but Cadillacs and Mercedes. With regard to mandated benefits that exist only because of rent seeking, one can hardly hope that enriching the shareholders of commercial sperm banks hardly contributes to equality.

At this point, it is worth making one further comment on reforms aimed at leveling the playing field between individual and employer-provided health care. Judged purely in terms of efficiency, the playing field could be leveled either by removing the tax advantage of employer-paid plans or by extending the same tax advantages to individual plans. If health care is thought to be just another consumer good like any other, it would be more logical to take away the tax advantage for both kinds of plan. Doing so would probably reduce the demand for health insurance across the board. This, in turn, would shift the entire health care demand curve to the left, for reasons discussed in Chapter 3.

On the other hand, if health care is viewed as a merit good, it makes more sense to extend tax benefits to all health care plans equally—insurance, MSAs, and HMOs, whether purchased individually or by employers. Doing so would preserve efficient market incentives in most major respects while broadening access to health care.

No matter how cleverly market reforms are designed, some people will still fall through the cracks. These will include people who barely participate in the market at all—the unemployable, the mentally ill, substance abusers, habitual criminals. It may well be decided, as a matter of public policy based on the merit good concept, to extend health care coverage to these people in some way. If so, the economists' advice is to use narrowly targeted programs to aid just these people, rather than to burden the entire health care system with inefficient regulations.

Liberty By now it should be clear what kinds of reforms are consistent with the standard of liberty. The libertarian ideal is a market-based system in which relationships between patients and health care providers are, to the greatest extent possible, based on voluntary, mutually beneficial agreements. Health insurance has a place in such a system, as do MSAs, HMOs, and perhaps other ideas yet to be thought of. Compulsory community rating, mandated benefits, and one-sided tax privileges have no place.

Toward a common ground on health care reforms This chapter and the previous one have ranged widely. They have not touched on every issue of health care economics, but they have hit the central ones. In a surprising number of cases, advocates of efficiency, equality, and liberty can agree about what is wrong with our health care system. In particular:

- The system is too strongly oriented toward serving the interests of health care providers and not enough toward serving the needs of patients.

- It contains many perverse incentives that lead to overtreatment of some conditions while leaving other health needs unmet.

- The degree to which health care coverage is tied to employment serves neither the goal of efficiency nor that of universal access.

Based on this agreed diagnosis, there are certain core reforms that should find favor among advocates of efficiency, equality, and liberty alike. These include:

- Tax changes to level the playing field between employer-provided and individual plans, and among conventional insurance, MSAs, and HMOs.

- Narrowly targeted, subsidized programs to aid the very poor, substance abusers, and the chronically ill.

- Reforms that return insurance to the job it can do well—protecting against fortuitous, acute, and catastrophic health risks—rather than turning insurance into a system for prepayment of all health care expenses.

It is not likely that any one reform or act of Congress will resolve all of our health care problems at any time soon. Expect the ideas discussed in these chapters to remain on the political agenda for years to come.

Questions for thought and discussion

1. If you buy an extended service agreement on your new car from your dealer, the agreement requires that you have the work done there or at another authorized dealership. The dealer determines what work is necessary and the charges that will be made. Why does the agreement not let you take the car to any mechanic you choose to have any work done you think necessary, with the dealer paying the cost of the work? Compare with the situation of HMOs vs. fee-for-service insurance policies. Include the concept of moral hazard in your discussion.

2. In the abortion debate, some people draw a distinction between therapeutic abortions, performed when the life of the fetus or mother is in danger, and discretionary abortions, performed for family planning purposes. Do you think this is a purely moral distinction, or does it also have economic content? In particular, do therapeutic abortions more closely fit the concept of an insurable risk? Discuss.

3. In his science fiction classic, *The Moon Is a Harsh Mistress*, writer Robert Heinlein describes a society in which the insurance function is performed by bookies. For example, a homeowner could go to a bookie and place a $100 bet, at 1,000-to-one odds, that the owner's house will burn down in the next year. If the house does not burn down, the homeowner loses the bet and the $100. If the house does burn down, the owner wins the bet and receives $100,000. Are such bets really the same

as an insurance policy? What kind of bet, placed with a bookie, could protect you from health risks? What restrictions might the bookie place on the kinds of bets that would be accepted?

4. Our discussion of lunch insurance focuses on the moral hazard problem, that is, the problem that the insured is likely to eat more because of the coverage. Do you think lunch insurance would also be subject to an adverse selection problem? Would there be an information asymmetry that would prevent lunch insurance underwriters from classifying customers into separate risk groups? Discuss, and compare lunch insurance to health insurance in this respect.

Suggestions for further reading

Butler, Stuart M. and Edmund F. Haislmaier, eds. *A National Health System for America.* Washington, D.C.: Heritage Foundation, 1989. *This collection of essays covers many relevant topics, including the history of the health care system (Ch. 1) and ways of providing care for the poor, unemployed, and chronically ill (Ch. 5).*

Goodman, John C. and Gerald L. Musgrave. *Patient Power: The Free Enterprise Alternative to Clinton's Health Care Plan.* Washington, D.C.: Cato Institute, 1993. *Chapters 4 and 6 discuss a variety of health insurance reforms.*

Robbins, Gary, Aldona Robbins, and John Goodman. *Inefficiency in the U.S. Health Care System: What Can We Do?* NCPA Policy Report No. 182. Dallas, Texas: National Center for Policy Analysis, 1994. *This report discusses the ways in which our current insurance system causes inefficiency and discusses a number of proposed reforms.*

Key terms

Risk pooling. A principle of insurance according to which risk is spread among a large pool of individuals facing similar risk of loss.

Insurable risk. A risk that fits certain characteristics: It should be fortuitous, many similar units should be exposed to it, the loss should be measurable, the loss should strike at random, and the probability of loss should be small.

Moral hazard. A situation in which an insured party, knowing that a loss will be covered, takes fewer precautions to avoid loss.

Underwriting. In insurance, the process of classifying risks into similar groups and calculating appropriate premiums.

Adverse selection. The tendency of people most likely to suffer a loss to be most likely to seek insurance.

Information asymmetry. A situation in which one party to a contract (such as the holder of an insurance policy) has information not available to the other party (the company issuing the policy).

Merit good. A good of which it is thought that everyone deserves a fair share, regardless of ability to pay.

5

Illegal Drugs: The Unintended Consequences of Prohibition

On a sunny spring afternoon, five young men with troubled pasts and dim futures stand on a street corner in northeast Washington, D.C. Each of the men, whose ages range from 22 to 25, has served prison time for drug offenses, mostly distribution of crack cocaine. Three of them have been shot. Eleven others in their neighborhood, all of them known to these five, have been murdered in the last 18 months. Not one of the five has a job.

J.L. Harris, a local Baptist minister, approaches them. He cajoles, pleads, and offers biblical warnings trying to get even one of the men off the streets and into his church. But the fisher of men has no luck this day.

After witnessing Harris's fruitless encounter, a reporter draws the five men into further conversation. Why do they continue to inhabit the violent underworld of drugs and guns?

It's not so easy to get out, they explain. They see themselves as no more able to avoid prison or a violent death than a fish can avoid water. "Once you have an adult felony [conviction]," one says, "your life is over." A juvenile conviction is not a problem, because the records are sealed, but once you have an adult conviction, you can't even get a fast food job. There's no way out.[1]

---

1 Based on Ruben Castaneda, "In City's Toughest Areas, A Worn Path to Violence," *Washington Post*, June 21, 1994, p. B1.

Drugs destroy lives, we are told. Just say "no" to drugs. But as the case of these five young men indicates, drug prohibition destroys lives, too. Is it time to say "no" to prohibition? A remarkable array of commentators from left, right, and center, including William F. Buckley, Jr., David Boaz, Hodding Carter III, Russell Baker, Anthony Lewis, and Richard Cohen think that it is time at least to consider ending prohibition. Is there any other issue they come so close to agreeing on? Kurt L. Schmoke, as Mayor of Baltimore, called on the U.S. Conference of Mayors to debate the issue. Former Surgeon General Joycelyn Elders thinks that ending prohibition should be among the options considered in setting national drug policy. Nobel laureate economist Milton Friedman thinks repressive measures only make a bad situation worse.[2] Former New York City police commissioner Patrick Murphy thinks we need radical changes in the way the war on drugs is conducted, with an emphasis on treatment rather than law enforcement.[3]

What lies behind the thinking of all of these people is a recognition that no other policy, in both its historical and modern forms, has so clearly failed to achieve its intended goals while producing such a devastating array of unintended consequences. In this chapter, we employ some simple principles of economics to show why this is so.

A Short History of Prohibition

There is nothing new about prohibition as a response by government to the consumption of potentially addictive, psychoactive substances. In the sixteenth century, rulers of Egypt banned coffee and ordered all supplies of beans burned. In the seventeenth century, the Tsar of Russia and the Ottoman Sultan executed tobacco users. Alcohol has, at times, been banned in many countries and is still prohibited by a number of authoritarian regimes in the Middle East.

By contrast, laws regarding alcohol, tobacco, cocaine, opiates, marijuana, and their derivatives were relatively permissive in the United States until early in this century. Cocaine and opium were not only legal and available, but were often viewed as less harmful alternatives to alcohol consumption. Coca-Cola, which got its name from the cocaine that it contained in small quantities, was considered a milder beverage than wine. Doctors prescribed opium to counteract alcoholism.

---

2 All of those listed except Elders are contributors to David Boaz, ed., *The Crisis in Drug Prohibition,* 2nd ed. (Washington, D.C.: Cato Institute, 1991).

3 Patrick Murphy, "The War on Drugs Is Over (Drugs Won): What to Do Now," *Washington Post,* December 4, 1994, p. C3.

Opiates and coca derivatives came under control only with the Harrison Act of 1914.[4] On its face, the act seemed to aim only at controlling and taxing the drugs in question, but as time went on, it was increasingly interpreted as a general prohibition on even their medical use. Marijuana remained legal until 1937. No medical evidence was presented to Congress at the time it was banned; some people think that its addition to the list of banned substances was a result of its association with "undesirable social elements," such as jazz musicians.

By far the best known historical example of prohibition, however—so well known that we spell it with a capital "P"—was the prohibition of alcohol in the United States in the years from 1920 to 1933. Because the American founding fathers never contemplated a government intrusive enough to deny its citizens a drink, implementation of Prohibition required a constitutional amendment. The hope of doing away with the social and medical problems of alcoholism by legislative fiat was strong enough to generate the necessary majorities.

At first the results were as hoped—drinking declined. However, tens of millions of Americans continued to drink, and soon Prohibition's unintended consequences began to be felt. The most spectacular was the takeover of the liquor industry by organized crime, symbolized in the public mind by the notorious Al Capone and his Chicago-based gang. The murder rate rose every year during Prohibition. Official corruption became widespread as policemen, sheriffs, and prosecutors accepted bribes to turn a blind eye to the alcohol trade going on under their noses. Medical problems surfaced, too. Prohibition was most successful in suppressing the production and sale of relatively bulky beer and wine, so more and more drinkers turned to hard liquor. Quality control and laws against adulteration of liquor with methanol and other poisons ceased to operate. The death rate from alcohol poisoning soared to 40 per million, ten times its level today.

Backers of Prohibition responded with calls for greater law enforcement efforts. The enforcement budget was doubled between 1921 and 1932. The number of convictions for violation of Prohibition rose from 18,000 to 61,000. The number of stills seized increased from 32,000 to 282,000. But drinking did not stop and the murder rate continued to rise.

Eventually, sober, serious-minded people began to understand that the costs of Prohibition outweighed its benefits. The views of John D. Rockefeller, Jr., an early supporter of Prohibition, are illustrative. After seeing the effects of the policy in action, he wrote "that a vast array of lawbreakers has been recruited and financed on a colossal scale . . .; that respect for all law has been greatly lessened; that crime has increased to an unprecedented degree—all this I have slowly and reluctantly come to believe."

The Constitution was amended again, and by 1934, Prohibition, as national policy, was dead. Drinking in general may have increased as Prohibition ended, and

---

4 For a discussion of the Harrison Act and its background, see James Ostrowski, "Thinking About Drug Legalization," Cato Policy Analysis No. 121, May 25, 1989, pp. 3-5.

drinking of wine and beer certainly did. (Firm numbers are hard to come by because no one kept accurate data on illegal liquor consumption during Prohibition.) Deaths from drinking declined, however, and the murder rate began to fall and continued to do so for the next 11 years. The "noble experiment," as alcohol prohibition had been called, was a failure. Drug prohibition lingered on, however, with similar unintended consequences that affect American society to this day.

Tracing the consequences of drug prohibition

Why is it that the unintended effects of prohibiting alcohol and drugs are so spectacular, while successes in actually suppressing use are so modest? A large part of the answer lies in the economic concept of *elasticity of demand*. The elasticity of demand (more precisely, price elasticity of demand) for a good means the percentage by which the quantity demanded by customers changes in response to a given percentage of change in the good's price. Figure 5-1 illustrates the notion of elasticity for two goods, matches and donuts.

Part (a) of Figure 5-1 shows a demand curve for matches at an imaginary small convenience store. If the store sets the price of matches at $.10 per box, it will sell twenty boxes per day. If it doubles the price of matches to $.20 per box, it will sell just fifteen boxes a day. In percentage terms, that is only a moderate decrease in the quantity sold. In a case such as this, where the percentage change in quantity is small in relation to a given percentage change in price, an increase in price will increase *total revenue* (the quantity sold multiplied by the price of the good). Demand for the good in question is then said to be *inelastic*. In this example, raising the price from $.10 to $.20 raises revenue from $2.00 per day (10 cents times 20 boxes) to $3.00 per day (20 cents times 15 boxes).

Donuts, as illustrated in Part (b) of Figure 5-1, provide a contrasting example. The same increase in the price of donuts, from $.10 to $.20, has, in percentage terms, a much greater impact on the sale of donuts than was the case with matches, because it is easy for customers to substitute other sweet snacks. At $.10, the store sells thirty donuts per day, for a revenue of $3.00. Doubling the price cuts donut sales to just ten per day, and revenue falls to $2.00. In such a case, where the percentage change in quantity is large in relation to a given percentage change in price, an increase in price will decrease total revenue. Demand for the good in question is then said to be *elastic*.

Elasticity and prohibition To see why elasticity is important for drug policy, look at Figure 5-2. Part (a) of the figure shows how the market for a good with inelastic demand responds to prohibition. The example used is cocaine. The figure shows a hypothetical demand curve for cocaine and two supply curves. The lower of the two supply curves shows the situation that would prevail if cocaine could be produced and sold legally, just like coffee, cocoa, or tea. Given this supply curve,

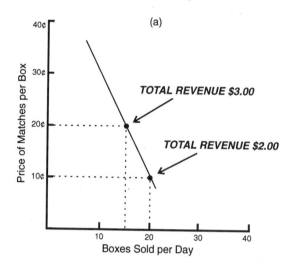

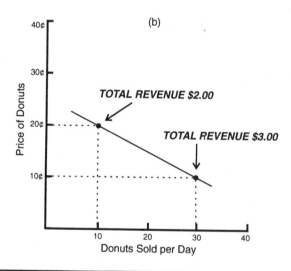

Figure 5-1 Elastic and Inelastic Demand Curves

the market would establish an equilibrium price of about $10 per gram (even less, by some estimates), as shown by Equilibrium Point E₁. For the sake of illustration, annual sales are shown as 3 million grams, for a total revenue of $30 million.

A policy of prohibition pushes the supply curve sharply higher because it greatly raises the costs of importing and distributing cocaine. In our example, the equilibrium price in the cocaine market rises to $100 per gram under prohibition,

Market for Cocaine

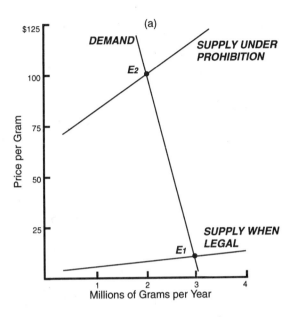

Market for DDT

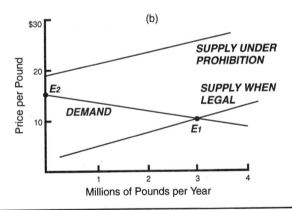

Figure 5-2

with the quantity sold falling to 2 million grams per year. Because the percentage decrease in quantity is less than the percentage increase in price, total revenue increases, from $30 million per year at Point E_1 to $200 million per year at Point E_2.

What happens to the extra $170 million of revenue generated as a result of prohibition? Popular descriptions of the drug trade often refer to the "fabulous profits" earned by drug kingpins, and no doubt many individuals do earn large profits. Economic analysis suggests, however, that most of the added revenue goes not to profit, but to cover the added cost of doing business under conditions of prohibition. These costs take a variety of forms. Drug authorities succeed in confiscating some of the product before it reaches the market (an estimated 11 percent of the total supply, in the case of cocaine), thus adding to the average cost of product that does get through. To reduce the risk of confiscation, smugglers use high-cost means of transportation, including airplanes and even landing strips that are used for a single shipment and then abandoned. The risk of jail terms further raises the cost of the drug trade, both as a personal threat to organizers of the trade and as a factor that raises the cost of hiring subordinates.

When prohibition is introduced in a market where demand is elastic, the effects are different. This case is illustrated in Part (b) of Figure 5-2 using the example of DDT, a once-common pesticide that is now banned because of its harmful environmental effects. In the market for DDT, as in the market for cocaine, the effect of prohibition is to push up the supply curve. Any pesticide suppliers who wanted to continue to produce and distribute the banned substance would, like drug dealers, incur the higher costs of keeping their operations secret, risking fines and jail sentences, and so forth.

But because there are good substitutes for DDT that cost only a little more to use, the demand curve is much more elastic than that for cocaine. As a result, the upward shift in the supply curve drives DDT off the market altogether. It just isn't worth anyone's time to incur the costs and run the risks associated with illegal supply.

Intended and unintended effects of drug prohibition How do we know that cocaine, heroin, and other illegal drugs better fit the model of inelastic demand than that of elastic demand? The criminal nature of cocaine, heroin, and marijuana make collection of reliable quantitative data difficult. Good data do exist for legal substances that are both psychoactive and addictive, especially alcohol and tobacco. It is well established that demand for both is strongly inelastic. This suggests, but does not prove, that the same is likely to be true for illegal drugs. However, the preceding discussion of cocaine versus DDT suggests that we can indirectly determine the elasticity of demand for a banned substance by analyzing the unintended as well as the intended consequences of prohibition.

The intended effect of prohibiting drugs like cocaine and heroin is to reduce their use. In any market, prohibition will be partly successful in achieving this intended result, but the more inelastic the demand for the product, the smaller the effect of prohibition on use. Some evidence is available that suggests that prohibition has not dramatically reduced drug use. For example:

- The percentage of the population using opiates regularly is not much different today than it was in 1915, at the time the Harrison Act first came into effect.[5]

- From 1981 to 1987, the federal drug control budget increased from $1.2 billion to $4 billion. The amount of cocaine consumed in the United States doubled during that period, according to a report by the General Accounting Office.

- The rate of use of marijuana is not lower in the United States than in the Netherlands, where it has been decriminalized, nor is it significantly higher in Alaska, where marijuana laws are less strict than in other states.[6]

- From the 1920s to the late 1960s, British doctors could legally prescribe heroin to addicts. The number of addicts rose during this period, but not more rapidly than in the United States. A change in the British law that prohibited legal prescription of heroin did not stop the increase in heroin use.[7]

The failure of prohibition to accomplish its intended effect of reducing use in these cases is consistent with inelastic demand. Let's consider next some of the unintended effects of drug prohibition and their linkage to inelasticity of demand.

First, if demand for drugs is inelastic, prohibition will increase total expenditures by users. For users and their families, this unintended consequence of prohibition means impoverishment, as a $10-a-week recreation becomes a $1,000-a-week obsession. For the communities in which the people live, the high price of drugs means an increased exposure to crime as users in poor neighborhoods steal from their poor neighbors, high-income professionals rob their companies, and middle-class users rob college tuition money from the family budget. In contrast, in markets where demand is elastic, prohibition will cut expenditures. People will have more money to spend on other goods—not less.

Second, if demand for drugs is inelastic, prohibition will mean more jobs and higher incomes for people employed in producing, smuggling, and selling drugs. Everyone knows that such employment opportunities exist. In fact, in some communities, drug dealing has come to be seen as the best employment opportunity around. Forget finishing high school, learning a trade, holding a job; the people with the gold jewelry, the fancy cars, and the best clothes didn't get those things through honest work. Of course, there are risks—the risk of jail, the risk of murder in a drug deal gone sour. But so long as prohibition-constrained supply and inelastic

---

5 See Ostrowski, p. 27.

6 See Arnold Trebach, *The Great Drug War* (New York: Macmillan, 1987), pp. 103, 105.

7 *Ibid.*, pp. 36-39.

demand keep drug prices high, new recruits can always be found to replace the casualties. If drug demand were, instead, elastic, prohibition would dry up employment opportunities. How many people do you know who are getting rich dealing in black-market DDT?

Third, in the market for illegal drugs as in other markets, high prices and fat profit potentials act as a spur to innovators and entrepreneurs. In the elastic-demand market for DDT, innovation and entrepreneurship have taken socially productive directions, as better and better substitutes for the banned products have been developed. The same has been true in the market for octane-raising gasoline additives since lead-based additives were banned. However, in the market for drugs, prohibition-induced innovations have been far less socially beneficial.

One direction that innovation has taken has been the replacement of long-established, naturally occurring drugs such as cocaine and opium with cheaper, laboratory-modified, or entirely artificial substitutes. An early example concerns the opium derivative heroin. Heroin was first invented in 1898, but before implementation of the Harrison Act, the usual form of opiate consumption was smoking natural opium or drinking laudanum, a solution of opium in alcohol. Heroin use became widespread only after opiates were prohibited. A similar example is the isolation of cocaine from the coca leaf. In areas where the coca plant is grown, people simply chew the leaves, from which they get a mild high. In nongrowing areas, purified cocaine was introduced more than a century ago. (The fictional detective Sherlock Holmes was one noted user.) More recently, crack cocaine, an even more concentrated drug, has become popular. Some powerful drugs—PCP, for example—are entirely laboratory-made, and have no natural equivalent. They were first introduced after drug prohibition was in force.

Without suggesting that naturally occurring drugs like coca and opium are harmless, it is fair to say that many experts find the synthetic substitutes to be even more hazardous. They produce very strong, rapid effects from very small doses. They thrive under conditions of prohibition, partly because they give "more bang for a buck," partly because the concentrates are easy to smuggle and conceal, and partly because they require fewer imported raw materials—in some cases none.

At the same time that prohibition has spurred technical innovations such as crack and PCP, it has also given rise to organizational innovations. One is the increasing use of young children to carry out many tasks of drug retailing. This sometimes begins with the employment of children as young as nine or ten as lookouts for street vendors. By their early teens, they become full-fledged dealers. Because they are shielded by the juvenile justice system from the full force of the law when apprehended, they are ideally suited to carry out many of the riskier and more-exposed tasks of the drug trade. The fact that by the age of fifteen, such young people may have thrown away their chance for a productive life is of little concern to the heads of the big drug cartels.

When only outlaws sell drugs A listing of the unintended effects of drug prohibition would be incomplete without mentioning one fact so obvious that it is easy to forget: Because drugs are outlawed, only outlaws sell drugs. The negative consequences, for participants in the trade and for drug users, are profound.

For growers, processors, and retailers in the drug trade, normal contractual relationships based on law and enforced by the court system are replaced by relationships based on fear and intimidation, enforced by violence and murder.

For users, the outlaw nature of the drug trade has equally negative consequences. Aside from the danger of getting caught up in drug-related violence, it means that there are no guarantees of product quality. The buyer of, say, a loaf of bread is protected from the danger of buying a loaf made from sawdust by laws regulating product quality and by the seller's need to protect a reputation in the community. In contrast, the buyer of a marijuana cigarette that turns out to be laced with paraquat, or the buyer of a bag of heroin "cut" with quinine, has no such protection. Doctors who treat drug users report that a significant percentage of medical problems, including "overdose" deaths, arise from the consumption of substances whose composition or purity was misrepresented to the buyer.

In popular discussions, the unintended effects just listed are often treated as if they were unique to the drug culture. To an economist, however, they are simply the rational, predictable responses of market participants to the combination of prohibition and inelastic demand. All of the same phenomena appeared in the United States during the era of alcohol prohibition. They largely disappeared from the alcohol market when prohibition ended. On the other hand, the phenomena of crime, impoverishment, fraud, and murder do not appear when the government prohibits the sale of products, such as DDT or lead additives for gasoline, that are subject to elastic demand.

Evaluating drug prohibition

In examining the effects of prohibition, we have seen that the intended effect, reduction of product use, is greatest when demand is elastic, whereas the unintended effects are greatest when demand is inelastic. The well-known problems associated with illegal drugs—persistent, widespread use despite vigorous antidrug campaigns, impoverishment of users, criminal activity by suppliers, and unreliable product quality—are consistent with those to be expected when demand is inelastic. We turn now from the task of tracing the effects of drug prohibition to that of evaluating the policy. As usual, we do so in terms of the standards of efficiency, equality, and liberty.

Efficiency Economists often approach the question of the efficiency of a policy by asking whether its benefits exceed its costs. This test is difficult to apply in the case of drug prohibition, in part because of disagreements about the nature of the costs and the benefits of the policy.[8] However, we can try to apply the language of benefits and costs in a way that will at least give us some feeling for the issues involved.

We can begin by dividing society into three groups affected differently by prohibition of any given drug. First there are the nonusers—those who would not use the drug under any conditions, whether legal or not. Second, there are the conditional users—those who would use the drug if it were legal, but do not use it under prohibition. And third, there are the unconditional users—those who would use the drug, legal or not.[9] In discussing costs and benefits of prohibition, we will first consider effects on nonusers and then the effects on conditional and unconditional users.

The effects of drug prohibition on those who do not use drugs and would not do so even if they were legal can be framed in terms of the economic concept of **external effects** or **externalities**. An externality is said to exist when activities of the producer, seller, or consumer of a good have effects on other people who do are not parties to the activities in question. Air pollution by a steel mill that harms downwind residents, or noise pollution by a student whose loud stereo keeps dormmates from studying, are examples.

A parallel can be drawn between drug prohibition and laws prohibiting pollution: To the extent that use of drugs by some people harms others who are nonusers, a case can be made for government controls, just as government controls might be justified in the case of large-scale air pollution or noise pollution. The externalities argument, however, must be applied with care.

Clearly, the most feared externality associated with illegal drugs is the possibility of becoming a victim of violent crime. Here it is important to distinguish between two different types of crimes: first, those that result from the inherent psychopharmacological properties of drugs, which can, in certain circumstances, induce violent behavior or lower inhibitions toward violence, and second, crimes that are a by-product of drug prohibition.

As is the case in other questions related to drugs, the fact of illegality has hampered research. However, some studies have been done. In his book, *The Heroin Solution,* Arnold Trebach concludes that "there is nothing in the pharmacology, or physical or psychological impact, of the drug, that propels a user to crime."[10] The authors of a study of cocaine conclude that "personality and setting as usual make all the difference."[11] Just as the Prohibition-era gangster Al Capone

---

8 In 1988, at the height of the Reagan administration war on drugs, James Ostrowski wrote to a number of high government officials, including Vice-President George Bush, then head of the South Florida Drug Task Force; Education Secretary William Bennett, and the information directors of the FBI, the Drug Enforcement Administration, the GAO, and other agencies, to ask if any of them knew of any cost-benefit analyses of drug prohibition showing the benefits of the policy to be greater than its costs. None of these officials knew of any such studies.

9 Some writers claim there is a fourth group, motivated by a "forbidden fruit" effect, who use drugs only because they are prohibited.

10 New Haven, Conn.: Yale University Press, 1982, p. 26.

as usual make all the difference."[11] Just as the Prohibition-era gangster Al Capone did not murder his enemies because he was drunk, today's cocaine dealers do not gun down their rivals because of cocaine-induced paranoia. Of all drugs, the most widely studied and most frequently associated with violent crime is alcohol. According to federal data, more than 50 percent of all people in prison for violent crimes report having used alcohol just prior to commission of the act for which they were arrested.[12] Marijuana, by contrast, is rarely associated with violent behavior. Thus, if a change in policy caused some people to switch from alcohol to marijuana (as happened to some extent during Prohibition), we could expect a net reduction in violence.

Crimes of the second type—those committed as a by-product of prohibition—are much more common than those committed under the influence of illegal drugs. Muggings and robberies committed by drug users seeking money to support their habits fall into this category, as do acts of gangland violence by drug dealers. Police active on the front lines of the drug wars know that this is the more common form of drug crime. Noting that 38 percent of murders in New York were drug-related, Deputy Police Chief Raymond W. Kelley explained that "when we say drug-related, we're essentially talking about territorial disputes or disputes over possession . . . We're not talking about where somebody is deranged because they're on a drug."[13]

On balance, fear of violent crime provides the strongest single argument against drug prohibition, just as it was the decisive element in ending alcohol prohibition six decades ago.

Accidents caused by people operating cars, trains, or airplanes while under the influence of drugs are another category of externalities. To the extent that full prohibition of drugs reduces drug use, it can be expected to produce benefits in terms of accident reduction. Legalization would move cocaine, heroin, marijuana, and other substances into the same category as alcohol: It would be illegal to drive or operate machinery under their influence. As the case of alcohol shows, such measures do not entirely control the problem, but then, neither does prohibition.

Let's turn now from the impact of prohibition on nonusers to its impact on users. We can begin by considering the group we have called unconditional, that is, those who can be expected to use drugs whether they are legal or not. This group is clearly made worse off by prohibition. Users of illegal drugs not only suffer

---

11 Lester Grinspoon and James B. Bakalar, *Cocaine—A Drug and Its Social Evolution*, rev. ed. (New York: Basic Books, 1985), p. 227.

12 Data cited by Ethan A. Nadelmann in David Boaz, ed., *The Crisis in Drug Prohibition*, p. 29.

13 *New York Times*, March 23, 1988, p. B1, cited in Ostrowski, p. 13.

find their lives made more miserable by the numerous unintended effects of prohibition. Among these effects are the following:

- They are impoverished, and often drawn into crime, by drug prices that may be 10 to 20 times as high as those that would prevail under legalization.

- They run severe medical risk from poor quality control, unknown purity, and dangerous adulterants in the drugs they buy. It is estimated that four-fifths of drug deaths stem from these causes, rather than the inherent effects of the drug.[14]

- They run further risks, especially the risk of AIDS, from using contaminated needles. Under legalization, not only clean needles but also oral forms of many drugs would be widely available.

- They may be arrested, dismissed from work, deprived of professional licenses, or suffer other penalties for using drugs, suffering severe economic hardship as a result.

An objective analysis of "lives ruined by drugs" must conclude that a very large part of the ruin comes from these unintended effects of prohibition rather than from the inherent psychopharmacological effects of the drugs themselves.

The remaining group to be considered are those we have called conditional users—those who do not now use drugs but would do so if they were legal. Arguments in favor of prohibition focus primarily on this group. In order to judge whether the benefit of prohibition to conditional users outweighs its costs to other groups, we would want to know how large this group is, and how much they would be harmed by access to legal drugs.

Neither kind of information is easy to quantify. Earlier, we discussed evidence that prohibition has not been very effective in decreasing drug use. Nevertheless, some proponents of prohibition contend that prohibition has stabilized drug use or slowed the rate of its increase. They claim that without prohibition, use of not just marijuana, but also heroin and cocaine, would become much more common. But how much more common?

Currently, about 100 million Americans use alcohol and about 60 million use tobacco, compared with an estimated 5 million users of cocaine and 500,000 users of heroin. Many people argue that alcohol and tobacco are much more strongly ingrained in Western culture than cocaine and opiates, and were always much more popular even when all of these substances were legal, so that it is likely that even

---

14 See Ostrowski, Appendix, for a detailed discussion.

without prohibition, the currently legal substances would remain more popular than their now-outlawed competitors. However, between the extremes of no increase in drug use after legalization and equal popularity with alcohol and tobacco, there is room for considerable growth of drug use. Some harm would no doubt be felt by users as a result.

One admittedly imperfect measure of this harm is the number of people who die from use of drugs. It has been estimated that today, under prohibition, about 2,000 people die each year from use of heroin and about 1,000 from use of cocaine. These numbers are small compared with the current 390,000 annual deaths from tobacco use and 150,000 annual deaths from alcohol use in the United States, but 3,000 deaths is nevertheless a matter for serious concern.[15]

To know the impact of legalization on drug deaths, we would need to weight the increase in quantity of drugs used against the relatively greater safety of using quality-controlled legal drugs. For example, if 80 percent of drug deaths at present are the result of adulterants, unknown potency, dirty needles, stray bullets from dealer shoot-outs, and so on, anything less than a five-fold increase in drug use would result in a net decrease in deaths. Of course, the individuals dying would in some cases be different. Thus, parents of a non-drug-using child might rationally refuse to accept even a small probability of their child's death from legal drugs, despite being told that several strangers in some other part of town might have to die as a consequence of continued prohibition.

Some people could suffer harm from use of legal drugs short of death. They could injure themselves, lose interest in work, fail examinations taken while under the influence of drugs, and so on. In the case of nonlethal effects, however, the harm from drug use must be weighed against whatever pleasure users get. A matter of great controversy is whether one should accept the user's own judgment as a basis for the evaluation. A gourmet sipping a glass of Chateau Lafite in a fine restaurant might argue passionately that the enjoyment of a fine wine outweighs any small risk. Another person watching the alcoholic self-destruction of a loved one might argue just as passionately that the drug itself destroys the ability to make a rational comparison of costs and benefits. If we cannot resolve this issue for the familiar drugs, alcohol, and tobacco, we can hardly hope to do so for cocaine, heroin, and marijuana, which provoke much stronger fears and about which there is less good scientific knowledge.

Ultimately, then, an evaluation of the efficiency of prohibition on a cost-benefit basis must be based on a combination of information that is inherently subjective, and information that is potentially quantifiable, but difficult to obtain under conditions of prohibition. All that can really be accomplished is to draw up a list of the potential benefits and costs. The benefits consist primarily in saving a certain

---

15 These estimates are assembled from various sources by Ostrowski. See *Thinking About Drug Legalization*, Appendix.

number of conditional users from the consequences of their own bad judgment. The costs are those borne by users of illegal drugs (greatly increased health risks, impoverishment, and involvement in crime), and those borne by nonusers (the tax cost of attempts to enforce prohibition and the risk of becoming a victim of crime).

Almost the only conclusion that can be drawn with certainty from this list is that the less elastic demand is, the greater will be the costs of prohibition and the less its benefits. Circumstantial evidence strongly favors the hypothesis of inelastic demand, but without an actual experiment in legalization, no definitive conclusion can be drawn.

Drug prohibition and equality Effects on equality do not always figure strongly in discussions of prohibition versus legalization. As in the case of other issues in this book, however, they deserve our consideration.

Superficially, the availability of drug dealing as a get-rich-quick opportunity for young people might suggest that prohibition reduces poverty. Stories are told of kids who earn enough in the drug trade to buy Porsches and BMWs before they are old enough to get a license to drive. How ever, the fact that drug dealing is a path to quick riches for a few people from low-income backgrounds by no means suggests that it makes income distribution more equal within the neighborhoods they come from, or within society as a whole.

On balance, the effects of the illegal drug trade appear to worsen the problems of inequality. For each person who gets rich dealing in drugs, many find their poverty made worse by the side effects of prohibition. Drug users are impoverished by the cost of their habit. If they turn to crime to support their addiction, their victims are disproportionately often their poor neighbors. The crime associated with the illegal drug trade has additional adverse effects on poor neighborhoods, driving out legitimate businesses, reducing availability of insurance and financial services, and destroying job opportunities.

The story with which this chapter opens illustrates an especially painful aspect of prohibition's impact on poor youths. Many of them, like the group encountered on a Washington street corner, get involved in the drug trade at a low level that produces occasional income but leaves them far from wealthy. Once they have a conviction for a drug-related felony, they lose any opportunity to get a legitimate job. They are permanently trapped in an underclass life even if they later decide that involvement in the drug trade was a career mistake.

Familiarity with the devastating effects of drug prohibition on inner city minority communities is a major reason why Baltimore Mayor Kurt Schmoke decided to urge serious consideration of decriminalization as a policy alternative. As he put it, "it is very easy for people living in communities where drugs are not a problem to argue that drug-related violence cannot justify decriminalization. But if you have to live with that violence day in and day out—as millions of people in large urban areas do—and live in terror of being gunned down, robbed or assaulted, or having the same occur to one of your loved ones, you soon start wanting results."[16]

Prohibition and liberty The standard of liberty provides the least support for a policy of drug prohibition. Drug prohibition contradicts American traditions of freedom and privacy in three ways.

First, and most obviously, drug prohibition runs against the tradition that people should be able to live their lives as they choose, so long as they do no harm to others. This tradition has always had its enemies. In some times and places, the enemies have used the government's powers to burn witches or suppress the practice of unorthodox religions. In other times and places, they have suppressed unpopular modes of political or artistic expression.[17] Sexual practices, even those between husband and wife, have been the subject of government regulation. Today in the United States, tolerance is considered the norm in all of these areas, to the great benefit of freedom. Yet in the area of substance use and abuse, a society that tolerates self-destruction by means of tobacco, alcohol, and high-cholesterol, low-fiber diets is not ready to tolerate heroin, cocaine, or marijuana—even when used under conditions where no harm is done to others.

Second, drug prohibition offends liberty by subsidizing crime. As more and more resources are invested in enforcement of prohibition, inelastic demand induces criminals to invest more and more resources in their own armies. The dangers to the life and liberty of innocent bystanders are very real.

Third, as the failure of prohibition to eliminate drug use has become more and more obvious, increasingly desperate enforcement efforts themselves become a threat to liberty. Take, for example, proposals for widespread random drug testing. Civil libertarians see such tests as a violation of constitutional protections against illegal searches. Law-abiding, non-drug-using citizens would be subject to humiliating invasions of privacy. For example, under current military regulations, officers, including female officers, and including those not suspected of drug use, must not only submit urine samples for drug testing, but must produce the samples under direct observation by medical personnel. Worst of all, people find their lives and careers placed in jeopardy by "false positive" results on drug tests. Statistically, false positives are few, but as testing spreads to the general population, they will become an increasing problem.

Law professor Steven Wisotsky characterizes the war on drugs as in fact a war on civil liberties.[18] He notes an increasing willingness of the court system to recognize a "drug exception" to the Bill of Rights. Drug offenders are subject to

---

16 "Drugs: A Problem of Health and Economics," in *The Crisis in Drug Prohibition*, p. 11.

17 William J. Bennett, formerly director of the Office of National Drug Control Policy, expresses the prohibitionist view in these words: "I remain an ardent defender of our nation's laws against illegal drug use and our attempts to enforce them because I believe that drug use is wrong. A true friend of freedom understands that the government has a responsibility to craft and uphold laws that help educate citizens about right and wrong." "A Response to Milton Friedman," *The Wall Street Journal*, September 19, 1989, p. A30.

18 *A Society of Suspects: The War on Drugs and Civil Liberties*, Policy Analysis No. 180 (Washington, D.C.: Cato Institute, 1992).

searches and seizures under circumstances that would not be allowed for other crimes. They are made the targets of wiretapping and military surveillance. They are subject to long prison terms without parole for minor, nonviolent offenses, and increasingly, to administrative penalties, such as confiscation of assets, without trial and conviction. Even freedom of religion gives way when it clashes with drug prohibition, as has been shown in the case of native Americans' use of mild hallucinogens during religious rituals.

Between prohibition and legalization It should be noted that drug prohibition is not an all-or-nothing affair. At one extreme are such "zero tolerance" options as random testing of the whole population, compulsory jail terms for possession of the slightest trace of controlled substances, and death penalties for dealers. At the other extreme is full legalization, so that drugs would be sold like chewing gum. In between are many other options: reduced enforcement without full legalization, as in the Netherlands; use of taxes, age limitations, and advertising restrictions to manage demand as with alcohol and tobacco; dispensation of drugs at low cost from clinics that also offer drug counseling—the alternatives are limited only by one's imagination.

Viewed in economic terms, the optimal policy would not necessarily be the same for all drugs. It would have to consider the inherent risks of using the drug and the elasticity of demand. Lower inherent risks and inelastic demand would favor greater toleration; higher inherent risks and elastic demand would favor more forceful prohibition.

The easiest choices would occur when both risk and elasticity considerations point in the same direction. One example is coffee, which contains the mildly psychoactive and potentially addictive drug caffeine. Demand for coffee is known to be inelastic. The risks of caffeine use, although not zero, are small. Full legalization is surely the proper policy.

At the other extreme, consider the synthetic drug PCP. Many authorities consider PCP to be one of the riskiest drugs, and one of the most likely to induce violence as a psychopharmacological effect. It also appears that demand for PCP is fairly price-elastic. Evidence for this is the fact that the drug made its appearance on the street as a cheap substitute for traditional drugs whose prices were driven up by prohibition. If the price of PCP were driven up by strict enforcement while greater tolerance permitted the price of traditional drugs to fall, PCP use would very likely fall as well.

The difficult cases are those of drugs that carry potential health risks but are subject to inelastic demand. Four major traditional drugs—cocaine, opiates, alcohol, and tobacco—fall into this category. The first two are subject to the strictest prohibition of any substances, while the last two are legal but subject to some governmental management of demand. It is difficult to imagine that benefit-cost considerations justify such disparate treatment of substances which, inherently, appear to pose such similar problems. By treating alcohol and tobacco as issues of public health rather than law and order, positive results have been achieved. Per capita consumption of alcohol has declined. A decreasing percentage of the population smokes. And even though alcohol and tobacco use and abuse remain widespread, the problems associated with these substances are not seen as a threat to the whole fabric of society.

The politics of prohibition

Despite misgivings raised on grounds of efficiency, equality, and liberty, drug prohibition enjoys great political popularity in the United States. In recent decades it has been one of the most consistently bipartisan issues, with Democrats and Republicans usually arguing only over who will make the greatest enforcement efforts. Elected officials, like Mayor Schmoke, who openly question prohibition, remain quite rare. Why is this the case?

It might seem enough to note that the U.S. political system is, after all, based on majority rule, and that all opinion polls show strong majorities in favor of prohibition. If the issue is viewed in terms of the economics of public choice, however, such an answer is not enough. Even under majority rule, we have hundreds of laws that benefit minorities. This is true, both in the favorable sense of laws that protect the rights of racial and religious minorities and also in the less favorable sense of pork-barrel, tax-loophole, and protectionist laws that favor special-interest groups. Why is it that cocaine snorters or marijuana growers cannot obtain the same benefits or protections that, say, small aircraft owners or sugar beet farmers are able to secure? There is probably no single answer to this question, but some elements of an answer suggest themselves.

First, public choice economics teaches that a politically successful minority must be able to mobilize a large proportion of its membership. In the case of sugar beet farmers, small aircraft owners, trade unions, and the like, the mobilization process begins with knowing who the members of the group are. They can then be reached through newsletters, assembled in conventions, and asked for contributions. The fact that drug use is illegal makes it difficult to conduct such interest group activities. At least one active group does exist, the National Organization for the Reform of Marijuana Laws, but its membership and political clout are small in view of the percentage of the population that has at least occasionally used marijuana.

Second, if the issue is viewed in term of rent seeking, we are led to the conclusion that the current suppliers of drugs would actually favor prohibition. Why would criminals who are making fortunes from producing and distributing illegal drugs welcome laws that would open the market to wide legal competition? No doubt, even with the low prices that full legalization would bring, cocaine, heroin, and marijuana would still be big businesses. But these businesses would no longer be controlled by the underworld gangs that now dominate them. Instead, they would be run by ordinary legitimate businesspeople just like those who now sell beer, cigarettes, and coffee.

Third, although we have argued that drug users are harmed by prohibition, that does not automatically mean that they are inclined to become active lobbyists for legalization. Here we have in mind not only those with serious addictions, whose health, jobs, and social relations have been destroyed by their habits, but also those who have established more stable patterns of drug use. Studies of drug users often associate drug use with apathetic attitudes toward work, school, and personal relationships. Some observers believe this apathy to be a clinical effect of drug use, while others think that aimless, apathetic people are the ones who find drugs attractive in the first place. In either case, such people would hardly be material for a successful political movement.

For all of these reasons, it seems unlikely that any movement toward decriminalization of drugs will come at the initiative of users' or producers' interest groups. If current policies are ever to be changed, it will probably be because people who are neither users nor producers become convinced that the unintended damage done by prohibition outweighs its intended benefits. The issue is well summed up in the words of columnist William Raspberry, a person who admits to "serious—perhaps irrational—misgivings about legalization." "Drugs kill," writes Raspberry. "They destroy minds. They stifle ambition. They account for billions of dollars in lost productivity. We are right to worry about these things. But I suspect that the drug-related problems we worry most about are less the result of drug abuse than of our efforts to control drugs."[19]

Questions for discussion

1. Cartoonist Al Capp once drew a series of comic strips that parodied prohibition. In the parody, beans were outlawed. The production and marketing of beans was immediately taken over by underworld gangs. Secret basement restaurants serving beans were the scene of wild shootouts between police and gangsters. Bean-craving fathers stole their families' rent money to buy a can of the illegal fruit. Corrupt politicians took bribes from bean farmers. Chaos reigned. Looking at the matter from an economic point of view, would you expect prohibition of beans actually to have such effects or not? Discuss.

2. Which of the standards—efficiency, equality, or liberty—do you consider most important in determining drug policy? Are there other moral or ethical standards that bear on this issue? If so, what are they?

---

19 William Raspberry, "Would Drugs Be So Dangerous If They Were Legal?" *Washington Post*, July 11, 1988, p. A11.

3. Can you think of any measures that would relieve the unintended harm that prohibition does to drug users without posing a risk that more people would be attracted to using drugs? Discuss.

Suggestions for further reading

Bannie, Richard J., and Charles H. Whitebread. *Marijuana Conviction: A History of Marijuana Prohibition in the United States.* Charlottesville, Va.: University of Virginia Press, 1974. *Covers the most popular prohibited drug.*

Boaz, David, ed. *The Crisis in Drug Prohibition,* 2nd ed. Washington, D.C.: Cato Institute, 1991. *In this collection of essays, writers from many different backgrounds find many different reasons to be skeptical of prohibition.*

Musto, David F. *The American Disease: Origins of Narcotic Control.* New Haven, Conn.: Yale University Press, 1973. *A scholarly, historical study.*

Weil, Andrew, and Winifred Rosen. *Chocolate to Morphine: Understanding Mind-Active Drugs.* Boston: Houghton Mifflin, 1983. *A user-oriented guide to the effects, risks, and possible pleasures of a broad range of psychoactive substances.*

Key terms

Elasticity of demand (price elasticity of demand). The percentage by which the quantity of a good demanded changes in response to a one percent change in the good's price, other things being equal.

Total revenue. The quantity of a good sold multiplied by its price.

Inelastic demand. A situation in which a one percent increase in price results in less than a one percent decrease in quantity demanded, so that total revenue increases.

Elastic demand. A situation in which a one percent increase in price results in more than a one percent decrease in quantity demanded, so that total revenue decreases.

Externality (external effect). A situation in which the activities of a producer, seller, or buyer of a good have effects on other people who are not parties to the activities in question.

6

Farm Policy:
Welfare for the Rich?

In the mid-1980s, as the manufacturing sector of the U.S. economy enjoyed an export-led resurgence, the farm economy faltered. The farm crisis made lovely television footage. Reporters visited auction yards where tractors, combines, and Ma's old washtub went on the block at distress prices. Hollywood cashed in with popular dramatizations of the death of the family farm. Rock groups held concerts to aid stricken farmers.

Congress, of course, responded to the crisis. Farm subsidies soared to an all-time record level. But somehow, Congress didn't quite get Ma's old washtub and the Hollywood version of the family farm in proper focus. Instead, Congress arranged to pay the Crown Prince of Liechtenstein, a partner in a huge Texas rice farm, the princely sum of $2 million. It gave one California cotton farmer more than $12 million in Commodity Credit Corporation payments. And agribusiness giant Archer Daniels Midland received a whopping $29 million subsidy in 1986 for distilling grain into ethanol. Thanks in part to congressional largess, Archer Daniels Midland made record profits that year.

In the years that followed, new crises hit the nation's farmers. In 1988 a record-breaking drought devastated their crops. Five years later the worst floods of the century put millions of acres under water. Each time, weather-beaten men in John Deere caps came alive in American living rooms. As they talked stoically with TV reporters amidst burned-out or flooded-out cornfields, Congress called hearings to help them out. Each time they did so, a clangorous bazaar ensued, with lobbyists lining the hallways. One especially productive day, House Agriculture

Committee members churned out 53 special-interest amendments to a drought-aid bill, and Senate committee members came up with 31. These pinstripe Santa Clauses found room to aid beekeepers, ethanol producers, sunflower seed exporters, and the Kentucky horse industry.[1]

What is going on here? Given widespread public sympathy for maintaining a rural way of life epitomized by the "family farm," why does the government instead give billions to foreign princes and giant agribusinesses? This chapter will seek an answer by tracing the unintended consequences of a half century of U.S. farm policy.

The foundations of U.S. farm policy

The foundations of U.S. farm policy were laid in the Great Depression of the 1930s. At that time, more than 20 percent of the labor force was engaged in farming, the bulk in small-scale operations where a single family provided all or most of the labor and management. The economic and climatic disasters of the Depression and the Dust Bowl hit this rural population hard. The average income of farmers dropped to less than 20 percent of that of the nonfarm population. After many years of legislative effort, the problems of the American farmer were finally addressed in the landmark Agricultural Adjustment Act of 1933.

At that time, price instability was seen as the root of the farmers' plight. Price instability in agriculture stems from a combination of variable output and inelastic demand, as shown in Figure 6-1. There, we see that a given shift in supply—produced, say, by a change in weather—has a much greater effect on the price when demand is inelastic (first panel) than when it is elastic (second panel).

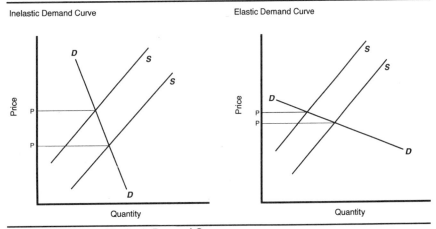

Figure 6-1 Elastic and Inelastic Demand Curves

---

1 Ward Sinclair and Bill McAllister, "Drought Aid Plan Withers in Congress," *Washington Post*, July 14 1988, p. A3.

Inelastic demand combined with variable output means that there is never a year when all farmers do well. When the weather is good, output soars and prices plummet. Lower prices, with inelastic demand, mean less total revenue for farmers. Thus, a year of good yields means low income for all farmers. When the weather is bad and output falls, total farm income rises. The problem is, it doesn't rise equally for everyone. In 1988, for example, the drought hit the upper Midwest especially hard. Some farmers on the fringe of the drought area had normal crops and high incomes, but that did not help those who lost their wheat and corn to the dry weather. In the great flood of 1993, those in wet areas lost while those in areas of normal rainfall were better off than usual.

The 1933 act introduced two basic mechanisms to stabilize farm prices: price supports and acreage restrictions. In 1965, a third price stabilization mechanism was introduced—target prices. Let's look at how each of these affects the supply and demand for farm products.

Price supports Figure 6-2 shows how price supports work. The supply curve in this diagram is shown to be positively sloped, reflecting the fact that at higher prices, more of the product—wheat, in this case—will be produced.

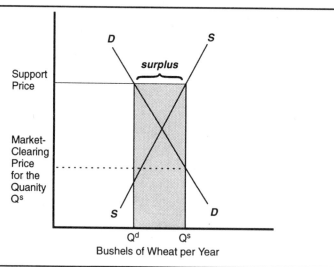

Figure 6-2 The Annual Market for Wheat with Price Controls

There are several reasons for the positive slope of the supply curve. In the first place, not all land is equally fertile. The cost of producing wheat on very fertile land is lower because with a given amount of labor, fertilizer, and machinery, more wheat can be grown per acre than on less fertile land. Second, an acre of land of given quality will produce more wheat with better fertilizer, better cultivation, and better harvesting techniques. And third, land can often be used to produce a variety of goods. As the price of wheat rises, farmers are induced to switch from growing corn or soybeans to growing wheat. All this means that when the price of wheat goes up, the quantity supplied can be expected to increase.

Under a price-support program, the government in effect guarantees wheat growers that they will receive a certain price for their crop. If consumers choose not to buy all of the wheat produced at this price, the government stands ready to buy the remainder and store it. (The actual mechanism is a little more complicated, and varies from one farm product to another, but this is the essential effect.) In Figure 6-2, the support price is clearly higher than the equilibrium free-market price. This means that a surplus develops, with quantity supplied exceeding quantity demanded.

The most obvious effect of the price support system is that total revenue and net income to farmers are higher than it would have been with free-market pricing. With price supports, income to farmers is divided into two parts: income from consumers and income from government. Consumers pay the support price multiplied by the quantity they purchase. Receipts from government are indicated by the shaded area.

The nonfarm sector suffers in two ways. First, consumers are clearly hurt by higher prices. Since the demand for most agricultural products is very inelastic, consumers will spend more on these goods than they would at free-market prices. In return, they receive smaller quantities. But consumers are also taxpayers; therefore, they must also pay an amount equal to the shaded area plus the costs of storing the surplus that government accumu lates.

The amount of grain stored under such programs has at times been enormous. From 1986 to 1987, the annual carryover stock of all grains was over 200 million metric tons. The government couldn't sell the wheat without ruining the market price, so it tried to give it away as foreign aid and once even experimented with using wheat instead of gravel to pave roads.

Output restrictions If price support had been the only tool of farm policy in the past, surpluses would have been even greater than they were. To keep surpluses under control, another technique has been used: output restrictions. There are several variations, but the most interesting—and the most objectionable to nonfarmers—was to pay farmers not to produce. Thus, farmers were given paychecks for retiring part of their land and for not growing wheat or other crops. Others received payments for not raising hogs. In one program, dairy farmers have begun receiving subsidies in return for not milking cows. This Alice-in-Wonderland system inspired a lot of jokes, but it was really a serious policy.

In all of the various forms of output restrictions, the objective is to reduce the quantity produced and thus reduce the surplus. Figure 6-3 shows how such policies work. As this figure is drawn, the free-market quantity would be Q_1. Suppose the government wants to raise the price to a higher desired level, as shown. If this were done through a support price without output restrictions, the quantity supplied at the desired price would rise to Q2, leaving an enormous surplus. To reduce the surplus, the government could pay farmers to remove a portion of their acreage from wheat production. Such a policy could potentially save a lot of money; the farmers would not have to be paid as much not to grow wheat on a given acre as to grow wheat, since it costs less not to grow wheat than to grow it. It also costs less not to store wheat than to store wheat. If enough acreage were taken out of production, output could fall all the way to Q3, and the surplus would disappear.

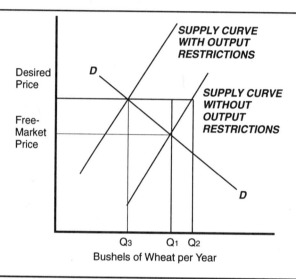

Figure 6-3 The Annual Market for Wheat with Price Supports and Acreage Controls

For some crops, like peanuts, acreage controls are the primary means used to raise the price above the market level. In other cases, a support price is maintained, with less stringent acreage controls acting to partially reduce, but not eliminate, the surplus.

Target prices Output restrictions and price supports were originally intended to aid farmers through price stabilization. In years when crops were large, these mechanisms would keep prices high. Surpluses would be added to carryover stocks. In theory, market prices would rise above the support level in years when crops were small. Grain could then be sold from accumulated stocks, moderating the rise of market prices. Farmers would avoid the problems of unstable prices, and over a period of years, consumers would pay the same average prices that they would have without stabilization policy.

However, the original notion of price stabilization gradually evolved into a policy of *price enhancement,* under which supports and output restrictions were set to produce prices above market-clearing levels in good years as well as bad. Price enhancement had several undesired results. First, accumulated surpluses were not automatically sold during years of poor crops. Second, because prices were raised above the average level they would have reached in a free market, consumers suffered. And third, high prices hurt farm exports.

In the hope of mitigating these undesired results, a third element was added to farm policy in 1965: the mechanism of **target prices**. Under this policy, farmers are assured of receiving a set target price, even if the market price falls below the target level. But unlike a policy of price supports, a target-price policy does not require the government to buy surplus crops. Instead, the government makes a **deficiency payment** directly to farmers, equal to the difference between the market price and the target price. Figure 6-4 shows the operation of the wheat market under a target-price policy. As in the case of price supports, the revenue that farmers receives comes partly from consumers and partly from government, but the division between the two is different. Payments received from government are shown by the shaded area.

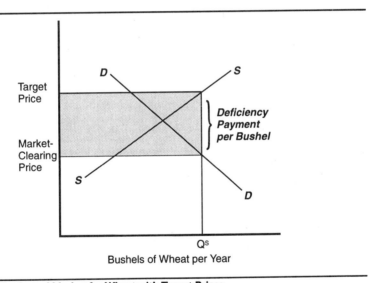

Figure 6-4 The Annual Market for Wheat with Target Prices

The target-price policy did not altogether replace price supports and output restrictions. Instead, farm policy since 1965 has included elements of all three in varying mixtures. During the 1990s, for example, a greater emphasis on target prices and deficiency payments, combined with changing market conditions, largely eliminated the government's once enormous stocks of surplus grain, and reduced total farm commodity subsidies to about half their peak level of the mid-1980s.

An evaluation of farm policy

In discussing the mechanics of farm policy, it is easy to lose sight of why we have a farm policy in the first place. The purpose is to help farmers, that's clear enough, but why? To help decide why we should have a farm policy—and if so, what kind,—let's look at existing policy in terms of our three standards. This time, however, we will *begin* with the standard of equality.

Farm policy and equality Public support for federal farm policy, outside the farmbelt itself, is based largely on the Hollywood image of the family farmer in distress. The family farmer is seen not only as economically disadvantaged but also as the representative of a uniquely valuable way of life in which much of American culture and mythology is rooted. For many city dwellers, protecting that way of life is worth a few pennies more for a loaf of bread.

The problem with basing a farm policy on such a combination of nostalgia and compassion is that farms fitting the Hollywood image don't play as big a role as they used to. Consider some numbers:[2]

- Some 58 percent of all "farms"—those with less than $20,000 sales per year—are really better described as rural residences or "hobby farms." They produce just 4 percent of all farm output. Their net income from farming is, on average, negative. But off-farm income of these rural residents averages a healthy $36,000 per year, well above the nonfarm average. As in the case of other farm units, official data on cash income do not take into account substantial value of food raised on the farm and consumed there.

- The Hollywood concept of a family farm probably more closely fits farms in the range of $20,000-$100,000 in sales. These are 26 percent of all farms, producing 16 percent of farm output, and on average are profitable. Even so, their owners rely on off-farm sources for more than 60 percent of their total cash income, which averages $47,000 per farm.

- The really representative American farms of today are those with over $250,000 in annual sales. Just 5 percent of all farms, they produce 60 percent of all farm output. On average, they generate a handsome $317,000 of net farm income, after meeting expenses, each year.

- Ma's washtub is safe from the auction block on the vast majority of U.S. farms. The government classifies a farm as "vulnerable" if it has negative net farm

---

2 USDA data, 1993.

income and a debt-to-assets ratio of 40 percent or more. Just 5 percent of
farms fit this profile in 1994. (Exactly comparable data are not available, but
undoubtedly a higher percentage of gas stations, beauty shops, or restaurants
would be "vulnerable" by this definition.)

- The average income of farm families has risen steadily since the black days
  of the 1930s when U.S. farm programs were begun. As Figure 6-5 shows,
  farm families are now substantially better off, on average, than nonfarm
  families.

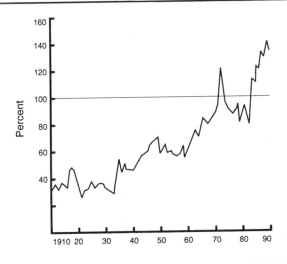

Figure 6-5 Per Capita Income of Farmers as Percent of Nonfarmers

Despite the fact that the average farm family is rather well off, generous farm
subsidies could still be justified on grounds of equality if they were narrowly targeted
on the minority of poor farmers. But they are not. Vulnerable farms receive just 5
percent of all government payments to farmers. The reason is that all of the major
farm programs—price supports, output restrictions, and target prices—aid
farmers by raising prices. That means, roughly, that farmers benefit from
government generosity in proportion to how much they grow. As of 1992, only
about a third of all farms received any government payments at all. Half of those
(16 percent of all farms) received less than $4,400 each. A third of all subsidies went
to 5 percent of recipients (that is, less than 2 percent of all farms). Payments for
these averaged $35,000. By law, one person can receive no more than $50,000 in
farm aid payments, but lawyers and accountants have proved very ingenious in
finding ways to turn a single farm into as many "persons" as are needed to collect

subsidies. For example, one California rice farmer leased his land to 56 "tenants," each of which collected the full $50,000, and then split the loot with their landlord.

Small wonder that farm aid has come to be called "welfare for the rich!"

Farm policy and efficiency The original concept of stabilizing prices without raising them on average could arguably be defended on grounds of efficiency. By saving farmers from boom-and-bust cycles, a pure stabilization policy would encourage farm investment and create a stable environment for long-term planning. But having long ago left price stabilization behind in favor of price enhancement, farm policy today fares no better by the standard of efficiency than by that of equality. As in other cases, we can trace the unintended effects of farm policy on efficiency by looking at farmers' responses in terms of maximization and entrepreneurship.

Farmers, like all business owners, are maximizers. Whether they go by the smell of the soil or by computer printouts, they try to combine inputs of labor, machinery, fertilizers, and pesticides in a way that will maximize their net income per acre. In the absence of governmental controls, their efforts have an unintended benefit for consumers—the nation's crops get produced at the minimum possible cost.

When governmental policy changes the constraints, farmers rework their calculations. They alter their input mix, given the new constraints, with the same objective of getting the highest net income (subsidies included). Consider, for example, the effects of acreage restrictions. Suppose the government offers a 25 percent higher price to farmers who will take 20 percent of their land out of production. Taking the new price and acreage constraints into account, the farmer makes new calculations. Given the higher price, it pays to farm those acres that remain in production more intensively. Extra inputs of labor, machinery, fertilizers, and pesticides are poured on, to the point where the marginal cost rises to the new, higher price level.

But the farmer's new solution to the maximization problem means a continuation of overproduction and, at the same time, an increase in the cost of production. Both consumers (who have to pay higher prices) and taxpayers (who foot the bill for subsidies) are the losers. Who are the winners? The farmers, of course—and the equipment and fertilizer manufacturers.

The preceding example involves simple maximization and just one farm program. When entrepreneurial responses by farmers to many interacting farm programs are taken into account, the unintended results of farm policy can be truly bizarre.

Take the case of California's pastureless dairy farms.[3] The average U.S. dairy farm milks 70 cows a day. But at one point a farm owned by the Maddoxes, of Fresno County, California, was milking 3,100 a day, and their neighbors the

---

3 Example based on Ward Sinclair, "Dairy Farms That Don't Need Pastures," *Washington Post*, March 28, 1988, p. A4.

Zonnenvelds were milking 4,000. Milking machines on these farms ran 22 hours a day. Whereas the average Wisconsin cow yields 13,800 pounds of milk a year, the Maddox and Zonnenveld cows averaged 21,000 pounds. And the numbers aren't the only thing that's odd about these California dairy farms. There are no pastures. The cows spend their days packed tightly into pens, munching high-quality alfalfa hay.

These pastureless dairy farms are marvels of entrepreneurial ingenuity, yet they are far from efficient economically. They are, instead, artifacts of two interacting government subsidy programs: price supports that keep milk prices high, and irrigation subsidies that keep the cost of growing alfalfa low. Without these programs, comparative advantage in milk production would revert to the more traditional (although still technologically sophisticated) dairy farms of Wisconsin.

The inefficiencies attendant to growing the wrong crops in the wrong places using the wrong technologies means that the cost of farm programs to consumers and taxpayers far exceeds the farmers' gains from these programs. One set of calculations by the President's Council of Economic Advisers indicated that losses to consumers and taxpayers exceeded gains to producers by some $7 billion per year.[4]

Farm policy and liberty Not surprisingly, farm policy scores poorly by the standard of liberty. There is, first of all, the enormous involuntary transfer from consumers and taxpayers to farmers. Other aspects of farm policy involve restrictions on international trade, thus limiting the freedom of consumers to obtain products from low-cost sources and also the freedom of foreign producers to earn a livelihood. And finally, farm policy also restricts the freedom of farmers to choose their crops and manage their businesses in a rational, cost-effective manner.

Many farmers are uneasy with the existing system, especially when it leads to the waste or destruction of crops they work hard to raise. Steve Maddox, manager of one of California's pastureless dairy farms, admitted that "we are not happy that part of our production goes to the government." A California orange grower, after seeing tons of fruit left to rot on the trees by government order, commented that "even the Communists don't do what we're doing—destroying good food." Farmers who serve markets that remain relatively free of controls, like those for poultry and beef cattle, are not all that eager to give up control over their operations in exchange for joining the governmental gravy train. And they resent being whipsawed when changing government policies raise the cost of their inputs and subsidize competing products. But, as one editorialist put it, "American farmers are trapped by policies that encourage dependency, price U.S. farm commodities out of the world market and largely subsidize wealthy or inefficient farmers."[5]

---

4 President's Council of Economic Advisers, *Economic Report of the President*, (Washington, D.C.: Government Printing Office, 1987), p. 146.

Prospects for change

If farm policy scores so poorly according to the standards of equality, efficiency, and liberty, why not change it? [6] To begin with, it must be pointed out that there have been changes. Although the basic framework of farm policy has remained intact, changes in details have reduced the total size of farm subsidies considerably. In 1986, farm subsidies peaked at $26 billion, or 2.6 percent of the federal budget. By 1994, helped by changing world market conditions as well as program changes, subsidies had declined to $12 billion, just 1 percent of the budget. The government's carryover stocks of major grains had virtually disappeared.

Critics would like to see the farm aid budget reduced still more. But before examining some of their proposed changes and discussing their prospects for success, we should consider why the present mix of policies has been so durable politically. As in other cases, the principles of public choice economics provide some insight.

Public choice and farm policy First, farm subsidies are a classic case of a policy whose benefits are concentrated and whose costs are spread widely. Take price supports for milk, for example. According to the President's Council of Economic Advisers, price supports for milk cost taxpayers about $1 billion and cost consumers another $1.6 to $3.1 billion in the form of higher prices. These are, in the aggregate, enormous sums. However, when spread over the population as a whole, they come to less than $20 on each family's annual tax bill and perhaps $1 a week on its grocery bill.

For most consumers, that is not enough to overcome the opportunity costs of political action. Few of them write to their senators, change their votes in national elections, or join political action groups on behalf of lower milk prices. For that matter, few of them even find it worthwhile to become informed about what happens to their tax and grocery dollars. Many have no idea that government price supports add to the cost of every gallon of milk they buy. Many consumers still believe the myth—that U.S. agriculture is dominated by the Hollywood vision of the family farm and that saving those farms is the primary function of farm policy.

To dairy farmers, however, things look quite different. Currently, federal programs are thought to keep milk prices about one cent per pound higher than the market-clearing level. Translate that into 4,000 cows giving 20,000 pounds of milk a year each, and that penny a pound comes out to $800,000 a year in benefits for an operation the size of California's Zonnenvelts'. These operators find it very

5 "Sacred Farmers," *Wall Street Journal*, March 5, 1987, p. 28.

6 Special thanks to Virginia N. Taylor, Executive Secretary, Office of the Assistant Secretary for Economics, U.S. Department of Agriculture, for supplying much of the material on which this section is based.

worthwhile to support the political activities of groups such as Associated Milk Producers, Inc.; Dairymen, Inc.; and Mid-America Dairymen, Inc.

The combination of dispersed costs and concentrated benefits create the conditions in which rent seeking by special-interest groups can flourish. Milk price supports provide an ample illustration. In the early 1980s, for example, a coalition of consumer groups, with support from producers of milk-based products, made a push to lower milk price supports. Dairymen's political action committees responded by giving over $1.3 million to more than two-thirds of the House membership. They were careful to give generously to congressmen from urban areas as well as those from dairy farming districts. As an Associated Milk Producer's press release put it, "The great majority of U.S. congressional districts have no significant milk production." But noting that 92 percent of representatives receiving dairy money were elected, the press release went on to boast that "the dairy farmers have proved that they can have a substantial impact nationwide on the decision-making process."[7] If the proof comes in the voting, it is hard to argue with this boast. Of 21 city and suburban members who got $5,000 or more each from the dairy political action committees, only one voted in favor of cutting milk price supports.

The importance of money to effective political action in Washington also helps explain why 19 out of each 20 farm-aid dollars go to farmers who are not suffering financial distress. The explanation, quite simply, is that lobbying groups and political action committees raise money primarily from their more prosperous members. The little guys are not in a position to contribute to congressional campaign funds, hence the strong resistance to proposals for targeting farm programs more narrowly at farmers in need. It makes much more sense politically, if not economically, to devise subsidies that benefit farmers in proportion to their output than in proportion to their need.

Proposals for change A growing number of critics think that farm subsidies should be phased out altogether by the end of the century. Even if this goal is accepted, however, the question remains how best to accomplish it. In principle, Congress could simply repeal the laws that authorize price supports, production controls, and deficiency payments, but given the political realities described in the preceding section, this seems unlikely to happen. As debate began on a scheduled 1995 farm bill, critics of current programs focused on the possibility of cutting or eliminating outright subsidies while retaining some federal programs aimed at stabilizing farm incomes.

One widely discussed proposal of this type is that put forward by David H. Harrington of the USDA Economic Research Service and Otto C. Doering of Purdue University.[8] The H-D proposal (as we will call it) is designed to protect farm income

---

7 Brooks Jackson and Jeffrey H. Birnbaum, "Dairy Lobby Obtains U.S. Subsidies With Help From Urban Legislators," *Wall Street Journal*, November 18, 1983, p. 33.

both from yield shortfalls and from low prices. If crop yield fell below a certain point, say 70 percent of normal, farmers would receive a crop insurance payout to make up the difference. If the price fell below a target level, say 80 percent of normal, they would receive a deficiency payment equal to the difference between the target price and the market price. Some individual farmers might experience years when both yield and price were below the designated threshold, and thus qualify for both kinds of payments at the same time. But the logic of supply and demand is such that for the farm sector as a whole, low yields are usually accompanied by high prices and high yields by low prices.

The H-D proposal contains several features designed to make the program as nearly self-financing as possible and to minimize the distortion of incentives. First, the yields on which crop insurance payments are to be based are the historical yield of each crop for each participating farm. Second, target prices are to be based on an average of prices over a period of time, say, the most recent 10 years. And third, the costs of the program are to be covered by a premium paid by participating farmers themselves, although a provision is made for government subsidy of the program's startup costs.

The proposal is, in effect, a form of insurance. That being the case, one might ask why does the government have to be involved at all? Why can't farmers just buy insurance against price and yield risks from private insurance companies? The answer appears to be that low crop yields and low farm prices are not insurable risks in the normal sense.[9] The biggest problem is that the risks tend to be catastrophic—a drought or change in world market conditions is likely to affect most or all farmers at once, or none at all, unlike the risk of, say, fires in farm buildings, which affect a small and predictable percentage of farmers each year. Insurance against risks of low crop yields and low prices also carries problems of adverse selection and moral hazard, as we will see shortly. Thus, farm income insurance falls into a category together with unemployment insurance that cannot easily be provided by conventional private insurers.

It is quite possible that the H-D proposal, or similar proposals aimed at ending subsidies while retaining income stabilization, would represent an improvement over present policy. However, programs of this sort are by no means free of problems. A few of these deserve mention.

First, there is the problem of whether to base crop insurance on each farmer's own average yield, or the average yield of farms in the area. If area yields are used (as in an existing and somewhat similar Canadian scheme), the plan is open to adverse selection: Only farmers on land of quality below the area average would find it worthwhile to join. But tracking each farmer's individual yield record for each

---

8 The program is outlined in *Choices: The Magazine of Food, Farm, and Resource Issues*, First Quarter 1993, p. 14 ff.

9 The characteristics of insurable risks were discussed in Chapter 4.

crop would be administratively difficult and create opportunities for fraud and "farming the program." In addition, a program based on the historical yield of each farm introduces an element of moral hazard.

The moral hazard comes from the fact that any scheme like the H-D program will pay more to a farmer with variable yields than to one with constant yields, given the same average yield. Suppose Farmer A gets 50 bushels per acre every year without fail, while Farmer B gets 100 bushels in odd years and no crop at all in even years. Farmer A would be paid for 50 bushels each year, whereas Farmer B would be paid for 100 in the good year and for 35 in the bad year (70 percent of the average 50-bushel yield). The average of payments received by Farm B would be the equivalent of 67.5 bushels per year, although the actual average harvest on Farm B, as on Farm A, would be only 50 bushels. The problem here is not so much that farmers might purposely ruin their crops half the time (although some dishonest participants might do just that), as that they would be encouraged to use risky farming methods or plant crops on land unsuited for them in any but ideal conditions.

Other incentive distortions could be at work as well. It is hard to design a crop insurance program that gives the optimal incentive to salvage partly destroyed crops in a bad year. And if technology constantly lowers costs while target prices are based on historic prices, there could be an upward bias in the target price relative to the market level.

But perhaps the biggest risk of the H-D proposal, or any other like it, is political. After all, 60 years ago the original U.S. farm program was billed as one of income stabilization, yet it soon turned into income enhancement. Under the H-D proposal, decisions about target prices, historic yields, fair premium payments, and so on would be made by Congress, not by a disinterested committee of agricultural economists. If the parameters of the program were made generous enough, the program could end up being just as much welfare for the rich as are current programs.

Is the 1995 farm bill likely to include a move away from subsidy and toward stabilization in some form? It is not impossible that it may. As the downward trend of farm subsidies over the last 10 years shows, the farm lobby's power is not as strong as it used to be. And some major farm groups have broken rank to back substantial (although perhaps not radical) reform. An example is the Iowa Farm Bill Study Team, backed by a number of major Iowa farm and agribusiness groups. The Iowa proposal is different in technical details but similar in spirit to the H-D proposal. It will be interesting to watch how farm legislation fares in the new Republican-controlled Congress in 1995.

Questions for thought and discussion

1. Farmers favor price controls and output restrictions in part because demand for farm goods is inelastic. Are there conditions of greater price elasticity of demand under which these mechanisms would cease to benefit farmers? If so, how would you characterize those conditions?

2. Farmers are not the only economic group whose earnings are subject to sharp year-to-year variations. Construction is another example of an industry subject to highly variable earnings. Why do you think the government has not developed an equally elaborate program for stabilization and support of the construction industry?

3. Studies of household budgets suggest that farm goods are subject to low- income elasticity of demand as well as low-price elasticity of demand. That is to say, when a household's income doubles, its expenditure on food increases but does not double. As a reflection of this fact, low-income households tend to spend a larger percentage of their budgets on food than wealthy households. What are the implications of this fact for an evaluation of farm programs in terms of the standard of equality?

4. This chapter was written in late 1994. As of that time, it was expected that Congress would debate and approve a new farm bill some time before the end of its 1995 session. Review news sources in your library to find out what changes in policy, if any, were made. What proposals were considered? approved? defeated?

Selected references

Bovard, James. *The Farm Fiasco.* San Francisco: Institute for Contemporary Studies, 1989. *An expose of fraud, waste, and abuse in farm policy.*

Choices: The Magazine of Food, Farm, and Resource Issues. Ames, Iowa: The American Agricultural Economics Association. *This quarterly publication is a good place to look for discussions of farm policy. The Harrington-Doering proposal discussed in the text is presented in the issue for the first quarter of 1993. Following issues contain discussions of the proposal.*

Learn, Elmer W. "Agricultural Price and Income Policy: A Need for Change." *Contemporary Policy Issues,* January 1986, pp. 49-61.

President's Council of Economic Advisers. *Economic Report of the President.* Washington, D.C.: Government Printing Office, 1987, 1991. *These two reports contain material on the last two rounds of farm policy revision. Watch the 1995 and 1996 Economic Reports for a discussion of the proposed 1995 farm bill.*

Key terms

Target price. A policy under which farm commodities are sold at the market equilibrium price but farmers receive a *deficiency payment* equal to the difference between the market price and a higher target price.

Deficiency payment. A payment the government makes to farmers reflecting the difference between the market equilibrium price, at which a commodity is actually sold, and a higher *target price*.

7

Regulating Safety: How Safe Is Safe Enough?

A few years ago Federal Judge Stephen Breyer, later to become a justice of the Supreme Court, was jogging near the Charles River in Cambridge, Massachusetts. When he came to a place where the jogging path ran through a tunnel under busy Storrow Drive, he found the tunnel closed. In compliance with federal regulations, workers were removing asbestos, thought to pose a health hazard.

When they came to the blocked tunnel, joggers had two choices. They could turn back for half a mile along the path and take a different branch to another safe crossing, or they could dash through the traffic directly across Storrow Drive, rejoining the path on the other side. Breyer observed that most runners chose the second option.

This episode set Breyer to thinking. Why were federal regulators intent on removing the tiny risk that asbestos in the tunnel posed for joggers when the joggers themselves willingly took the much larger and more immediate risk of dashing through traffic? Were the regulators imposing excessive precautions, or were the joggers not cautious enough? How safe *is* safe enough, and why do different decision makers come up with such seemingly inconsistent answers?

These questions are important because safety regulation affects so many areas of our daily lives. Federal safety regulations help design the cars we drive and the gasoline with which they are fueled. They affect the safety of the equipment we work with and the food we buy on the way home from work. Preventable accidents burden the economy with billions of dollars in costs each year, but compliance with regulations costs billions, too. Many observers, including Justice Breyer, think that the process through which the costs and benefits of safety regulation are weighed in the United States is seriously flawed. This chapter will examine some of the arguments and policy alternatives.

Measuring the
economic value of safety

The concept of expected value provides a starting point for almost any discussion of risk and safety. As explained in earlier chapters, the expected value of loss from any risk is the size of loss if it does occur multiplied by the probability that it will occur. To use an example from Chapter 4, a health insurance company might determine that the average cost of heart bypass surgery is $50,000 and that one insured person out of each thousand will need such surgery each year. The mathematically expected cost of surgery to any one patient is $50. The company must charge a premium of at least this amount (plus something extra for administrative costs) to provide its customers insurance coverage for this particular health risk.

This concept suggests one possible answer to the question, How safe is safe enough? Any safety precaution that reduces the expected value of loss by more than the cost of the precaution could be considered worthwhile. Precautions that cost more than their payoff in terms of reduced expected value of loss could be considered excessive. We will call this the *expected value standard*. But before it can be applied to any safety issue involving a risk to life, we need an answer to another question: What, in economic terms, is the value that should be assigned to the loss of a human life?

The value of life in labor markets The most reliable way to determine the economic value of something is to find a market where it is freely bought and sold. For example, the heroes of the television series *Star Trek* had a device that allowed them to "beam up" to their ship whenever they were faced by a mortal hazard, such as an exploding volcano or a berserk enemy warrior. If a beaming-up service were commercially available on our own planet, the price people would willingly pay for it would be a good measure of the value to them of avoiding the risk of death, just as the price of cellular telephone service provides a good measure of the value people place on keeping constantly in touch with their friends and business associates.

Although no company currently offers a beaming-up service, there are other markets where we can indirectly observe the price that people attach to the risk of loss of life. The most thoroughly studied are labor markets, in which we can observe the market wages for more and less dangerous occupations.

Suppose, for example, that we compare the wages of two types of construction welders. One group welds assemblies of steel beams together at street level. The assemblies are then hoisted hundreds of feet in the air, where other workers, using identical skills and equipment, weld them in place. The only difference between the jobs: If a street-level welder trips and falls, the result is a bruised knee. If a high-level welder does the same, the fall is fatal.

Suppose that our study finds that there are no fatal on-the-job accidents among street-level welders, whereas there is one fatality per 1,000 high-level welders per year. Furthermore, the study shows that firms must pay an extra $10,000 in wages per year to induce welders to work at the high level. Applying the expected value standard, we can conclude that if people will accept a 1-in-1,000 risk of death for a compensation of $10,000, they value their lives at no more than $10,000,000 ($10,000,000 ÷ 1,000 = $10,000).

In practice, things are not quite so simple. It is hard to find pairs of occupations that require exactly the same skills, differing only in terms of safety. And, if we compare jobs without taking other factors, like skills and experience, into account, we may paradoxically find that dangerous jobs often draw lower pay than safer jobs. For example, if we look at crash statistics, we find that the job of piloting a small commuter airliner is more dangerous than that of piloting a large jetliner. Yet airlines put their best paid and most experienced pilots in the big jets and their less experienced, lower paid pilots in the smaller planes. Furthermore, because piloting even a commuter jet takes special skills and training, all pilots will be found to earn more than farm tractor drivers, even though the chance of getting killed by rolling over while driving a tractor is greater than the chance of crashing in a plane.

Researchers have used a variety of sets of data and methods of holding other things equal when studying wages and job safety. Because none of the data sets or methods are perfect, their estimates of the implicit value of life also differ. However, a comparison of many such studies finds that estimates of the implicit value of life cluster in the range of $3 million to $7 million.[1]

Implications for safety regulation The approach to estimating the value of life that we have just outlined suggests a refined answer to the question, "How safe is safe enough?" This answer has two parts, as follows:

(1) "Safe enough" means a level of spending on safety measures that can be justified by the reduction in the expected value of loss of life. For example, if we assign a value of $7 million to the loss of one life, it would be worth spending $70,000 to avoid a 1-in-100 risk, $7,000 to avoid a 1-in-1,000 risk, $7 to avoid a 1-in-1,000,000 risk, and so on. The logic behind this is that if a person's labor market behavior shows a willingness to *accept* a 1-in-1,000 occupational risk of death in return for $7,000 in additional wages, we would not expect the same person to be willing to pay more than $7,000 to *avoid* a different risk of the same magnitude. If the person

---

1 For a comprehensive survey, see Kip Viscusi, "The Value of Risks to Life and Health," *Journal of Economic Literature*, December 1993, pp. 1912-46, especially Table 2.

were willing to sacrifice more than $7,000 to avoid such a risk, he or she would already have revealed that willingness by taking a safer job in the first place.

(2) Once the value of safety is established, it should be applied consistently to all categories of risk. For example, suppose that it would be worthwhile, but only barely so, to spend $7 million on better ventilation to avoid one death from a coal mining accident. It follows that it would be a mistake to pass up an opportunity to save one traffic accident death by spending just $1 million on new traffic signals, but it would also be a mistake to spend $100 million to avoid only one cancer death by removing asbestos from elementary school cafeterias.

Critics of safety regulation, Stephen Breyer among them, are quick to point out that existing safety regulations do not at all conform to this two-part test based on the expected value standard. Consider the examples shown in Table 7-1. There we see that a Consumer Product Safety Commission (CPSC) ban on unvented space heaters carries an estimated cost per life saved of just $100,000, which looks like a very good bargain. Farther along the list, but still a relative bargain, at $1.5 million per life saved, are standards set by the Occupational Health and Safety Administration (OSHA) for trenching and excavation safety. OSHA standards set in 1972 for protecting occupational exposure to asbestos cost $8.3 million per life saved, near the upper end of the reasonable range implied by labor market estimates of the value of life.

Hazard-regulated (date)	Cost per Life Saved ($ Millions)
Unvented space heaters (1980)	0.1
Auto seat belt standards ((1984)	0.1
Underground construction standards (1989)	0.1
Service of auto wheel rims (1984)	0.4
Auto side-door supports (1970)	0.8
Trenching and excavation standards (1989)	1.5
Grain dust explosion prevention (1987)	2.8
ethylene dibromide in drinking water (1991)	5.7
Asbestos occupational exposure (1972)	8.3
Electrical equipment in coal mines (1970)	9.2
Uranium mill tailings at inactive sites (1983)	31.7
Uranium mill tailings at active sites (1983)	45.0
Asbestos occupational exposure (1986)	74.0
Ban on DES in cattle feed (1979)	124.8
Dichloroproane in drinking water (1991)	653.0
Formaldehyde occupational exposure (1987)	86,201.8
Atrazine/Alachlor in drinking water (1987)	92,069.7
Hazardous waste listing for wood preservatives (1990)	5,700,000.0

Source: Adapted from Breyer, *Breaking the Vicious Circle*, Table 5.
Original data taken from United States Budget for Fiscal Year 1992, Table C-2, Part 2..

Table 7-1 Cost-Effectiveness of Various Health and Safety Regulations

But the list also includes some regulations that are very costly per statistical life saved. An Environmental Protection Agency (EPA) regulation related to mill tailings at active uranium processing sites costs $45 million per life saved. A Food and Drug Administration (FDA) ban on the chemical DES in cattle feet has a price tag of $125 million per life saved. And an EPA regulation relating to safe disposal of waste wood-processing chemicals is estimated to cost a huge $5.7 trillion ($5,700,000,000,000) per life saved.

Clearly, something is very wrong, either with the process of safety regulation, or with the labor market studies and the expected value standard on which the critics rely, or both.

Explaining the pattern of safety regulation

After considering many examples, ranging from his casual observations of joggers at the Storrow Drive tunnel to elaborate cases presented in thousands of hours of testimony before his federal court, Judge Breyer concluded that the inconsistencies implied by the data in Table 7-1 reflect flaws in the process of safety regulation. His analysis reflects the thinking of public choice theory, in which irrational results can be traced to the rational response of decisionmakers acting within the constraints of imperfect government institutions.

The vicious circle of regulatory failure Breyer presents his analysis in the form of a "vicious circle" consisting of three elements: distortions in public perceptions of safety risks, congressional reactions to those perceptions, and bureaucratic procedures used to implement laws passed by Congress.

The vicious circle begins with what Breyer calls *random agenda selection*—a tendency to set priorities for safety regulation not on the basis of scientific evaluation but rather, on the basis of public perceptions, which are, in turn, heavily influenced by chance events. People react much more strongly to events that stand out from the background than to everyday events. Thus, an event like the accident at the Three Mile Island nuclear power station in Pennsylvania, which stands out from the background, creates a strong public perception of danger, even if no one is killed. This perception of danger may rank much higher in the public mind than such everyday dangers as those associated with motorcycles or fatty foods, although the latter kill people by the thousands every year.

The tendency for some dangers to stand out from the background is amplified by the tendency of the news media to feature the unusual. Even a small accident at a nuclear power station is newsworthy, whereas motorcycle accidents or deaths from heart disease are usually not. Thus, chance events put first one category of risk, then another, on the agenda for public discussion and political action.

The second element of Breyer's vicious circle lies in the way Congress reacts to public perceptions of risk. Because individual members of Congress are interested in votes, and votes are based on perceptions, public perceptions of risk are naturally more important than expert statistical assessments. Similarly, creating a perception in the mind of voters that something has been done to make their lives safer is more important than actually reducing the risk. Finally, Congress cannot, in any event, actually act to reduce risk, but instead, can only pass a law directing some executive agency to act.

Breyer emphasizes that laws are not precision weapons in the war against risk. More often than not, they miss their target, sometimes on one side and sometimes on the other. Some laws contain language that is inappropriately precise or absolute. A frequently cited example is the Delaney Clause, which prohibits the addition of any carcinogen to foods, regardless of how minute the quantity, how small the risk, or how great the cost of compliance. But in other cases, laws are written so broadly that they give hardly any guidance to the executive bureaucracy. For example, a law may direct regulators to "apply all applicable standards," or to act in a way that is "relevant and appropriate." Neither the overly broad nor overly specific type of law encourages (let alone requires) balancing costs and benefits of various risk reduction strategies across a broad spectrum, for example, balancing the dangers of food additives against problems of airline safety.

The third element of the vicious circle lies in the implementation of legislation by the federal bureaucracy. One problem is that each agency tends to develop what Breyer calls *tunnel vision,* that is, a tendency to pursue its own agenda to the limit without balancing the costs against broader social goals. For example, as shown in Table 7-1, OSHA set an occupational exposure standard for asbestos in 1972 at a level involving an estimated cost of $8.3 million per life saved. This is not far from the range of what can be justified by the expected value standard. However, in 1986, it issued further occupational asbestos regulations that raised the price to $74 million per life saved. This reflects a general feature of measures to improve safety: Getting rid of the first 90 percent of risk is often cheaper than getting rid of the last 10 percent.

Another problem hampering efficient decision making within the bureaucracy is the high premium placed on following certain procedural rules. According to Breyer, this problem has become worse over time. As an example, he notes that as recently as the 1970s, a regulator, faced with a question of scientific uncertainty, could simply telephone an appropriate specialist and ask for an off-the-record opinion. The regulator might ask, for example, whether saccharin poses a major health risk. The informal answer might be, "We're still doing research on that, but from what we've found so far, I don't think saccharin looks like a high priority." Today, rules require regulators to communicate with scientists only through formal, on-the-record procedures. This can greatly inhibit the expression of candid views regarding risk and scientific uncertainty. In one actual case, scientists debated at length whether their report should say that "available evidence does not indicate that saccharin is useful in weight control," or instead, that "scientific evidence does not permit an assessment of the role that saccharin plays in weight control." It is difficult for a lay person to tell the difference between the two statements, and neither statement provides any really useful guidance to bureaucrats.

Faced with inadequate scientific evidence and vague congressional directives, bureaucrats construct safety regulations that serve their own interests. One of these is to avoid threats to their own job security by opting for excessive caution where the optimal degree of caution is unknown. If a dam breaks, and I wrote the standards for dam safety, I am likely to become the target of investigative journalists and lose my job. If the dam doesn't break and I wrote regulations that made it cost more than needed to make it adequately safe, my error is much less likely to get me in trouble. Another bureaucratic interest is often to raise the budget of one's own department. Thus, I may interpret congressional directives in a way that require a maximum number of inspectors and clerks.

In sum, the vicious circle gives rise to a pattern of regulation that is too lax here, too stringent there, and rarely finds the right balance between costs and benefits. Yet, following the logic of public choice, it is the product of decisions which, each considered in its own narrow context, may be perfectly rational.

The psychometric approach to safety The preceding critique of safety regulation, which is the mainstream view among economists and is shared by many noneconomists like Breyer, is itself not above criticism, however. An alternative approach begins by challenging the underlying assumptions of the expected value standard: that the value of life implied by labor market studies is relevant to regulatory decisions, and that efficiency requires a uniform cost per life saved across widely differing risk categories. The alternative explanation is rooted in *psychometric* studies of attitudes toward risk, that is, in attempts to measure people's actual subjective perceptions of various kinds of risks.[2]

One finding of psychometric studies is that people tend subjectively to overestimate the likelihood that mathematically unlikely events will happen to them. One familiar example concerns lotteries. For a lottery to be profitable, tickets have to be sold for a price that is greater than the expected value of winnings. Lottery operators have found that it is easier to make a profit on tickets that give a 1-in-a-million chance of winning a million dollars than on tickets that give a 1-in-10 chance of winning 10 dollars. Even though the expected value of winnings is the same in both cases, people can't easily grasp how small the chance is of winning the million-dollar prize. Similarly, many people have a greater fear of the very small chance of dying along with hundreds of others in a plane crash than of dying alone in a car crash, even though statistics show that cars produce more fatalities per passenger mile.

Another psychometric finding is that subjectively, not all risks are alike. Some risks make people lie awake at night worrying while others are never given a thought.

---

2 For a survey of psychometric studies of risk, see Paul Slovic, "Perception of Risk," *Science* 236 (April 1987): 283.

Some are confronted calmly and rationally, others with strong emotions. Two groups of factors in particular affect subjective perceptions of risk.

One group of factors relates to how well the risk is understood. If the risk is a new one, if scientific understanding of it is poor, if a person can be exposed to the risk without knowing it, and if the effects are delayed, the risk will be seen as greater. Risks from microwave ovens or oral contraceptives share these characteristics. On the other hand, risks that are familiar, well understood, and have effects that are immediately perceived are subjectively minimized relative to their statistical probability. Dangers of alcohol and car accidents fall in this category.

Another group of factors together define a category known as **dread risks** because of their power to inspire special apprehension and discomfort. One key element of dread is the degree to which exposure is voluntary. Another is the degree to which a person subjectively feels the risk can be controlled. Thus, the risks of skiing, which are voluntary and subject to control, are less dread than risks of pesticide exposure, which are involuntary and less subject to control. The degree of dread also varies according to who is subject to the risk. Risks that affect innocent parties, like children, are less dread than risks that affect responsible adults. Risks that affect future generations may be more dread than those that affect people now living. And risks that are potentially catastrophic, killing many people at once, are more feared than risks that are mathematically likely to kill the same number of people a few at a time. Thus, the risk of earthquake may be more feared than the risk of death in household fires, and the risk of an asteroid collision may be feared more than earthquakes. Finally, risks are more dread if they are increasing, even though now small, than if they are now large, but decreasing. Thus, risks of nuclear accidents may be more dread than risks of infectious disease, even though disease kills far more people.

When these factors combine, they can produce choices that seem completely out of proportion to objective measures of expected value. Breyer's observations of the Storrow Drive joggers provides a perfect illustration. The danger of running through traffic, although objectively high, is familiar and easily understood. It is voluntarily undertaken and puts only the individual at risk. In addition, the individual has the perception (perhaps false) that the risk can be controlled by choosing the right moment and having quick reactions. The danger of asbestos lies at the other end of the scale. It is poorly understood. It can affect people without their knowing it, and its effects are long delayed. Innocent victims, including children, may be affected. And when asbestos is present in public places, it may not be easy voluntarily to avoid the risk.

When economics and psychometrics are combined, the result is a different standard by which to judge risk regulation. Now the objective becomes not one of balancing the statistical number of deaths against the costs of regulation, but one of producing maximum subjective peace of mind per dollar spent. It becomes reasonable to make relatively greater regulatory effort to reduce new, poorly understood, dread risks, like global warming or carcinogenic food additives, and to devote relatively less attention to familiar risks like those of traffic accidents, to which exposure is at least partly voluntary.

It is sometimes objected that people are *irrational* to fear nuclear power and global warming more than cigarettes and motorcycles. However, to say this is to use the concept of rationality in a different way than it is usually applied in economics. For example, suppose that a colleague from the chemistry department tells an economist that a test shows expensive, Absolute-brand vodka to be chemically indistinguishable from a cheap generic brand. Observing that many consumers nevertheless buy Absolute, economists do not draw the conclusion that their behavior is irrational. On the contrary, they conclude that the two brands, although objectively identical, are subjectively different enough that consumer satisfaction is maximized by buying the more expensive brand. If rationality in the liquor store consists in balancing subjective valuations against costs, regardless of "objective" facts, why not apply the same standard to safety regulation?

But there is a risk of pushing the psychometric argument regarding safety regulation so far as to make it tautological. That is, it would be wrong to interpret the pattern of safety regulation revealed by Table 7-1 as an actual *measure* of subjective valuations of risk. For example, regulations mandate spending a million times more to eliminate a death caused by careless disposal of wood-preserving chemicals ($5.7 trillion per life saved) than to eliminate a death caused by ethylene dibromide in drinking water ($5.7 million per life saved), but we would be hesitant to take this as evidence that wood preservatives are subjectively a million times more fearful than ethylene dibromide.

In short, it is likely that psychometric considerations are one among many factors that influence the pattern of safety regulations. They most likely operate at at the level of agenda selection and congressional response to public perceptions. They may, in a way that is not fundamentally unreasonable, justify stricter regulation of mysterious cancer-causing substances than of familiar risks like construction ditches and space heaters. Nonetheless, government regulation remains an imperfect mechanism for responding to subjective perceptions of risks. Where applicable, other, more market-oriented approaches to dealing with risk deserve consideration. We will return to this issue in the last section of the chapter.

An evaluation
of safety regulation

We have now looked at the pattern of safety regulation in the United States and at possible explanations of that pattern. Next we turn to an evaluation of safety regulation in terms of the standards of efficiency, equality, and liberty that we have applied in other chapters.

Safety regulation and efficiency   Much of what needs to be said about the efficiency of safety regulation has already been covered in the preceding section. If the expected value standard is accepted at face value, the evidence of Table 7-1, which shows a wide variation in cost per life saved over different areas of regulation, suggests substantial inefficiency. Furthermore, reliance on labor market studies, which imply a value of $3 to $7 million per human life, suggest that efficiency could be increased by relaxing regulations that carry a greater cost, and possibly tightening up on those whose cost per life saved is less.

Bringing psychometric evidence into the balance complicates the analysis. Efficiency no longer requires exactly equal expenditures per life saved in different risk categories. Furthermore, it is likely that labor market studies, which often deal with familiar risks to which workers voluntarily expose themselves, may understate the amount that can reasonably be spent to reduce dread risks.

But even taking psychometric factors into account, the arguments of public choice theory suggest that government regulation is no more likely to produce a perfectly efficient pattern of safety regulation than it is to produce a perfectly efficient pattern of highway construction. Pressure-group politics, partisan battles in Congress, and bureaucratic self-interest all act to filter and distort the public demand for safety during the process that produces a supply of regulation to meet that demand.

In particular, efficiency cannot justify regulations like the Delaney Clause that completely exclude a balancing of benefits and costs. Similarly, regulations that impose widely different standards on risks falling into apparently similar psychometric categories (like wood preservatives and ethylene dibromide) are suspect on efficiency grounds. Finally, psychometric evidence suggests that risks to which people voluntarily expose themselves should be less strictly regulated than involuntary risks, which is not always the case.

Safety regulation and equality All people are exposed to risk, all value their own lives, and thus all benefit, to one degree or another, from government actions to improve safety for workers and consumers. However, these benefits are not distributed equally and do not come without costs. An evaluation of safety regulation in terms of equality must take the distribution of both costs and benefits into account.

We can begin noting that the optimal degree of safety for each person is a matter of opportunity cost: How much of other goods or satisfactions is a person willing to forego in order to reduce risk to life? The answer varies from one person to another. We, your authors, are both willing to run the risks of skiing to capture its pleasures. Neither of us is willing to run the greater risk of hang gliding, even though, judging from films we have seen, it looks like at least as much fun as sliding down a hill on plastic boards. Similarly, some people willingly sign up for risky jobs like helicopter pilot or police quick-response squad in return for the extra pay, while others are happy with a desk job and a more modest standard of living.

These variations in attitudes toward safety are partly random and subjective, like preferences for watching basketball instead of baseball. But they have a systematic component as well. The systematic component comes from the fact that safety is a normal good, that is, one that people are willing to spend more on as their incomes rise. As we saw in Chapter 2, economists use this term in contrast with that of an inferior good, one like hot dogs or bus travel, on which people tend to spend less as their incomes rise.

Suppose, for example, that the head of a construction crew asks for a volunteer to do a job that is dangerous but requires no special skill, say, climbing to the top of a church steeple to bolt on the cross that belongs there. She offers a $200 bonus. Who is more likely to volunteer, a skilled electrician, for whom $200 is less than a day's pay, or a laborer, who takes home barely $200 a week? If safety were an inferior good, the electrician would be the first to volunteer, being willing to sacrifice safety in return for a smaller payment. If safety were a normal good, we would expect that a smaller bonus would be needed to get the laborer to climb the steeple than to get the electrician to do so. Evidence from people's behavior in labor markets suggests that safety is a normal good, that is, that higher-paid workers are less willing to sacrifice safety in return for gains in pay.

Much the same goes for safety regulation. Suppose a factory faces the issue of how much to spend removing benzene from the air. To reduce the benzene level to 10 parts per million would cost $100 per worker per year, to cut it to five parts per million would cost $500 per worker per year, to cut it to one part per million would cost $2,000 per worker per year, and so on. If safety is a normal good, a point would eventually be reached beyond which low-paid workers would no longer be willing to make the sacrifice in wages to gain added safety, although high-paid workers might still consider the trade-off worthwhile. Similar reasoning applies in the area of consumer safety: A Mercedes is safer than a Ford Escort, but low-income consumers might object to regulations that made all cars as safe, but as expensive, as a Mercedes.

The tendency of safety regulation to benefit the well-to-do more than the poor could, in principle, be offset if regulations automatically imposed a greater share of the costs of regulation on the well-to-do, but this is not typically the case. Instead, regulations more frequently impose equal burdens on all. Poor communities are expected to meet the same standards for removing asbestos from schools as are wealthy communities. Low-income and high-income consumers both pay the same added cost for required safety features on lawnmowers, space heaters, and kitchen appliances. And employers are required to meet the same standard of protection for the lowest-paid as for the highest-paid workers. In fact, the added cost of protecting each worker may even give the employer an incentive to replace two low-skill, low-paid, workers with one high-skill, high-paid worker.

During Stephen Breyer's confirmation hearings as a Supreme Court Justice, Senator Joseph Biden criticized his views on regulation as "elitist." He contrasted "Harvardese" cost-benefit analysis with "American cultural values" that made people willing to spend money to avoid risks that were objectively small. But it may be that the real elitism lies elsewhere, among professed guardians of public safety who assume that a poor, hungry person is just as willing as a well-fed, wealthy one to see the cost of food driven up by regulations requiring the removal of tiny traces of suspect chemicals.

Safety regulation and liberty An evaluation of safety regulation in terms of liberty can be divided into two parts, according to whether exposure to the risk in question is voluntary or involuntary.

When exposure to risk is voluntary, it is difficult to reconcile mandatory safety regulation with freedom of choice. Libertarians are content to let motorcyclists choose whether or not to wear helmets. Similarly, they are content to let workers decide whether to work in a plant where the level of benzene in the air is high and the pay is also high, or in a different plant where both are lower. This does not, of course, justify fraud or deceit. An employer or product manufacturer who fails to disclose a known hazard violates the workers' or consumers' freedom to make an informed choice.

On the other hand, the standard of liberty does not automatically exclude regulations that prevent one person from involuntarily exposing another to risk. People have no right, for example, to dispose of hazardous wastes in a way that pollutes their neighbors' air or water. Similarly, regulations that prohibit driving while intoxicated, because of the danger to other motorists, are justified by the standard of liberty, even though prohibition of drinking for protection of the drinker's own health is not.

However, the standard of liberty does encourage the search for means of dealing with safety problems that are least intrusive on individual liberties in the circumstances. Mandatory government regulations are not necessarily best in this regard. Alternative public policy approaches to managing risk, which are the subject of the final section of this chapter, are often more attractive to libertarians than regulation.

Alternatives to
mandatory safety regulation

Our discussion to this point has shown that safety regulation is subject to many doubts and dangers. It is not clear what should be the proper goal of such regulation-reducing risk at any cost, minimizing the expected value of loss of life, or enhancing people's psychological perception of safety. Achievement of any goal that is chosen may be frustrated by imperfect institutions of public choice at the stage of voting, legislation, or bureaucratic rulemaking. Even when regulation leads to some measurable improvement in safety, it may do so in a way that is inefficient, inequitable, or inconsistent with individual liberties.

These drawbacks of regulation make it worthwhile to look for alternative means of enhancing safety. This section considers two such alternatives, one based on certification and disclosure, the other on legal liability. In some cases, these offer advantages by each of our three standards of evaluation—efficiency, equality, and liberty.

Certification and disclosure Not everyone values safety equally, as we have seen. Regulations that impose a uniform degree of safety on everyone are likely to violate one or more of the standards of efficiency, equality, or liberty. Such regulatory failure can be avoided by allowing everyone to choose his or her own preferred level of safety, after balancing costs and benefits, provided the exposure to risk is voluntary and the choice is well informed.

Certification and disclosure are ways of creating the conditions for informed, voluntary choice in the area of safety. The two are closely related. *Disclosure* refers to information about risk provided by the seller of a good. *Certification* is a statement by an independent third party to the effect that certain safety standards have been met.

Cigarettes are an example of a product whose risks are handled through disclosure. The government requires cigarette makers to label their product with specific warnings of health hazards, including those of cancer and heart disease. But, at least when smoking is done at a time or place where others are not involuntarily exposed to undue risk, the choice of risk versus pleasure is left to the individual.

The hazards of bacterial infection from meat illustrate the use of certification to control risk. Although it is impossible to reduce the risk to zero, the U.S. Department of Agriculture uses inspectors to verify that reasonable steps are taken to minimize the risk. Consumers are informed that a product meets USDA standards by a seal printed on the package or, in some cases, stamped directly on the meat.

Disclosure and certification can be combined. In the case of over-the-counter medications, for example, the USDA requires disclosure of any hazardous side effects and also certifies that the medication meets its standards of safety and effectiveness.

All of the examples just given concern mandatory certification or disclosure. This means that they do not give consumers complete freedom of choice. You cannot go into your local grocery store and choose between packages of steak that are certified by the USDA and others (possibly cheaper) that are not certified, nor can you choose between painkillers that are certified effective by the FDA and others that have not been reviewed for effectiveness. Nevertheless, even mandatory certification or disclosure gives consumers somewhat more choice than the strictest forms of regulation. For example, lead-based paints are completely banned. Instead, the government could require cans of lead-free paint to carry a seal saying "Certified Lead-Free," and/or require cans of lead-based paints to say "Warning! May cause brain damage! Do not use on surfaces accessible to children!" Similar labels could be required on painted objects. People could then choose for themselves whether or not the risks of lead-based paint were balanced by its advantages of cost and quality.

Certification and disclosure do not have to be mandatory, however. Private organizations certify some goods and services. For example, some products carry a label that says "Union Made." Some consumers take this as an indication of likely superior quality, or prefer union-made goods out of a feeling of solidarity because they themselves are members of labor unions. But nonunion goods are free to compete with them; consumers can take their choice. In this case, there is no issue of safety, but suppose there were no government safety regulations or mandatory certification and disclosure laws. It is then likely that private consumer protection groups would emerge with labels like "U.S. Consumer Safety Association Approved" that shoppers could choose to heed or ignore as they saw fit.

Legal liability Another mechanism that encourages firms to provide safe products and services is their legal liability for harm done by unsafe products. This area of law is called **tort liability**; the word "tort" is a legal term that means "harm." Under tort law, a person poisoned by an improperly packed can of mushroom soup or injured when a defective tire sends a car off the road can sue the manufacturer for compensation. In the case of death, the victim's heirs can sue. Unreasonably hazardous services, such as incompetent medical practice, as well as unsafe products, can be the basis for lawsuits.

Tort law, like regulation, provides an incentive for safety. Lawsuits for defective products or incompetent services are expensive in terms of lawyers' fees, damages paid to victims, and harm to a firm's reputation. In some cases tort liability provides a better mechanism than regulation for balancing the costs and benefice of safety precautions.

An important part of the balancing mechanism in tort law is the concept of **negligence**, which means the failure to take reasonable precautions. For example, suppose a consumer is injured in a fall when a chair breaks. If the leg of the chair broke because of a knot in the wood, the manufacturer may be found negligent, because a reasonable company would have inspected its materials for defects. But if the chair was made properly but broke because it was, say, used to support a car that the victim was repairing, the manufacturer will probably not be found negligent. Thus, chair makers are encouraged to take reasonable, cost-effective precautions to ensure that their products will be safe for sitting, but are not required to take the inefficiently expensive measures needed to make them strong enough to support a car.

Tort law also encourages disclosure. Suppose a consumer is injured by fumes that accumulate when painting furniture in a small, closed room. If the paint can contains a label that says, "WARNING! HAZARDOUS FUMES! USE ONLY WITH ADEQUATE VENTILATION!," the victim may have no grounds to sue. But if the firm fails to take the reasonable and inexpensive precaution of a warning label, it may be found negligent and be required to pay damages to the victim.

Often tort law permits consumers with differing attitudes toward risk to choose greater or lesser degrees of safety. A consumer can, for example, read product labels and decide whether to use safer water-based paint, even though it might not adhere as well to the object being painted. Or, after listening to warnings given by a doctor (who has been advised by a lawyer to give such warnings), a consumer can choose whether or not to undergo a hair transplant or try a weight-loss medication.

Tort law has the further advantage of protecting victims from risks to which they may be exposed involuntarily. Suppose that the blowout of a tire causes a car to crash into another car. Victims in either car can win a lawsuit against the manufacturer if they can show that reasonable precautions were not taken when the tire was made. This deters manufacturers from selling unreasonably low-quality, but cheap, tires that some people with limited budgets might risk buying, thereby endangering other drivers.

Tort law is not a perfect solution to all safety problems. The high costs of bringing and defending against lawsuits is one problem. These costs may sometimes make it impractical for a victim suffering a fairly small harm to sue, with the result that there is inadequate safety incentive. In other cases, the potential cost of suits may induce firms to take extremely expensive safety precautions that are not cost-effective, or even withdraw a product from the market altogether. For example, firms that produce small, private airplanes are often sued by families of crash victims. To defend against such a suit may cost as much as half a million dollars, even when it can be shown that the crash was caused by bad weather or careless flying, not a defective airplane. The cost of such suits has contributed to the near collapse of the small-airplane industry.

Despite these problems, tort law is an important mechanism protecting people from avoidable risks. Like certification and disclosure, it offers an alternative to the regulatory approach to risk management—an alternative that operates within the context of the market system rather than attempting to replace markets with government bureaucracies.

Questions for thought and discussion

1. One argument for safety regulation is that if people become sick or disabled, "society will have to take care of them." Apply this argument to the case of motorcycle helmet laws. Should a very wealthy person, who will not become a public dependent in case of disability, be allowed to ride a motorcycle without a helmet? Should people be exempt from the helmet law if they demonstrate to the Department of Motor Vehicles that they have adequate private health and disability insurance? Discuss.

2. A study by Rachel Dardis (cited by Kip Viscusi—see References) looked at consumer purchases of smoke detectors. Using the expected value model, and based on objective measures of fire danger and the price of a detector, Dardis found an implied value of human life of just $600,000 in this case. Why do you think

consumers place so little value on the protection given by smoke detectors, which objective cost-benefit analysis suggests are a great safety bargain? What implications would you draw from this study for regulation?

3. In the fall of 1994, Washington, D.C. schools opened several weeks late because the school board, contrary to a judge's order, had not corrected certain fire hazards. Some of the hazards were minor, such as a burned-out bulb in an exit sign, and others major, such as missing fire doors. Meanwhile wealthier suburban school districts opened on time. Do you think the judge was right to require the relatively poor D.C. schools to meet the same safety standards as wealthy suburban schools? Why or why not? Discuss.

4. Federal regulations prohibit the sale of raw (unpasteurized) milk, because of the danger of disease. Some people prefer the taste of raw milk, however, and others think it has higher nutritional value. Would you favor a change of law to allow stores to sell raw milk alongside pasteurized milk, provided both were clearly labeled and the possible dangers of raw milk were disclosed? Discuss.

Selected references

Breyer, Stephen G. *Breaking the Vicious Circle: Toward Effective Risk Regulation.* Cambridge, Mass.: Harvard University Press, 1993. *Breyer's views on safety regulation, especially on the ways that well-meaning regulation can bring about counterproductive results.*

——. *Regulation and Its Reform.* Cambridge, Mass.: Harvard University Press, 1982. *An earlier, more systematic exposition of Breyer's views regarding government regulation in general.*

Slovic, Paul. "Perception of Risk" *Science* 236, p. 283 (April 1987). *A good introduction to the psychometric approach to perceptions of risk.*

Viscusi, W. Kip. "The Value of Risks to Life and Health." *Journal of Economic Literature,* December 1993, pp. 1912-46.

Key terms

Psychometrics. An approach to risk assessments that attempts to measure people's subjective perceptions of risk.

Dread risk. A risk having an ability to inspire apprehension and discomfort that is large in relation to the actual mathematical expected value of loss.

Tort liability. A legal principle under which a person who causes a harm (tort) to another person, for example, by negligence or by selling an unsafe product, can be made to pay damages to the harmed party.

Negligence. In tort law, the failure to take reasonable, cost-effective precautions to avoid harm to another.

8

Schools, Garbage, Buses, and the Economics of Privatization

Where did you attend school? If you are like most children in the United States, you went to the public school nearest your home, and had little choice about it. If you lived in impoverished East Harlem, you probably also went to a public school, but your parents would be more likely to have had a choice between a traditional school, the district's B.E.T.A. school (Better Education Through Alternatives), or the prestigious East Harlem Performing Arts School, among others. If you lived in Milwaukee, your range of choice may have been even greater, with the possibility of attending a public school or using public money to attend a private school.

Who picks up your trash? If you live in a small town, your trash is probably picked up by a private firm. If you live in a city, chances are that the garbage collector is a public employee. But some urban communities, like Wichita, Kansas, and Pelham, New York, have found that they can save money by turning trash collection over to private firms.

Do you ride a bus to work or to campus? Who owns it? In almost any city in the United States, chances are that the government owns the bus. Chances also are that your local government got into the bus business less than 30 years ago. But if you live in Buenos Aires, your bus won't belong to the city; more likely, it will belong to the person who drives it.

We think of some services as "naturally" the business of government. The army, the navy, the courts, and the police are common examples. Other services such as laundering shirts or giving haircuts, seem "naturally" private. Only the most thoroughgoing Communist systems have used government-owned firms to provide these services. But in between, as the examples of schools, trash collection, and urban transit show, there are many kinds of service often provided by government but often also provided privately. Policy determines which. But what determines that policy?

Over the first three-quarters of the twentieth century, there was a trend for government to provide more and more services. A major reason for doing so was to promote equality by ensuring that all members of society have fair access to these services. For a long list of public services, along with the decision to *provide* the service to citizens, another decision was also taken: to *produce* those services. So governments became producers of schooling, trash collection services, transportation, police and jail services, library services—you name it.

Meanwhile, private businesses were also growing. They too wanted to provide more goods and services to their customers, and often also, to their employees. But for businesses, the decision to provide was never automatically linked to the decision to produce. To make or to buy was treated as a matter of efficiency, quality control, and maximum consumer satisfaction.

For example, an automobile manufacturer wants to provide its customers with cars—should it make its own engines? Its own radios? Should it make its own steel? Mine the coal and ore from which the steel is made? Henry Ford once built a fully integrated plant that made everything that went into his cars, even the steel. He couldn't make it operate efficiently. It was one of that industrial genius's mistakes.

Suppose the automaker wants to provide its workers with cafeteria services so that they don't have to leave the plant at lunch time. Should it own and operate the cafeteria, or contract out the work to a restaurant operator like Marriott or McDonalds? Some firms do it one way, some the other, although contracting out is becoming more popular.

In the last quarter of this century, governments have started to review the make-or-buy decisions to which they once gave little thought. The result has been a worldwide trend toward **privatization** of government services. The trend, which consists of selling government facilities to private owners or turning government services over to private contractors, has been spurred by the realization that government operation of public services can have unintended negative results that more than accompanied the attempt to equalize provision of goods and services through government.

In this chapter, we will use some basic economic tools, including some elements of public choice theory and the notion of rent seeking, to examine the consequences of government provision of services and the reasons for the privatization movement.

The economics of
incentives and monitoring

Before looking at actual case studies of privatization, we need some background in the economics of incentives and monitoring. To give someone an incentive means to reward that person for behaving in one way rather than another. To *monitor* someone means to watch how the person is behaving. Problems of monitoring and providing incentives are very important considerations in deciding how the production of services should be organized.

We can use the very basic task of trash removal to show that monitoring and incentives are problems of social interaction. They would not exist for a castaway like the fictional Robinson Crusoe, living alone on an island. Suppose Robinson wants to remove a mess of old banana peels from his hut. He doesn't have to worry about monitoring how the job is carried out—he himself, after all, is the one who must do it, and he has an incentive to do it quickly and well to leave himself more time for fishing.

Economic interactions where only two people are involved are hardly more complicated. Suppose you hire a worker to clean up some brush in your yard for a fixed payment of $20. Monitoring simply consists of looking to make sure the brush is gone before you hand over the money. And the worker has the same incentive Robinson Crusoe did—the quicker the job is done, the more time for other things.

In a complex modern city, however, things may be different. Very often workers and supervisors can get by with inefficient work habits and can escape any penalty for doing so. Sanitation workers, for example, are usually paid according to the number of hours they spend on the job. Within certain boundaries, they are often able to slack off on productivity without fear of retaliation. On the other hand, if they act to raise productivity, they may get no personal reward.

Suppose a work crew decides to perform a job at a more leisurely pace. Suppose they take extra-long rest breaks or fail to maintain their truck or tools properly. Why not do these things, so long as no loss of income or job results? By contrast, a worker may be especially diligent or may discover a new, more productive way of doing the job. But why do so unless a reward is provided in terms of promotion or increased pay?

Here we have problems of both monitoring and incentives. If information were costless and immediately available, we would always be able to reward and penalize workers according to how well they did their jobs. We could construct an ideal incentive system: Each worker would be able to reap the full rewards of good decisions and bear the full costs of bad ones.

Unfortunately, information is not costless. This means that in order to monitor worker behavior we often need a manager. But managers rarely monitor perfectly. For one thing, complete monitoring of worker behavior could very well cost more than the benefits. For another, the monitor may not be a good monitor. The monitor's decisions will also affect the efficiency of production. Ideally, the monitor should reap the benefits of good decisions and bear the cost of bad ones. But how can we assess the contribution of the monitor unless there is someone else who monitors the monitor? And who will monitor the monitor's monitor?

Monitoring workers is not the only problem that affects how production can best be organized. Monitoring and incentives concern the behavior of consumers as well. For example, if the price consumers pay for garbage removal is independent of the quantity they put out for collection, they have no incentive to reduce the volume of garbage they generate. Should one buy a trash compactor? Purchase disposable bottles or returnable ones? Throw away aluminum cans or sell them to reprocessing companies? If price is independent of trash volume, consumers will tend to make these choices based on their own convenience.

What is true of households is even more true of commercial enterprises, for whom the options of waste disposal are typically wider. But if businesses and households are charged on the basis of the volume of garbage they generate, someone must monitor that volume.

Let's look briefly at how monitoring and incentive problems are handled in the private sector. Then we will turn to the public sector.

Monitoring and incentives in the private sector Most private refuse companies are small and are typically owned and managed by only a few people. They are either organized as proprietorships or as corporations with very few stockholders.

Because the companies are privately owned, separate contracts are signed between the owners and each of the workers. The workers are guaranteed a fixed compensation in return for their services, but the owners have the right to hire and fire or to renegotiate salaries in accordance with their assessment of worker productivity. The owners, of course, receive the difference between the firm's revenues and its expenses. If the difference is positive, they realize profits; if the difference is negative, they suffer financial losses.

In such a firm the owners have strong incentives to engage in efficient monitoring. They realize the full financial rewards of good managerial decisions and suffer the full financial penalties for bad ones. Through experimentation, they discover how much monitoring of worker and consumer behavior pays off. Inefficient techniques are discarded in favor of efficient ones as owners strive to increase their income.

The owners are also spurred to efficiency by another force: competition. Private companies typically operate under one of two types of arrangements—either they sign contracts with individual homeowners and business firms or they sign a contract with a city government. In either case they run the risk of having their bids undercut by aggressive competitors.

Competition does not always work perfectly, however. Competitors have been known to collude on bids and artificially raise the prices for their services. They appear to be more successful at this when dealing with a city government than when dealing with private customers, but consumers have also been gouged on occasion. Even so, the existing competition seems to keep prices well below the cost of government-operated services. Let's see why.

Monitoring in the public sector At first glance, it may seem that a company owned by a democratically elected government and managed by civil servants is not altogether different from a large corporation owned and managed by private citizens. After all, each voter appears to be similar to a shareholder. Voters are entitled to vote for political officeholders, just as shareholders are entitled to vote for members of the board of directors of a corporation. Moreover, just as shareholders share in the profits and losses of corporations, so voters share in the profits and losses of governmental enterprises through higher or lower taxes needed to finance other government services.

True, the single voter's influence in any particular election is negligible, but the same may be said of many large corporations. For example, about 3 million people held shares of stock in American Telephone and Telegraph before its breakup into several parts. About half of these held fewer than 15 shares each; no single owner had more than 1 percent of the total. Since the breakup, ownership is even more widely fragmented. Nonetheless, such huge corporations can produce efficiently. They are certainly able to compete with proprietorships and smaller firms. Can government do the same?

Sometimes, perhaps—but there is an important difference between a government-owned firm and a private firm. In a democracy you cannot buy and sell your vote in the way you can buy and sell a share of corporate stock. This is not necessarily a defect of democratic society; we would probably not wish it to be otherwise. But this seemingly minor fact has a significant effect on the way government behaves.

To see why, let's briefly consider what incentive corporate managers have to make efficient decisions when ownership of shares is widely spread among millions of people. Who monitors the decisions they make, and what is the effect of the monitoring activity?

The monitoring works like this: Shareholders and potential shareholders, in search of personal gain, seek information about the probable future earning of various companies. They compare their own estimates with the evaluations made by others, as those are reflected in the market price of shares of each company's stock. When they believe a stock is overvalued, they sell shares; when they believe the stock is undervalued, they buy shares.

The motivation for each particular trader, then, is not to penalize or reward company managers for their performance. It is simply to beat the market by buying and selling shares at opportune times. There are many traders doing this, and their collective efforts determine the price of a share of stock at any time. We can be reasonably certain that at any given time on any given day, stock market prices are the best available estimate of the future earnings potential of any particular company. Those prices accurately reflect all known information about the future earnings potential of every large corporation.

How can we be sure of this? Simply because if anyone had better information than other market participants, he or she would buy or sell on the basis of that information. But that very buying or selling would eventually cause the price of the stock to rise or fall until it fully reflected the new information.

If stock market prices are the best available indicators of the current and expected future performance of large companies, stock market prices are also the best available evaluation of the behavior of managers. But how do these prices affect the incentives any particular manager faces?

The fact is that both managers and the boards of directors who instruct those managers are very sensitive to stock market prices. Low share prices (reflecting, say, poor management decisions) mean that a company will find it hard to raise additional capital by selling new stock issues or by borrowing. Low stock prices also encourage rebellions by disgruntled shareholders seeking a chance to profit by selling their shares to a takeover specialist who will install new management. And, of course, managers themselves lose because the value of their own stock, as well as the value of stock options they hold, depreciates as stock prices fall.

By contrast, in the political process, the typical voter has very little to gain by monitoring the behavior of the civil servant managers of public enterprises. Suppose a citizen has some special knowledge—such as a strong indication that the city Sanitation Department will run a deficit next year. There is no way that such knowledge can easily be turned to personal profit. In fact, the only way that such knowledge can be useful is if it is used to persuade a majority of voters to "throw the rascals out" and hire better managers.

But the cost of organizing a political movement to oust the sanitation bureaucracy could be enormous. And what conceivable monetary gain could the voter get in return for the effort? Thirty dollars? Forty? Fifty? Whatever the figure, it represents the upper limit of the voter's financial interest in the issue. Hence, although private investors will pay thousands of dollars to professional analysts to predict the future earnings of a private corporation, who among us would pay an analyst to predict future sanitation costs?

Not only do voters have very weak incentives to monitor the behavior of government managers, the managers themselves are largely insulated from the risks faced by the private manager. Government managers have no fear of takeover bids by other companies. Their ability to raise capital is not affected by stock prices. And since they do not own shares of stock in the government, they realize few of the rewards of good decisions. And, within limits, they bear none of the costs of bad decisions.

Rent seeking and government services But wait, you say. We are forgetting that voters engage in political action. They try to influence the behavior of politicians by campaign contributions, lobbying efforts, and the like. But voters who decide to invest in politics usually find that their returns are much higher if they direct their efforts toward policies whose effects are concentrated on a narrow interest group of which they are part, rather than broad efforts to make the bureaucracy more efficient. Indeed, efforts at general reform typically arouse tough opposition from interest groups who benefit from the very inefficiencies that the reformers attack. These interest-group activities are examples of rent seeking.

Government managers soon discover that the greatest threats to job security arise from the shifting influence of rent-seeking, special-interest groups, not from broad-based inefficiencies. For example, the standard of efficiency dictates that managers should pay workers the lowest wages necessary to bid their services away from competing private employers. But since employees vote, the standard of political survival often dictates that a much higher wage should be paid.

The economics of incentives and monitoring, and of rent seeking, then, suggests that an unintended result of public provision of a service like trash collection will be lower efficiency, compared with the private sector. Numerous studies seem to confirm that prediction.

A look at the evidence A number of studies of municipal garbage collection show that private carriers, on average, outperform the municipal carriers.

One study, conducted at the Columbia University Graduate School of Business under a grant from the National Science Foundation, surveyed over two thousand cities with a combined population of 52 million. The study found that twice-a-week curbside garbage collection cost the average municipal agency 69 percent more than it cost the average private firm. What's more, municipal collection takes twice as long per household, serves fewer households per shift, and involves larger crews and higher employee absenteeism than collection by private companies.

If anything, these figures probably understate the efficiency difference between the two types of organization. In many of the cities where private collectors are used, the collectors contract directly with the city rather than with individual households. Even when cities put these contracts out for bid, they often get gouged by price-fixing agreements among private firms. In fact, the record of government purchases of goods and services from others is not much better than the record of government production of goods and services. Many notorious price-fixing cases involve conspiracies to bid for government contracts.

In general, the propensity to rely on city collection rather than private collection seems to rise as city populations rise. Among cities with populations from 2,500 to 10,000, only 23 percent collect their own garbage. The proportion rises to 73 percent among cities with populations of 250,000 to 750,000. Very few of the largest cities rely on private services, although San Francisco, Portland, Boston, and Indianapolis are exceptions.

This seems to suggest that the larger the city, the easier it is for sanitation unions to secure a political foothold and the harder it is for the city to shop for less expensive alternatives. New York confirms the pattern, pro viding us with a classic example of rent seeking in action.

In 1971, a city-financed study showed that private collectors could pick up garbage at $17.50 a ton, compared to New York City's cost of $49. This result was hotly disputed by the sanitation workers' union, so New York City Environmental

Protection Administrator Jerome Kretchner proposed a test. City and private carriers would simultaneously work in comparable areas to determine the relative efficiency of each. The test was never conducted, however—apparently the sanitation workers' union put enormous pressure on the mayor to halt it.

A private test was done five years later by Professor Emanuel Savas, who also participated in the Columbia University study. Savas compared garbage collection in two sections of Queens with collection in a similar community in Nassau County that was serviced by a private firm. The pri vate firm charged $72 a year per household, while city collection costs were $209. Savas also compared New York City with other major cities, including San Francisco, which held costs to $40 a year per household by relying on private carriers.

The basic principle seems to be well understood in San Francisco if not in New York. S.M. Tatarian, director of San Francisco's Public Works Department, once said, "I shudder to think of what would happen if my department was responsible for collecting garbage. The rates would go through the roof." The reason? Because private enterprise, he explains, can do the job at a lower cost than can municipal employees, who have no incentive to do the job efficiently.

No one doubts that the salaries, fringe benefits, and working conditions enjoyed by New York City's municipal employees are the result of raw political power. It is believed that 250,000 of the 400,000 city workers live in the city; together with relatives, their voting strength is estimated at 500,000. That's over half of the 900,000 voters who normally turn out for the Democratic party primary and a good chunk of the 1.7 million who vote in general elections.

This power pays off. On average, the rate of salary increases for city employees has been twice the rate for federal employees. The biggest increases normally come in election years. Overall, city workers earn up to 25 percent more in straight salaries than do workers performing the same jobs in private industry. Moreover, they can typically retire after twenty years on pensions that are half their highest salary over that time period.

In explaining a particularly lavish settlement with several city unions, an aide to former New York Mayor John Lindsay put it this way: "In the final analysis it was a political decision. The unions had the clout; they were going to get it anyway. Lindsay decided he might as well get the credit."

The role of the bus in urban mass transit

Let's turn now from garbage to urban mass transit—another service provided by government almost everywhere in the United States. In particular, we will look at the case of buses, which, with the possible exception of subways in a few, very densely populated cities in the eastern United States, are the most economical and flexible form of urban mass transit.

As recently as the 1960s, most urban bus systems were privately owned. As time went on, however, these systems faced increasing competition from private cars. In no small part, this competition reflected government policies of providing private cars with free rights-of-way on public roads while making no special efforts to improve bus rights-of-way through construction of busways, designation of special bus lanes, or other measures.

In 1963, for the first time, the urban transit system as a whole faced an overall deficit, amounting to $880,000.[1] The next year, Congress passed the Urban Mass Transit Act, providing federal subsidies for urban mass transit. By 1980, the total mass-transit deficit had grown to $8 billion, almost ten thousand times the 1963 level. True, a good part of this deficit was attributable to losses on urban rail-transit systems, which tend to operate at much higher costs per passenger, but urban bus systems also contributed to the deficit on a massive scale.

In part, the inefficiency of city-owned bus systems stems from the same problems of monitoring and incentives that afflict city-owned garbage collection. Productivity is low. Pay scales reflect the political power of transit unions rather than the realities of the marketplace. Also, city officials have less incentive than private owners to resist costly union demands such as prohibiting employment of part-time drivers. But urban bus systems raise some unique economic issues of their own that bear on the issue of public-versus-private transportation.

Monopoly versus competition in bus service The privately owned and operated urban bus systems that dominated the urban-transit scene as recently as the 1960s failed in part, as we have said, because government policy favored their competitors: private automobiles. That is not the whole story of their downfall, however; they did not represent private enterprise at its competitive best. Instead, most systems operated as *franchised monopolies*, that is, monopolies having government-granted rights to provide exclusive service on specified routes or sometimes for a whole urban area.

As franchised monopolies, these companies faced many of the same incentive and monitoring problems that government bureaucracies face. They tended to be large, and a large scale complicates the process of monitoring in any organization. Also, they did not face the immediate threat of losing business to competitors if their costs rose or their service deteriorated. In principle, cities could, and sometimes did, seek competitive bids before granting bus route monopolies, but, as in the case of contracting for garbage services, this approach was not always successful.

What is more, when it came to issues such as route changes or union bargaining, the private monopoly bus companies were by no means free to make decisions on a dollars-and-cents basis. Instead, they were subject to constant pressures from

1 Gabriel Roth, "Private Sector Alternatives in Urban Transportation," National Center for Policy Analysis, Policy Report No. 125, January 1987, p. 7.

the politicians who granted their franchises and controlled the rights-of-way on which they operated. These politicians, in turn, responded to rent-seeking activities by neighborhood interest groups, real estate developers, unions, and others.

But why would a privately owned municipal bus service have to operate as a franchised monopoly? For example, why not let anyone buy a bus, jump in, and run along the street picking up passengers? The usual answer is that the minimum, technically feasible unit for a bus operation is not an individual bus, but a route. If competing companies operated on a particular route, it is said, there would be chaos. The predictability of service intervals and capacity on which users depend would disappear. In the confusion, all operators would go bankrupt. Sound reasonable? Well, experience abroad suggests otherwise.

One approach to distributing buses among routes and regulating service along routes depends entirely on market incentives. This is the "jitney" system. A jitney can be thought of as a multipassenger taxi that follows a regular route and schedule, but with the route and schedule determined individually by the owner-operator. If some routes become overcrowded with jitneys, operators will leave those routes in search of others where there are more passengers per vehicle. Such a system can adapt quickly to situations such as the opening of a new apartment complex or the addition of an evening shift at a factory.

The jitney system was invented in Los Angeles early in the twentieth century, but there and in most other U.S. cities it was soon outlawed. Today, however, jitney systems are reported to operate successfully in many major cities of the Third World. 2

In some cases, the market may demand more stability and predictability than is offered by fully independent jitneys. In such cases, owner-operators can band together into route associations. A jitney that joins a route association sacrifices some independence. The owner-operator must follow the agreed route, and must abide by association rules that enforce spacing of vehicles, so that operators can't "steal" passengers from a following bus by purposely dropping behind schedule. (Without close monitoring, drivers of city-owned buses have the opposite incentive—they try to make their job easier by carrying as few passengers as possible, which is best done by catching up as close as possible to the bus ahead.) Offsetting this loss of freedom, the greater service predictability of an association may attract a greater total number of riders to a route. Route associations are the basis of the urban bus systems of Buenos Aires and Calcutta, among other cities.

Either the pure jitney system or the route-association system offers benefits in terms of incentives and monitoring by comparison with either municipally owned or franchised monopoly systems. Owners do not have to worry that drivers will abuse the equipment—they are their own drivers. Labor-management problems are eliminated. And drivers have a direct incentive to provide courteous, reliable

---

2 See Roth, pp. 14-16. For more detailed descriptions, see Gabriel Roth and George Wynn, *Free Enterprise Urban Transportation* (New Brunswick, N.J.: Transaction Books, 1982).

service. Even though no major U.S. city currently allows jitneys to ply its streets as common carriers, van pools and charter bus service allow many commuters a limited opportunity to take advantage of these benefits of owner-operator transportation.

Freeways, taxways, and busways What's in a name? In California, multilane, limited-access highways are quaintly called freeways. How different the urban transportation scene might be if these roads were instead more truthfully labeled taxways. A citizen traveling to work on the Harbor Taxway in Los Angeles would then each day be reminded of the fact that urban rights-of-way have opportunity costs, that those opportunity costs reflect scarcity, and that scarce resources cry out for efficient use.

According to many urban transportation authorities, multilane highways open to all drivers without payment of tolls—so-called freeways—are not the most efficient use of taxpayers' dollars. Neither are costly new subway systems, which transportation economists disparage as nineteenth-century solutions to twenty-first-century problems. Instead, the most cost-effective right-of-way for urban transportation may be the busway.

A busway is nothing but a highway, or a lane of a highway, dedicated to mass-transit vehicles. The Virginia suburbs of Washington, D.C., for example, have three major routes that serve as busways. One of these operates on the two center lanes of the Shirley Highway, which are inbound in the morning and outbound in the afternoon. A second, Interstate 66, operates as a busway in the morning and evening rush hours and is open to all traffic at other hours. These two busways are open to private charter buses, jitneylike vanpools, and carpools as well as the municipal buses of the Washington-area Metro system. Buses share the third Washington-area busway, which runs from Route 66 to Dulles Airport, with taxis and private cars bound for the airport. Nonairport traffic is confined to other lanes, separated from the busway by a median strip.

Why do urban-transport economists so love busways? Not because they are high-tech. Not because they are beautiful. They are neither. The reason is that busways recognize that time is the most important opportunity cost of urban travel. And busways—in their low-tech, ugly duckling manner—combine the best features of cars and subways when it comes to economization of time.

Subways and other fixed-rail systems are fast, of course, for the line-haul portion of commuter travel. But the trade-off for rail systems is wide spacing of stations. In the typical, low-density U.S. suburb, the speed of rail commuting is offset by the drive to the station, the hassle of parking, or the time spent waiting for and transferring from a "feeder" bus. This assumes that work is within walking distance at the other end of the subway line; if not, the hassle begins all over again when the passenger leaves the station.

Even where rapid-transit rail systems exist, the opportunity cost of feeder travel to and from the station is so great for many suburban commuters that they drive to work instead, typically one per car. Nothing beats the car for door-to-door pick-up and drop-off, but when it comes to line-haul speed, rush hour driving ranks between snailback and turtle cart.

Busways, properly managed, can offer the best of both worlds. Buses travel a dense route network with many local stops, drive onto the busway for a high-speed, line-haul trip, and then exit to city streets for drop-off service.

In addition to these advantages, busways, unlike rail systems, need not operate on a monopoly basis. A system of busways populated by jitneys and route-association vehicles could potentially achieve high door-to-door speed while avoiding the incentive and monitoring problems of monopoly systems. With a system of tolls properly tuned to reflect the opportunity costs of busway construction, traffic congestion on feeder roads and city streets, air pollution, and other factors, such a busway system would have a better chance than most existing mass-transit systems of being self-financing. It would be tough not to come closer to breaking even than such alternatives as Miami's "metrofail" subway that has been reported to gobble tax dollars at the rate of a $20 subsidy per passenger!

School choice, privatization, and quality of education

Let's face it: the quality of trash collection service is not a hot-button issue for most American families. The cost and quality of urban transit may rouse the passions of city dwellers, but it is a matter of indifference for the millions who live in small towns. But the quality of education affects everyone. That's why school choice and privatization are among the biggest privatization issues we face.

Compared with the horse and buggy era, both trash collection and urban transit are better than they were at the beginning of the century. Many people believe that schools are not. For example, to earn an eighth-grade diploma in a small Kansas town in 1907, author Avis Carlson had to define words like "panegyric" and "talisman," and to find the interest on an 8 percent note running for 2 years, 2 months, and 6 days. Today, half of all high school seniors cannot answer the following question: "Which of the following is true about 87 percent of 10? (a) It is greater than 10; (b) It is less than 10; (c) It is equal to 10; (d) Can't tell." Of eight industrialized countries compared in one study, the United States was the only one in which people over 55 did better than recent high school graduates at a test of locating countries on a map.[3]

The inadequate quality of much American education is not even a matter of controversy. Liberals and conservatives, white, African-American, and Hispanic

---

3 These examples are cited by David Boaz, in "The Public School Monopoly: America's Berlin Wall," in David Boaz, ed., *Liberating Schools: Education in the Inner City* (Washington, D.C.: Cato Institute, 1991), pp. 2-3.

parents all agree on a laundry list of desirable changes: better school discipline, better math scores, lower dropout rates, more dedicated teachers. The controversies concern how to achieve these results.

For decades, establishment educational reformers have tried to achieve these results within the framework of the government-operated monopoly public school system. They have failed far more often than they have succeeded. Now a new generation of reformers is beginning to see privatization and school choice as the keys to success.

Monitoring and incentives in schools We can see why a change in the organizational structure of schools is needed for reform if we consider the extent to which poor educational quality stems from the same problems of incentives and monitoring that plague city-run trash collection and bus services. The issue of merit pay for superior teachers illustrates the problem.

Author Myron Lieberman suggests the following thought experiment.[4] Suppose you and some like-minded supporters of merit pay are elected to the local school board. Luckily, the teacher's union contract is up for renewal. You propose including a 10 percent merit pay bonus for the best 10 percent of teachers in the next union contract. It will add just 1 percent to the total salary bill but it will provide a big incentive for hard work and creativity, you say.

School administrators, who supported the reform when you ran for the school board, now start to drag their feet. They wanted to go on the record as backers of educational quality, but they are not so enthusiastic about monitoring their teachers to select the best 10 percent. For one thing, monitoring is hard work, and they're already busy enough. For another, they know that many teachers they pass over will be angry because they think their work is creative, too. Most frightening of all, if they, the administrators, are asked to monitor teachers more closely, it is likely that someone will begin to monitor their monitoring efforts. The life of a school principal is hard enough already without that!

Even without the administrators' full support, you go to the union. You try to sweeten the package by promising that the merit pay bonuses will be in addition to a scheduled across-the-board raise for all teachers. But the union won't buy it. At public meetings, they claim that "merit" pay will really be extra pay for political boot-lickers and school board favorites. But, in an off-the-record conversation, the union leader reveals her real concerns. "I'm not an administrator, you know," she says. "I'm elected by my members. Why should I support a policy that will make nine of my members angry for each one that is made happy? If I don't act in the interest of the majority, I'll be out of this job. Do you think the majority of teachers want closer monitoring and merit pay? If you thought a majority of teachers were outstandingly dedicated and creative, you wouldn't be proposing merit pay in the

---

4 See *Privatization and Educational Choice* (New York: St. Martin's Press, 1989), Ch. 1.

first place, would you? I don't really care what this proposal will do for the quality of education. Don't ask for my support!"

Voice versus choice as engines of reform The merit pay example illustrates a basic problem with pushing reform within the framework of public schools as they are now constituted. Such efforts rely entirely on the mechanism of *voice* as an engine of reform. Voice, in this case, means parents voting in school board elections, and perhaps also acting through parent associations like the PTA. But the voice of reformers runs into a brick wall of perverse incentives that are built into the public schools just as they are built into municipal transit systems and sanitation departments.

If we compare the private sector, we see that voice plays a minor role as a guarantor of consumer satisfaction. If the door falls off your new Chevy, you don't go out and buy some GM stock, then stand up at the next shareholder's meeting to voice a complaint. Instead, you go down the street and trade the Chevy in on a Ford. That's *choice*, a far more powerful engine of change.

Choice operates weakly in education as it is traditionally structured. There is the choice of tuition-supported private schools for the relatively well-to-do. There are less expensive private alternatives sponsored by some religious groups, but you might not adhere to their particular faith. In some areas, people have the choice of moving from one district or county to another in search of better schools. This does put some pressure on neighboring governmental units to keep quality up, but it is a clumsy form of choice. How well would it work if you had to move to a new house because you didn't like your current brand of refrigerator, instead of staying where you are and buying a new refrigerator?

In the 1990s, the country is alive with all kinds of experiments aimed at expanding the range of choices in schooling. These take many forms:

- Some experiments focus on the make-or-buy decision within the public educational system. School boards enter into contracts with private companies to provide bus services, cafeteria services, or special education services. Competition among providers who bid on the contracts provides an element of choice. The school board still has to monitor the quality of food served by the cafeteria, but the private contractor is responsible for monitoring the work or the individual cooks and dishwashers.

- Some experiments give parents a choice among public schools. Sometimes they simply let parents choose among districts. In other cases, they provide different kinds of schools within one district. East Harlem, with its special schools for children with discipline problems, those with artistic talent, and so on, is an example. Another popular variant allows groups of parents or innovative teachers to form *charter schools* that are financed by government but free of many of the usual bureaucratic restrictions. These approaches do not privatize the schools, but they do privatize the job of monitoring the schools. If parents see that school A is not doing a good job, they send their kids to school B, leaving A's teachers and administrators with fewer students and a smaller budget.

- Some of the boldest experiments, like Milwaukee's, provide parents with vouchers that can be used at either public or private schools. Vouchers represent a form of true privatization in which governments retain their role as providers of education but give up their monopoly as producers. The schools return the vouchers they receive from parents to the school district to get reimbursement. Parents monitor the schools, and express their views through choice. Administrators of both public and private schools are forced to monitor quality closely in order to attract the voucher-wielding parents on which their budgets depend.

An evaluation of privatization

We have already said most of what needs to be said about the benefits of privatization in terms of efficiency. The source of many of the gains of privatization, whether in schools, garbage collection, or mass transit, lies in the improvement of incentives and monitoring. In addition, privatization helps shield the provision of services from rent seeking by narrow interest groups.

Up to this point, however, we have said little about our other standards—equality and liberty. These deserve at least a few comments.

As we pointed out at the beginning of the chapter, a concern for equality is one reason that government has provided certain services in the first place. Take urban transit, for example. When the question of transit subsidies arises, so does the issue of providing affordable transportation for a city's low-income residents, especially those who do not own cars. Privatization of mass transit, it is feared, might mean price increases to cover the full cost of providing services. And how would poor people then get to work?

Proponents of privatization reply that subsidies to city services are not the only way to address the needs of low-income city residents, in transportation or other areas. There are at least two general approaches to reconcile the efficiency gains of privatization with a concern for equality. One is to retain taxpayer responsibility for the financing of certain services, but to contract out the actual operation of those services to private firms. With properly administered competitive bidding, this approach can produce tangible benefits. For example, municipal transit systems can gain from contracting out even small parts of their operations, such as maintenance. Another is to keep municipal trash service for residences while contracting out commercial services. Privatization does not have to be an all-or-nothing affair.

Another general approach to reconciling privatization with a concern for equality is the voucher concept. Under this approach, the education needs of the poor could be addressed through school vouchers, housing needs through housing vouchers, and so on. The food stamp program provides a model: The government attempts to meet the nutritional needs of the poor, but not through nationalization of farms and grocery stores!

The benefit of vouchers over general subsidies is that middle- and upper-income households can still be asked to pay their own way. Of course, some would ask, Why give the poor a grab bag of transit vouchers, housing vouchers, and food stamps—why not just give them cash? But that is another issue for another day.

Equality ties into the privatization debate in another way, quite different from the issue of subsidies and vouchers. One of the strongest arguments in favor of privatization is that government services do not always serve the interests of the poor, even if that is the intent. Instead, the benefits of tax dollars spent on services line the pockets of rent seekers—the contractors who build subway lines, the sanitation union members who receive wages twice those in the private sector, the teachers' union members who get paid regardless of how well they do their jobs. Getting the interest groups' hands out of the taxpayers' pockets can leave more resources for improving services that are more difficult to privatize, like police protection.

The equality issue is especially sensitive where education is concerned. Some reformers think that vouchers are just fine for middle-class white parents, but that low-income and minority parents still need the heavy hand of government monopoly to constrain their choices. Wisconsin State Representative Polly Williams, a strong backer of school choice, is one of a growing number of minority-group parents who get good and mad when they hear self-appointed reformers taking this line. Here is what she says:

"If your children come out of a home like my home-my husband and I divorced very early-they're supposedly doomed. My son is supposed to be in jail right now, if you listen to the social critics. . . . I am one of those people who is supposed to be very stupid because I am black, I live in the inner city, I am poor, and I raised my children in a single home. Well, those are all lies. . . . When you empower parents like myself, there is a major difference. We want to be responsible for ourselves. We are sick and tired of dependency on social programs that take away our will, motivation, and drive."5

Finally, consider the standard of liberty. Privatization advances the cause of liberty in several ways. First, it frees taxpayers from the demands made on them by interest groups. Second, by opening public services to competition, it gives citizens, as consumers, greater freedom of choice. And third, privatization opens new opportunities for entrepreneurs to seek their fortunes in areas such as mass

---

5 Polly Williams, "School Choice: A Vehicle for Achieving Educational Excellence in the African-American Community," *The Heritage Lectures*, No. 414 (Washington, D.C.: The Heritage Foundation, 1992), p. 2.

transit, trash collection, or security services that are closed to them in many cities. Privatization just may be an idea whose time has come.

Questions for thought and discussion

1. In U.S. higher education, one finds both public and private institutions. Can a case be made for privatizing all of higher education? What would be the possible drawbacks of doing so? Discuss in terms of efficiency, equality, and liberty.

2. Rent seeking by public-employee unions was mentioned as a factor in both trash collection and urban bus service. Why is rent seeking by unions more a factor in the public sector than it would be if trash collectors and bus systems were privately owned?

3. If subways and other rail-based transit systems are more costly to build and operate than busways—and if they provide slower service measured door-to-door, except in very-high-density areas—why are they so popular in political terms? Discuss, in terms of the concepts presented in this chapter, the nature of the coalition that might support rail transit over busways.

Selected references

Alchian, Armen, and Harold Demsetz. "Production, Information Costs and Economic Organization." *American Economic Review* 62 (1972). *A classic statement of the economics of incentives and monitoring.*

Boaz, David, ed. *Liberating Schools: Education in the Inner City.* Washington, D.C.: The Cato Institute, 1991. *A collection of the views of many authors on how to use choice as an engine of educational reforms.*

Liberman, Myron. *Privatization and Educational Choice.* New York: St. Martin's Press, 1989. *Discusses all aspects of privatization and school choice, ranging from contracting out educational services to vouchers to for-profit schools.*

Pirie, Madsen. *Dismantling the State.* Dallas, Texas: National Center for Policy Analysis, 1985. *A look at privatization around the world.*

Poole, Robert. *Cutting Back City Hall.* New York: Universe Books, 1980. *A study of opportunities for privatizing municipal services.*

Reason Foundation, Los Angeles, CA. This private research foundation publishes numerous case studies and how-to guides relating to every aspect of privatization.

Key terms

Privatization. Turning over government production of goods and services to the private sector through contracting out or sale of government enterprises.

Monitoring. The process of observing and evaluating the performance of an agent or subordinate.

Franchised monopoly. A private firm whose monopoly status in a given market is protected by laws or government regulations that prevent the entry of competitors.

9

Flying the Deregulated Skies

Several chapters in this book have dealt with policies that are inequitable, inefficient, and offensive to liberty but which have achieved apparent political immortality. In this chapter, we make a refreshing change of pace. We will look at a regulatory dinosaur from the 1930s that finally bit the dust: airline regulation.

The results of a decade and a half of airline deregulation have won wide approval among economists. Deregulation has also been endorsed by the public, which has cast its vote by purchasing record quantities of air travel. However, deregulation has brought change to the industry, and change always has its opponents. The changes that have occurred since deregulation have often surprised both its original backers and opponents, proving that good policy as well as bad can have unintended consequences. The surprises, the successes, and the continuing calls for reregulation from a minority of industry observers will all be discussed in this chapter.

Flying in the bad old days

Back in the bad old days, flying was different. Say you were a corporate executive wanting to make a quick trip from Chicago to Los Angeles. The day before your trip, you called your travel agent who gave you a choice of flights from the Official Airline Guide. They all cost about the same, and so what, the company was paying. You chose one airline over the others because it had an ad in that day's Wall Street

Journal boasting of extra wide seats and thick, juicy steaks. You took a taxi to the airport, arriving just a few minutes before the flight. There was no line at the check-in desk, so you made the plane in plenty of time. Even though you flew coach, you had plenty of room to spread your papers on the empty seat next to you. You were served by a flight attendant who was guaranteed to be a single young woman because the airlines openly discriminated against men and married women for this job category. As you sliced into your steak, you fell into a conversation with the executive sitting across the aisle, who turned out to be a potential customer.

Today, flying is different. Your travel agent gives you a bewildering array of routes and fares. If you wait to the last minute to book your flight, it may be sold out. You have to get to the airport well in advance of departure time because the place is jammed. In place of the juicy steak, you get a lukewarm chunk of turkey in an unidentifiable sauce, served by a flight attendant wearing a conspicuous wedding ring. You can hardly get your papers out of your briefcase because you are wedged into a center seat between a USC football lineman and a gum-chewing teenager plugged into a Walkman. As you try vainly to slice your lump of turkey with a plastic knife, you fall into conversation with the football player and are infuriated to learn that he paid exactly one-third as much for his ticket as you did. Oh, for the bad old days!

Each of these vignettes has an element of truth. The old system of regulation did tend to produce gold-plated service for business customers, even though it priced many others out of the market. The new system does have its annoyances—especially for those who were pampered before. Let's see how regulation worked and why it produced these results.

Origins of the CAB The Civil Aeronautics Board (CAB), like so many of our economic institutions, traces its origins to the Great Depression of the 1930s. The 1930s were terrible times. The economy virtually collapsed. The unemployment rate rose to a quarter of the labor force. Real GDP plunged by a third. And prices of just about everything fell dramatically.

For those of us brought up to regard inflation as the greatest threat to economic stability, it is hard to imagine that deflation was seen as just as great a disaster. Because prices fell, employers had to cut wages. Because wages were cut, people couldn't afford to buy the things that were being produced, so factories closed and workers joined the bread lines. Businesspeople said, "If prices were only higher, we could afford to put people back to work." Finding a way to raise prices became a national obsession.

We have already seen that raising prices was a central aim of the 1933 Agricultural Adjustment Act. Similar schemes were proposed for industry. A favorite theme of industrial policy was the organization of government-sponsored *cartels*; that is, associations of businesses working together to raise prices. These cartels were administered by governmental regulatory boards that would cooperate with the industries they regulated to restrict competition and limit output. Restricting competition, it was reasoned, would let firms raise prices; at higher prices, the firms could afford to hire more workers; and with more people at work, the Depression would soon be over.

This reasoning has long since been recognized as wrong-headed. Today, the Depression is understood to have been brought on by macroeconomic causes related to banking, monetary policy, investment, and international trade. No one now believes that the Depression was caused by an excess of competition. Yet many anticompetitive institutions survived the Depression and lived on for decades. One of them was the CAB, established in 1935.

The CAB's mission was to foster a strong and profitable airline industry—one in which competition was tightly controlled. It held the power to exclude new airlines, to limit the number of carriers serving any given city pair, and to maintain minimum fares on each route. It exercised these powers vigorously. For example, from 1938 to 1978, the CAB did not allow a single new long-haul airline to enter the market.

Intended and unintended results of regulation Despite vigorous control over entry and fares, one expected effect of regulation, high airline profits, never really materialized. The industry did grow rapidly, as air travel changed from a daring adventure for the rich to the standard form of business travel. However, airline profitability did not regularly exceed the average for nonregulated firms and often fell below it. There were two reasons for lackluster profits.

The first reason was a common problem of cartels: When a cartel restricts one type of competition among its members, competition breaks out in some new form. The CAB blocked two of the most obvious forms of competition—entry and fares. But doing so simply pushed competition into a new arena: service quality.

One dimension of service quality was frequency of departures. Because all airlines were required to charge roughly the same fares, the one with the most convenient departure times would get the most passengers. But scheduling more and more departures reduced the number of seats filled on each flight. In addition, airlines competed vigorously to offer the juiciest steaks, the widest seats, and the most generous drinks. Catering to every fantasy of their clients, mostly male business travelers, many airlines also used discriminatory hiring practices to ensure that all flight attendants would be young, female, and unmarried. But all these forms of service competition were costly, keeping profit margins thin.

The second reason for weak airline profits under regulation was the industry's vulnerability to rent seeking. The CAB's regulation of fares and entry did succeed in keeping airline revenues high, but not necessarily profits. The trouble was that airline stockholders did not always manage to make it to the front of the line when the time came for making claims on those revenues.

One competing claimant was labor. All major labor groups in the airline industry developed powerful unions that achieved wages well above the average for jobs of comparable skills in other industries. This was true for pilots, machinists, and flight attendants. Airline management granted these wages in the certainty that added costs could be passed along to customers through higher fares. The CAB, partly in deference to the unions' political clout, cooperated in this operation.

Rural and small-city interests also proved adept at rent seeking. Several regulatory policies benefited these interests. One was to set fares on long flights between major city pairs at a level well above the cost of providing service, while holding fares on short flights between smaller city pairs at or below cost—a policy known as *cross-subsidization*. A second policy was to limit the right of airlines to abandon service to small airports, even while limiting entry into long-haul markets. Finally, money-losing service to small communities was further supported through direct subsidies.

All in all, to think of the airline industry under the CAB as a cartel is only partly accurate. True, the CAB's restrictions on entry and fare competition were standard cartel practices. But the high revenues generated by these practices were not all allowed to flow to airline stockholders in the form of high profits. Instead, the airlines had to share them with other groups of rent seekers: unions, small-community residents, and business travelers more interested in service quality than low fares.

The end of regulation The coalition of owners, unions, business travelers, and small-community interests that supported airline regulation was, in political terms, a powerful one. For more than four decades, it ruled the skies. Economists criticized the system as inefficient, and consumer groups grumbled occasionally about high fares, but to no avail. But then came the inflationary 1970s. As if to prove the old saying, "It's an ill wind that blows no good," inflation proved to be a hurricane that swept regulation away.

Just as falling prices provided the impetus to establish regulation in the 1930s, inflation provided the issue that deregulators needed in the 1970s. The way to get prices down, they lectured, is to spur competition. Down with the regulatory dinosaurs! Legislators who had yawned when economists gave abstract testimony about the inefficiencies of regulation sat up and noticed. Casting a vote to end inflation looked like good politics.

Airline unions sent their top guns into action. Some of the airlines, some passenger groups, and some small-community interests offered supporting ground fire. But the effort failed. Other airlines broke ranks and favored deregulation. Testimony from consumer groups wanting low fares for ordinary folks offset the impact of testimony by business-travel interests. And small communities were bought off with a scheme to continue direct subsidies, even after regulatory cross-subsidies ended. In 1978, the deregulators won their first major victory with the Airline Deregulation Act. (In the next four years, they won comparable victories over regulation in the air freight, trucking, railroad, and intercity bus industries.)

Expected results of deregulation

Proponents of airline deregulation predicted a number of results: lower average fares and a changed fare structure; increased passenger volume; entry by new airlines and entry into new markets by existing airlines; changes in service quality; and changes in labor relations. All of these effects have materialized.

Lower fares Revenue per passenger mile is the broadest measure of air fares. Inflation-adjusted revenue per passenger mile fell from about 4.5 cents per mile in 1976 to about 3.5 cents per mile in 1986, and has not changed much since. But the decline did not affect all classes of fares equally. Recall, for example, that under regulation, airlines were forced to overcharge for long flights and undercharge for short flights. Not unexpectedly, under deregulation, standard coach fares on flights over two thousand miles decreased, and those on flights under two thousand increased. A great variety of discount fares also became available—a subject to which we will return later in the chapter.

Lower fares brought a huge surge in passenger volume. From 1978 to 1990, the annual number of passengers flying rose by 120 percent. The fact that this increase was accompanied by a much smaller increase in aircraft takeoffs reflects enormous efficiencies in terms of fewer empty seats and larger aircraft. Of the new passengers, tens of millions are nonbusiness travelers lured to the air by fares that are lower than bus fares in many markets. Before deregulation, 55 percent of passengers flew at company expense. Now almost 55 percent fly at their own expense for pleasure.

Immediately following deregulation, many new airlines entered the business. From 1976 to 1982, the number of airlines providing scheduled service rose from 28 to 61. Airlines made dramatic changes in their route structures, including the development of the hub-and-spoke system, about which we will have more to say shortly. Major carriers abandoned some short-haul and small-city markets, while regional and commuter airlines increased their service to such points.

Service quality There were also predictable changes in service quality. With higher passenger volume, the luxury of flying on half-full planes became a sometime thing. Business travelers found themselves having to pay business-class or first-class prices to enjoy roomy seating. Because airlines were now free to compete on the basis of price, low-price airlines predictably offered less elegant meals than the full-service carriers of the past. A few even invited passengers to bring their own meals in a brown paper bag. And a few aging male chauvinists no doubt regret the demise of employment discrimination that has brought men, mothers, and even grandmothers into the ranks of flight attendants.

As much as they have benefited the public at large, the combination of lower fares, higher passenger volume, and reduced service quality (on some flights) has generated calls for reregulation. Gregg Easterbrook, writing in *The New Republic,* put it this way: "The expense account class, beneficiaries of the old regulated airline system, are furious that their club now admits the unwashed. Air travel, once classy and pleasantly exclusionary, has become a madhouse of screaming kids and stalled queues."[1]

Labor relations Finally, deregulation has had predictable effects on airline labor. Some of the new entrants were nonunion operations with markedly lower wage scales than the incumbent carriers. Although average airline wages are still good compared to other industries, some employees have had to take salary cuts, and others have had to adjust to changed work rules. Some airlines introduced two-tier wage structures, under which recently hired workers earn less than those who were already on the job before deregulation. These schemes can be a source of labor tension. The most highly publicized airline labor dispute of all arose from the attempt to integrate unionized Eastern Airlines with largely nonunion Texas Air, parent of Continental Airlines. This dispute, together with other problems, eventually led to the bankruptcy and liquidation of Eastern. But even for labor, the picture has not been all bad. Total employment in the industry has risen by more than a third since deregula tion, and the jobs are still attractive enough that even the low-wage carriers have plenty of applications.

Safety: An expected nonresult During the debate, opponents of deregulation warned that safety would suffer if airlines were granted freedom to compete with one another. The argument was that competition would erode profit margins and that airlines, desperate to survive, would cut inspections, maintenance, and pilot training. Today, this argument continues to be raised by would-be reregulators whenever there is a crash or a near miss.

Economists did not expect safety to suffer from deregulation, and their expectation has been borne out. The principal reason is that safety is far from being a frill, like wide seats and juicy steaks, to be sacrificed as the intensity of competition grows. On the contrary: Competitive markets encourage adherence to rigorous safety standards. As a report by the President's Council of Economic Advisers puts it, "When an airline experiences an accident, the price of its stock suffers a loss. If carriers attempted to reduce safety precautions to an unacceptable level, they could be affected adversely by FAA enforcement actions, increased insurance premiums, increased cost of borrowing, and a loss of reputation."[2]

Economists Severin Borenstein and Martin Zimmerman have tried to estimate the size of the market penalty paid by an airline for a fatal accident. They found that the market price of the stock of an airline fell by an average of 2.3 percent, or $31 million, in the two days following a crash caused by pilot error. (If the carrier was

---

1 Gregg Easterbrook, "The Sky Isn't Falling," *The New Republic*, November 30, 1987, p. 20.

2 President's Council of Economic Advisers, *Economic Report of the President* (Washington, D.C.: Government Printing Office, 1988), pp. 211-12.

not at fault, the decline was somewhat less.) About a third of the decline was attributable to the expectation of increased insurance premiums and the rest to damage to reputation and lost passenger revenue.[3]

Broader data confirm that the long-term trend toward safer air travel was not reversed by deregulation, as the critics feared. In fact, the moment of deregulation cannot even be identified from the data shown in Figure 9-1. The good safety record after deregulation looks even better when one takes into consideration increased congestion of major airports and the serious disruption of the air traffic control system following the 1981 mass firing of controllers.

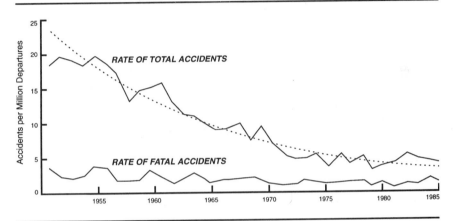

Figure 9-1 Actual and Predicted Accident Rates, 1955-1990

A complete discussion of safety should also take into account an estimated 7 to 14 percent of the increase in air travel that took place after deregulation represented trips that otherwise would have been made by car. Because air travel is about 20 times safer than automobile travel, this effect represents another 90 to 140 lives saved each year as a result of deregulation.[4]

---

3 "Market Incentives for Safe Commercial Airline Operation," *American Economic Review*, (December 1988), pp. 913-35.

4 For a discussion of several studies of this issue, see Nancy L. Rose, "Fear of Flying? Economic Analyses of Airline Safety," *Journal of Economic Perspectives*, Spring 1992, pp. 80-82.

Unexpected results of deregulation

Although most of the predicted effects of deregulation did take place, there have been other effects that neither the backers of deregulation nor its opponents expected. There is a reason for this. All of the effects listed above-lower fares, more passengers, changes in service, lower wages, continued safety gains-are based on the way airlines would be expected to respond as simple maximizers when the old constraints of regulation were removed. However, as we have seen in other chapters, policy changes also tend to call forth entrepreneurial responses. Since such responses consist of finding new ways of doing things that no one ever tried before, they are inherently less predictable. In this section, we will look at three unexpected entrepreneurial responses to deregulation.

The hub-and-spoke system The most noted innovation in the airline industry since deregulation has been the emergence of the hub-and-spoke pattern of airline operations. Under this system, airlines channel many flights into one or a few airports selected as hubs. From there, passengers continue their trips on flights leaving the hub. Thus, for example, a passenger traveling on Continental from Washington, D.C., to Salt Lake City would fly through Continental's Denver hub.

The hub-and-spoke system has advantages for both airlines and their passengers. For the airlines, it means superior utilization of equipment. Short flights feed into the hub and fill up large planes flying longer routes. Baggage-handling and catering facilities can be more centralized.

For passengers, the hub-and-spoke system means a dramatic decrease in the need to change airlines in mid-trip. In 1977, 68 percent of connecting passengers changed airlines; by 1987, that figure had fallen to 12 percent. Single-airline service is strongly preferred by airline customers. It means more convenient connection times, shorter transfers within a terminal, fewer missed flights, fewer lost bags, and better customer service from the airline in case weather or equipment problems do cause a missed connection. The percentage of all travelers who changed airplanes (as opposed to airlines) increased somewhat over this period, presumably reflecting the fact that connections were now quicker and more reliable. All the major carriers have now adopted the hub-and-spoke system. The improved quality of connections has helped offset some of the negative impact of deregulation on service quality, such as more crowded airplanes and airports.

Trends in concentration The hub-and-spoke system, itself an unexpected result of deregulation, has had some unexpected results of its own. Most importantly, it is thought to have been a major factor in the reconcentration of the airline industry that took place after the initial period of new entry. As shown in Figure 9-2, the reconcentration took the form of a wave of mergers involving both old-line carriers and new entrants: Delta merged with Western, Northwest with Republic; USAir acquired PSA and Piedmont; TWA took over Ozark; and Texas Air turned itself into an industry giant, combining all or parts of Continental, Eastern, People Express, and Frontier.

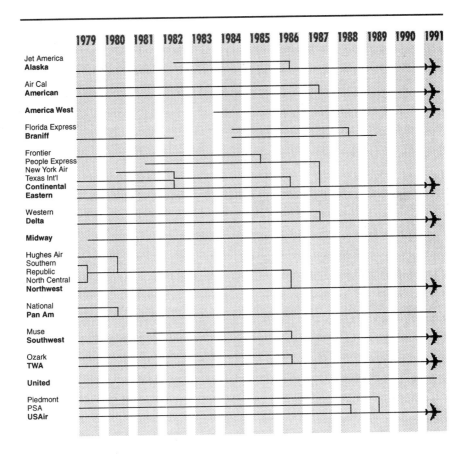

Figure 9-2 Chronology of Large U.S. Airlines Since Deregulation

In effect, the hub-and-spoke system seems to have changed the basic minimum unit of airline operation from the city pair to the hub. As long as the relevant market was the single city pair, airline markets were seen as highly contestable. By a **contestable market**, economists mean one where new competitors can enter at little cost, and if the entry doesn't work out, they can also leave at little cost. In the early days of deregulation, airlines like People Express and New York Air proved the contestability of individual city-pair markets by quickly entering and leaving many routes. This was possible because airplanes are inherently mobile and because a couple of gates and a ticket counter could be rented at any airport.

However, if the hub is the basic unit of operation, the market appears to be less contestable. Building a hub requires heavy investment in ground facilities, including maintenance centers, kitchens, and even new terminal buildings. These, unlike aircraft, cannot be moved around and, unlike gates and ticket counters, cannot be rented for just a few months. Furthermore, there are very few airports in the country with enough traffic to serve as hubs for more than two carriers.

Despite the tendency for one or two carriers to dominate most hub airports, broader measures of concentration show little or no increase for the national airline system as a whole. One widely used measure of concentration is the **Herfindahl index**. This measure of concentration has a value of 1.0 for a market that is completely monopolized by a single carrier, and approaches Ý as the number of competitors becomes large and their market shares become small.[5] The average Herfindahl index for the airline industry as a whole decreased from 0.106 in 1977 to 0.093 in 1982, and then increased to 1.21 by 1990. Most economists consider city-pair markets (e.g., New York-Chicago) to be a better measure of concentration. City-pair markets are more concentrated than the national market as a whole, but their degree of concentration has been falling, from an average value of 0.531 in 1984, at the peak of new entrant activity, to 0.506 in 1990. Short-haul markets became slightly more concentrated over this period, while long-haul markets became significantly less concentrated.[6]

Discounts and price discrimination The hub-and-spoke system has not been the only unexpected effect of deregulation. Another surprise, at least to some economists, has been the explosion of *price discrimination* in the form of discount fares, frequent-flyer plans, and other devices. Thus, Alfred Kahn, former head of the CAB and the "father of deregulation," wrote in 1979 that "much of the price discrimination will tend to disappear" under the impact of increased competition.[7]

For a time, it seemed that the prediction would come true. Several of the new entries right after deregulation were low-cost, nonunion carriers that offered across-the-board low fares on every seat. The best known of these, and for a time the most successful, was People Express. With fares like $19 for Washington, D.C. to Newark, New Jersey, not even the bus lines could compete, let alone the heavily unionized traditional airlines.

---

5 The Herfindahl index is equal to the sum of the squared market shares of the firms in the market. If the market shares are expressed in decimal terms (e.g., .5 for a firm with half of the market), the maximum value of the index is 1.0, its value for a market equally divided between two firms is .5, and its value for a market equally divided between 10 firms is .1. Sometimes the index is calculated for market shares expressed as percentages (e.g., 50 percent for a firm with half the market). In this case its value ranges from 10,000, for complete monopoly, to 0.

6 These data are from Severin Borenstein, "The Evolution of U.S. Airline Competition," *Journal of Economic Perspectives* (Spring 1992): Tables 1 and 2.

7 Alfred Kahn, "Surprises from Deregulation," *American Economic Review* May 1988, p. 320.

But the major carriers fought back successfully against the new entries. In a series of sometimes painful labor negotiations and management reforms, they cut their costs. More importantly, they developed targeted fare-cutting strategies that matched the low fares of the new airlines on selected routes. For one reason or another, the new entrants could not successfully sustain their position. People Express ran into trouble with too-rapid expansion. Its idiosyncratic management style, one of the sources of its early success, did not work well once the organization became large. In the face of selective fare cutting by the major airlines, the new entrants could not generate enough revenue to cover their costs with low fares across the board. One by one, the new entrants were absorbed into the expanding hub-and-spoke operations of the major carriers.

In retrospect, Kahn now thinks he should not have been surprised at the pervasiveness of price discrimination in today's deregulated airline industry. In fact, the industry meets the classic conditions for price discrimination.

First, it has high *fixed costs* and low *marginal costs.* Once a plane is flying, filling an empty seat costs the airline virtually nothing. At the same time, a uniform price high enough to cover average cost means that many planes will have many empty seats most of the time. When these conditions are met, the airline can increase revenues by filling empty seats at discount rates.

A second requirement for successful price discrimination is that the product be nontransferable. Otherwise, customers qualifying for the low prices will buy more than they need and resell the surplus to customers not qualifying for low prices directly from the supplier. (Imagine, for example, a bar that tried to sell beer to women at $1 a glass and to men at $2 a glass. Women would order all the drinks and pass them across the table to their male companions.) But airline tickets are nontransferable (for the most part), so price discrimination works.

There is a third necessary condition for price discrimination that airlines also meet: the ability to know which customers have inelastic demand and which have elastic demand. For airlines, the inelastic demand customers, who can be charged a high price, are business travelers. The elastic demand customers, who would stay home or drive at high prices, are vacation travelers, students, and so on. Of course, airlines are not so crude as to ask their customers whether they are traveling on business or pleasure. That would only encourage lying. Instead, they note that for the most part, business travelers like to get home by Friday night, book their flights only a few days in advance, often make intermediate stops, and often request refunds after last-minute changes of plans. By offering cheap tickets that require advance purchase, require a Saturday night stay, prohibit intermediate stops, and disallow full refunds, they separate the two groups of travelers fairly effectively.

Price discrimination by airlines sometimes draws complaints. Vacation travelers would like cheap tickets with no restrictions; business travelers would like more empty seats and less crowded airports. However, for the most part, discrimination in this market leaves everyone better off than average-cost pricing of all seats. Airlines gain revenue by filling more seats. Casual travelers who used to be priced out of the market now get a chance to fly, even though they have to put up with some restrictions. And although business travelers suffer from crowding of planes and airports, they gain from more frequent flights. Finally, more people flying ultimately means a more competitive industry. To date, competition has been sufficient so that even full-fare coach seats are often no more expensive, adjusted for inflation, than before deregulation.

Other effects: airports and air traffic control Airline deregulation, as we have seen, has had many positive results: lower fares, more efficient hub-and-spoke operations, and more frequent flights. It has also had some negative results, however. Most of the negatives have stemmed from the enormous rise in traffic volume over the last decade. To some extent these negatives reflect the fact that air transportation is really a three-part system, of which the airlines are just one part. While airlines have been deregulated, the second part of the system, airports, and the third part, the air traffic control system, remain government monopolies that are not subject to market incentives or the discipline of competition.

First, consider airports. While passenger volume has risen 120 percent, airport capacity has barely changed. Only one major airport, serving Denver, has been built since deregulations and no others are planned before the end of the century. Some airports have expanded runways and ground facilities, but many find it difficult to do even that.

In some cases, airport expansion has been slowed by bureaucratic restrictions and red tape. Washington, D.C.'s National and Dulles airports are examples. Rising traffic volume put a tremendous strain on these facilities, but Congress, which controlled the airports, was reluctant to spend any money to improve them because doing so would make the federal budget deficit look worse. Finally, after years of wrangling, these airports were transferred to a regional authority authorized to borrow money for expansion and renovation. But meanwhile, traffic volume has risen so much that even the expanded facilities will probably be crowded.

In other cases, airport expansion or construction has been slowed by opposition of local residents. Airports have serious negative externalities, especially in the form of noise and congestion of local roads. Ideally, a new airport should not be built unless the benefits to travelers outweigh the costs to local residents. If a new airport is to make everyone better off, local residents must somehow be compensated. For example, a new airport might promise to collect landing fees from airlines and use the fees to underwrite road improvements, schools, police, and other local services. Local residents would thus be compensated for airport nuisances through lower local taxes.

The politics of airport construction do not seem to favor such arrangements, however. Local opponents of new airports tend to be concentrated, politically effective groups. The travelers who would benefit from the airport are more numerous, but many of them would use the new facility only a few times a year. Thus, even when total benefits outweigh total costs, the large, diffuse group of beneficiaries is less effective politically than the small, cohesive group of local opponents.

In some cases, of course, the local negative externalities of a new or expanded airport would outweigh the benefits to travelers, and no compensation would be possible. In such a case, no new facility should be built. That situation is particularly likely to be the case with old "downtown" airports like Washington's National and New York's La Guardia.

When airport capacity is fixed in the face of rising demand, it is important that the scarce capacity be efficiently allocated. In the early years of deregulation, allocation of scarce capacity was handled poorly. In 1983, the FAA established new rules for four especially crowded airports—the two just listed and New York's Kennedy and Chicago's O'Hare. In these airports, airlines were assigned a fixed number of "slots" for landing and takeoff. To add a flight, an airline first had to obtain a slot.

At first, the slots were assigned by committee. That arrangement did not work well because there was no economic incentive for the committee to assign the scarce slots to the airline that had the greatest need. In 1986, the committee system was replaced by a market in which airlines buy and sell slots among one another. Some slots have sold for as much as $700,000.

The slot system has improved the efficiency of allocation of takeoff and landing rights. However, it is still not perfect. In particular, when airlines pay huge sums for slots, the money goes to another airline, not to the airport. Some economists have suggested replacing the slot system with takeoff and landing fees charged directly to airlines. (Actually, such fees are already charged, but at very low levels that do not reflect the true value of slots.) The fees would then be a source of revenue, both for airport expansion and for compensation of local residents.

Finally, a brief look at the nation's air traffic control system: The air traffic control system is a government agency, part of the Federal Aviation Administration. In the years since deregulation, the system has been plagued by problems. One was the 1981 strike which led to the firing of most air traffic controllers. It took years for the system to return to full staffing. Also governmental budgetary pressures and administrative problems have slowed the modernization of the vital air traffic control computer system. All in all, the air traffic control system operates with the low degree of efficiency one expects of a government bureaucracy.

Some observers believe that the full potential benefits from airline deregulation will never be realized so long as two of the three legs of the air travel system are inefficient government agencies. A possible solution: privatization of both airports and the air traffic control system. Both could be supported by user fees charged to airlines. Both could obtain funds for modernization by borrowing in private capital markets with repayment guaranteed out of future user fees. And both could operate more efficiently under private management, free of congressional meddling, complex governmental labor laws, and the other red tape that always snarls governmental monopolies.

Action to implement privatization may soon be taken. President Clinton proposed a partial form of privatization of air traffic control in his December, 1994, budget message. His plan would create a quasi-independent, government-owned air traffic control corporation to manage the system. Although not truly private, the new agency would finance itself through fees paid by airlines and would be free of some burdensome government personnel and procurement regulations. Some members of the new Republican-controlled Congress advocated going even further. They pointed to the models of New Zealand, Germany, and Switzerland, all of whom are in the process of full privatization of their air traffic control systems.

An evaluation

In terms of efficiency, airline deregulation has been one of the success stories of the 1980s. The hub-and-spoke system, fewer empty seats, and larger, more comfortable aircraft are manifestations of this. The ultimate confirmation of greater efficiency has been a steady drop in the average cost of airline tickets.

Despite its clear superiority over the CAB's former regulatory regime, however, the current system is far from perfectly efficient. As yet, governmental monopoly of airports and air traffic control has thwarted comparable efficiency gains in those parts of the system. And a scarcity of airport slots and other facilities has been a contributing factor in the reconcentration of the airline industry that has left many hubs with just one or two carriers.

In terms of equality, the impact of regulation has also been mostly positive. Superficially, it might seem that the increase in price discrimination runs contrary to the standard of equality. In fact, the opposite is the case. The real effect of price discrimination is to democratize air travel. It has made a once-elitist system accessible to the general public—grandmothers flying to visit their grandchildren, soldiers flying to visit their girlfriends, students flying home for vacation.

A major concern before deregulation was that small cities and short routes would lose service while large cities and longer routes would gain. In general, small cities have done better than expected. By some measures, such as total takeoffs and landings, service has actually improved. However, there are cases in which short-route fares have risen and others in which routes are now served by smaller airplanes.

But should the issue of service to small communities really be considered one of equality? It is not clear that it should. After all, incomes in small communities are not significantly lower than those in large cities. Also small town residents enjoy benefits such as relatively cheap housing and short commutes to work, so why is it so unfair that they pay more for a few things, including air travel? Sociologists could no doubt debate urban poverty versus rural poverty endlessly. However, even with today's low air fares, the truly poor are not major users of air travel. In short, the quality of air service to large cities as opposed to small towns appears largely neutral with respect to the standard of equality, broadly conceived.

Labor is a third area in which deregulation has had an impact on equality. The impact has been a favorable one. Airline employees have always been and still are well paid by comparison with wage earners in the economy as a whole. Those airline employees who have lost wages are the ones whose wages had been pushed highest above market levels by rent seeking under regulation. At the same time, tens of thousands of new, skilled, high-paying jobs have been created in the industry as passenger volume has expanded.

Finally, we come to the standard of liberty. One of the most important freedoms on which a market-based economy depends is the freedom for entrepreneurs to enter new markets in competition with firms already serving them. This freedom was denied under regulation, and it is the source of most of the gains from deregulation. In the future, privatization of airports and air traffic control could potentially bring the same gains to the remainder of the air travel system.

Questions for thought and discussion

1. Suppose that the Chicago city government decided to strengthen the profitability of the restaurant industry by establishing a Municipal Restaurant Board (MRB) with power to regulate entry and prices. No new restaurants could be started. A minimum price would be established, uniform for all types of restaurant and set at the price level of the city's finest restaurants before regulation. However, the MRP would not have power to regulate the quality of food or other aspects of service such as decor, music, or waiter training. How, do you think, would regulation affect the profitability of restaurants? The nature of competition? The average quality of meals served in restaurants? Who would gain, and who would lose from restaurant regulation? In particular, consider the effects on business-expense-account diners as compared with working-class families taking an occasional night out. Comment on parallels with airline regulation.

2. Airlines' frequent-flyer plans give their members points for each mile flown. The points can be cashed in for free travel; e.g., 100,000 points might get you two free tickets to London. In what sense do these plans constitute price discrimination? Who benefits and who loses from the plans? How do they affect efficiency, equality?

3. This chapter briefly discussed the issue of governmental support for rural interests as compared with urban interests. In your opinion, is it fair that deregulation has benefited urban-based travelers more than rural-based travelers and in some cases has actually reduced service to small airports? How would you feel if privatization of the postal service resulted in higher postal rates for rural delivery customers and lower rates for urban customers? If telephone deregulation raised rural phone bills and lowered urban phone bills? In general, when is it proper for urban customers to pay more than the cost of service, so that rural customers can enjoy service at less than cost? Discuss in terms of efficiency, equality, and liberty.

Selected references

Baily, Elizabeth E., David R. Graham, and Daniel P. Kaplan. *Deregulating the Airlines.* Cambridge, Mass.: MIT Press, 1985. *Covers the first five years of deregulation.*

Borenstein, Severin. "The Evolution of U.S. Airline Competition." *Journal of Economic Perspectives* (Spring 1992), pp. 45-73. *Discusses in detail the causes and consequences of changes in concentration in the airline industry since deregulation.*

Morrison, Steven, and Clifford Winston. *The Economic Effects of Airline Deregulation.* Washington, D.C.: Brookings, 1986. *Another early study, finding that many of the expected effects of deregulation in fact occurred.*

Poole, Robert W. *How to Spin Off Air Traffic Control.* Los Angeles: Reason Foundation Report No. 178 (August 1993). *Other Reason Foundation publications deal with privatizing airports.*

Rose, Nancy L. "Fear of Flying? Economic Analysis of Airline Safety." *Journal of Economic Perspectives,* Spring 1992, pp. 75-94.

Key terms

Cartel. An association of firms who cooperate to restrict output and raise prices of the product they sell.

Cross-subsidization. In a regulated industry, a policy of purposely charging one group of customers a price higher than cost to sell to another group at a price below cost.

Contestable market. One that competitors can enter and leave quickly and with little cost.

Herfindahl index. A measure of concentration, equal to the sum of squared market shares of firms in a market, having a value of 1° for pure monopoly and approaching 0 as the number of firms becomes large and their market shares small.

Price discrimination. A situation in which a firm charges different prices to different customers for the same service, with the price difference not reflecting a difference in cost.

Fixed Cost. An element of cost (e.g., rent on the company's headquarters building) that does not change in response to short-run changes in volume of output or number of customers served.

Marginal cost. The cost of serving one additional customer or increasing output by one unit.

10

Equal Pay for Comparable Work: Women in the Labor Market

In 1978 a group of nurses working for the city of Denver sued the city because they were being paid less than sign painters, tree trimmers, and parking meter repairers. They claimed that their work as nurses had a worth comparable to that of the other jobs in terms of training, responsibility, and contribution to society. The only reason they were being paid less, they said, was that almost all nurses were women whereas almost all of the painters, trimmers, and repairers were men. It looked to them like a case of illegal sex discrimination.

Nonsense, said the city. Wages for all city jobs are set by supply and demand. Sign painters are paid what they get because if they were paid less, not enough applicants would be attracted to fill the jobs. Nurses are not paid as much because plenty of people apply, even at a lower wage.

In the Denver nurses' case, the law of supply and demand held up in court. The judge ruled in favor of the city. But, as Eleanor Holmes Norton-then head of the Equal Employment Opportunity Commission—predicted, the issue of equal pay for work of comparable worth was not laid to rest in Denver.

In this chapter we will look at the economics of equal pay for work of comparable worth. We begin with a brief review of the facts of men's and women's pay that cause the issue to be raised in the first place. Next, we will look at the comparable worth controversy in terms of a standard labor market model based on supply and demand. We will then consider some problems of implementing comparable worth and end with an evaluation.

Trends in men's and women's pay

Trends in labor force participation One of the most dramatic developments in American society in the twentieth century has been the movement of women from unpaid work in the home into the paid labor market. In 1890, only 3 percent of white women worked outside the home. By 1980, the figure was over 60 percent. The labor force participation rate for nonwhite women has always been higher, but has also risen, from 22 percent in 1890 to 72 percent in 1980.

The increase in women's labor force participation has reflected changes in supply-and-demand conditions in the labor market over time, but also changes in the attitudes and cultural norms of successive generations. The latter show up in the interesting chart in Figure 10-1, taken from a book by economic historian Claudia Dale Goldin. Each line in the chart represents the labor force participation at comparable ages of **cohorts** of women, that is, groups of women born in the same time period, with birth dates from 1866-75 to 1956-65.

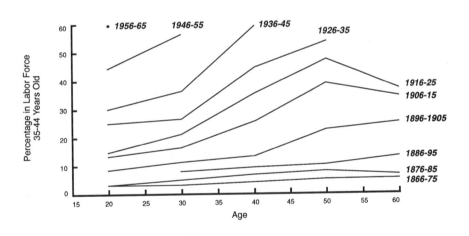

Figure 10-1 Labor Force Participation Rates by Cohort Married White Women, 1890 to 1980, for Cohorts Born 1866 to 1965

A number of interesting facts emerge from the chart. First, within each cohort, labor force participation increases with age, at least to age 50. Second, each successive cohort has an increased rate of participation at all ages. Third, we see that the generational effect is strong enough so at many (although not all) points in time, women of one cohort have labor participation rates higher than those of the next older cohort despite the tendency for rising participation rates within a given cohort. Thus, in the mid-1930s, when women born from 1906 to 1915 were in their 20s, they had higher labor force participation than did women born in 1896 to 1905, then in their 30s, and so on. Finally, it is interesting to note that the first surge in labor force participation represented entry (or re-entry) by women in their 30s and 40s, while participation of young women remained low. This is seen among women born as early as the turn of the century, while the sharp rise in labor force participation by younger women took place only among those who came of age during and after World War II.

Today, there is a tendency to view the increased role of women in the workforce in a positive light. It is seen as reflecting greater opportunities for women and the chance (still far from fully realized) to play an economic role equal to that of men. It is interesting to note, however, that "progressive" opinion of the earlier part of the century viewed working women as a social evil, similar to child labor. For a married woman to work outside the home was considered either a sign of desperate poverty, or of unconscionable exploitation by her husband. As recently as the 1930s, the expectation was that as society grew more prosperous and social attitudes toward women became more liberal and enlightened, women's participation in the labor force would decline.

Trends in earnings Trends in women's earnings are more complex. Table 10-2 reproduces another chart from Goldin's book. It shows that over the long term, and within many shorter periods, women's earnings have risen substantially relative to men's, although still falling well short of parity. However, it is possible to pick periods (periods often singled out for emphasis by women's rights advocates) when the ratio of women's to men's pay has stagnated, or even fallen. For example, the overall ratio of women's to men's earnings for full-time workers was no higher in

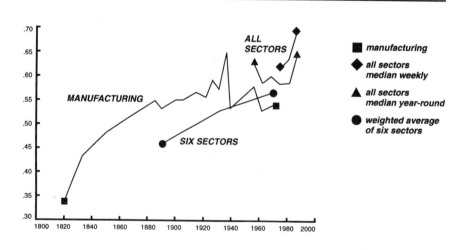

Figure 10-2 Ratio of Female to Male Earnings, 1815-1987

1985 than in 1955, and between those dates, it dipped considerably.

This "gender gap"—the earnings gap between men and womem—has been the focus of considerable attention. Does it represent discrimination against women by a male-dominated economic system? Does it simply reflect the voluntary choices that women make regarding education and occupation, as filtered through the workings of supply and demand in the labor market? There is no complete answer to these questions.

There are, however, some partial answers. All participants in the debate over women's earnings agree that about half of the earnings gap can be explained by quantifiable economic factors such as hours worked, education, experience, and years with the same employer. (For example, official data define a "full-time" worker as one who works more than 35 hours per week, but on average, men with full-time jobs work 10-15 percent more hours per year than women with full-time jobs.) These factors do not represent a flaw in the way the economy sets levels of pay. Even if it is viewed as the result of discrimination, rather than of women's voluntary choices, reduction in this part of the earnings gap must come, if at all, through measures such as ensuring equal educational opportunity and providing adequate day care, so that women wanting to work the same hours as men can do so.

The sources of the rest of the pay gap between men and women are more controversial. Consider, for example, the fact that the pay gap is much narrower for young workers than for older ones. In 1985, women aged 20 to 24 earned 85.7 percent as much as men the same age, whereas the earnings ratio for women aged 45 to 54 was just 59.6 percent. These data are subject to both optimistic and pessimistic interpretations. Optimists say they indicate that the earnings gap is solving itself and will disappear over the next generation. Indeed, the earnings ratio for young workers rose almost 10 percent between 1979 and 1985, and has narrowed further in the 1990s. However, pessimists say the wider wage gap for older workers reflects the fact that although men and women start out nearly equal, women are consistently passed over for promotion. There are data that seem to support this contention.

Then there is the fact that the earnings gap is strongly affected by marital status. Women who have never married earn about the same as men who have never married. Optimists see this as an indication that the earnings gap reflects women's voluntary choices: Women who choose not to marry do just as well as men who make the same choice. Pessimists have a different interpretation. They say that a male-dominated society forces a "career or family" choice on women, whereas men can more easily have both. Interestingly, although never-married women earn much more than married women, never-married men earn less than married men. In fact, the gap between earnings of married and unmarried men is wider than the gap between men and women. It is hard to believe that this reflects systematic prejudice of employers against unmarried men. More plausibly, complex social forces operating within the family tend to explain the "marriage gap."

Occupational segregation But no factor contributing to the earnings gap is as controversial as that of occupational choice. When occupation is included as a variable in statistical studies, up to 90 percent of the earnings gap between men and women can be explained. What this means is that male and female typists of comparable seniority earn about the same; so do male and female assembly-line workers; and so do male and female doctors. This does not mean that there are no differences within occupations. There are differences that reflect work experience, differences that reflect possibly discriminatory promotion policies, and so on. But these differences are fairly small. At least half of the wage gap is attributable to the fact that more women work in low-paid occupations and more men work in high-paid occupations.

Furthermore, the degree of occupational segregation is itself remarkable. One measure of occupational segregation is the percentage of women (or men) who would have to change their jobs to make the gender ratio equal in all occupations. If the whole labor force is split 60-40, men to women and each occupation is exactly 60 percent men and 40 percent women, the index of segregation is zero. If all the men work in one occupation and all the women in another, then the segregation index is 100. For the U.S. labor force as a whole, the index is about 65, meaning that two-thirds of all women (or men) would have to change their occupation to eliminate segregation. Incidentally, although the extent of occupational segregation by race has declined markedly in recent decades, occupation by gender has not changed much.

What is more, if the calculation is made by firm rather than occupation, the index increases. For example, among people who wait on tables in restaurants, about 85 percent are women, indicating substantial gender segregation. But if one looks restaurant by restaurant, one finds some that employ only waitresses and some that employ only waiters. Also, the firms that employ women in a given occupation tend to be the low-paying firms.

As Margaret Mead once observed with respect to Pacific island villagers, "There are villages in which men fish and women weave and in which women fish and men weave, but in either type of village the work done by the men is valued more highly than the work done by women."[1]

What is one to make of the data on occupational segregation and occupational pay differentials? Again, there are optimistic and pessimistic explanations.

To the optimists, all is as it should be. Women choose occupations that reflect their tastes and opportunity costs. Despite greater labor force participation overall, many women still prefer to split their lives between family and career rather than make an all-or-nothing choice. They thus choose occupations in which opportunities for part-time work are relatively great, hours are flexible, and it is easy to leave the labor market temporarily and then re-enter. There is an

---

1 Quoted by June O'Neil, in "Issues Surrounding Comparable Worth," Contemporary Policy Issues, April 1986, p. 1; original source not given.

opportunity cost to making such a choice, however. This is reflected in the fact that women with intermittent work patterns accumulate fewer, on-the-job skills valued by their employers. They are consequently paid less. Also, because women expect to work fewer hours over their careers, women rationally invest less heavily in education. And finally, is it really foolish for women to be less willing than men to accept dangerous working conditions in, say, construction or mining in exchange for somewhat higher wages?

But the pessimists look at the same set of facts and see things differently. In a male-dominated society, they say, men get to choose first when it comes to occupation. If they want to fish, they fish. If they want to weave, they weave. Women do whatever is left. But that is not all, say the pessimists. Once men have chosen which occupations to leave to women, they shape those occupations in a way that keeps women "in their place." Male managers make sure that women's jobs are "deskilled" by substituting capital for labor and by routinizing tasks, so that they require little training. A few men may work alongside women in occupations such as bank teller. But women quickly learn that the men are there as management trainees, whereas for women, teller is a dead-end job. In this version of the story, women opt for unpaid work at home and fail to pursue educational opportunities only because they realize that the labor market is rigged against them. In short, to the pessimists, the same facts tell a very different story.

The facts of earnings differentials and occupational segregation are the background for the comparable-worth debate. Optimists, who see the facts as reflections of free choices in free markets, think that tampering with wage structures can do only harm. Pessimists, who see invidious discrimination in the same set of facts, want action to correct the situation. Let's turn to the arguments advanced by each side and the likely effects of a comparable-worth policy.

The standard economics of gender and wages

According to standard economic theory, wages and salaries are set by supply and demand. The demand curve for workers of any given skill and occupation slopes downward, as shown in Figure 10-3, and the supply curve slopes upward.

There are two reasons for the downward slope of the demand curve. First, the demand for workers of a given type is a **derived demand**, which is to say, it reflects the demand for the goods or services they produce. (The demand for sign painters is derived from the demand for signs; the demand for nurses is derived from the demand for health care services.) If workers are paid less, the product can be sold at a lower price, and people will buy more of it. Thus, lower pay leads to more workers being hired because it affects the quantity of the product that consumers demand.

Demand curves for workers slope downward for a second reason: Many different inputs are used in producing any given good or service—skilled labor,

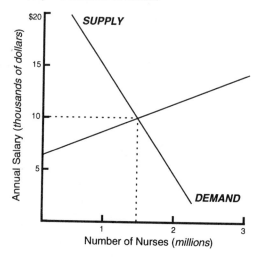

Supply and Demand for Nurses

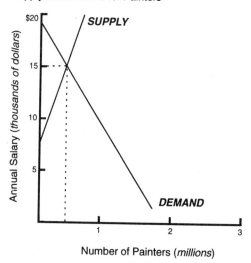

Supply and Demand for Painters

Figure 10-3

unskilled labor, machinery, energy, and materials. In many cases, inputs can be substituted for one another. Consider the case of health care services. Nurses are a key input in the production process. Because nurses on average are paid less than doctors, hospitals substitute nurses' services for those of doctors whenever the nurses' training permits. On the other hand, there are substitutes for nurses' services. Still-lower-paid nurse's aides, orderlies, and technicians can perform many routine tasks. Electronic sensors can monitor patients' conditions and send a signal to a central nursing station at the first sign of trouble. Such devices allow each nurse to look after more patients, with no sacrifice of quality of care. The incentive to substitute less costly inputs for more costly ones whenever possible would cause the demand curve for each input to slope downward, even aside from the fact that lower input costs mean lower output prices.

The supply curves in Figure 10-3 slope upward because the higher the wage rate offered, the more people are willing to work in a given occupation. One reason is that higher pay gives a greater incentive to invest in **human capital**, that is, to undertake the education and training required for a job. A second reason is that a high enough level of pay will attract workers from other occupations, even if the other jobs are more interesting or offer better working conditions. Finally, the supply curve for a given job category slopes upward in part because for higher pay, people will work more hours a week or more weeks a year.

For any given job, according to standard economic theory, pay is determined by the intersection of the supply and demand curves. In Figure 10-3, the equilibrium pay for nurses is shown as $10,000 per year, and that for sign painters is shown to be $14,000. Why are nurses paid less than sign painters, even though in equilibrium, the demand for nurses is greater? The graph makes the reason clear. Although there is a great demand for nurses, there is also a great supply. Even at the relatively low pay rate of $10,000 a year, enough people stay in the profession to fill all the jobs that are offered. The supply of sign painters is more limited—not so much because sign painters need rare skills or difficult training but because potential sign painters could do many other kinds of work. At less than $14,000 a year, some of the people currently working as sign painters would leave to become house painters, auto painters, truck drivers, or whatever else is available.

But why don't nurses also leave their jobs to become sign painters, house painters, or truck drivers when their pay drops below $14,000? Why do 1.5 million people—96 percent of them women—remain nurses, even at $10,000 a year? The economist's answer is that there must be something about the occupation that they like, even though the pay is low. Perhaps men and women who become nurses like to serve other people and would find painting signs unfulfilling. Perhaps they like the abundance of part-time work available in nursing, the availability of nursing jobs in all parts of the country, or even the relative ease of entering and leaving the field, once one has the training. From the point of view of supply and demand, it doesn't much matter why people want to be nurses (despite the lower pay) instead of painters or truck drivers. It is simply a fact that they do.

But isn't there another explanation for the low pay of nurses relative to sign painters? What about discrimination? What if employers refuse to hire women for any but low-paying jobs? Wouldn't that cut off higher-paying opportunities for women and force them to crowd into relatively few occupations, where pay would then be driven down by oversupply?

Economists agree that if there were systematic discrimination in hiring, these would be the effects. Still, far from all of them are convinced that the low level of nurses' pay is caused by discrimination.

The problem with the discrimination hypothesis, economists argue, is that in the private sector, which accounts for more than 80 percent of all jobs in the U.S. economy, discrimination tends to be unprofitable. To maximize profits, a firm must minimize the cost of producing any given level of output. If any job is paid more than the minimum needed to attract qualified applicants, the excess pay comes out of the owner's pocket.

Suppose, for example, that the going wage for painters is $7 per hour and that only men are hired as painters. Suppose too that a large pool of qualified women would be happy to lay down their hospital trays and pads and pick up a paint brush for any wage over $5 per hour. The first firm that broke with tradition and hired women painters would save $2 an hour. The savings would allow the firm to cut the price of its product a little and give it a competitive edge in the marketplace. More traditional employers might not like the idea of women painters, but they would have to follow suit if they did not want to see their market share eroded. As the tradition of men-only painters was abandoned, the increased supply of applicants for painting jobs would tend to drive the average level of painters' wages down. At the same time, the wider job opportunities for women would tend to force employers to pay a little more to keep their nurses on the job. The pay gap would shrink.

True, the profit motive only tends to eliminate discrimination. Some stubborn employers may hold out against the tendency, even if it injures their profits. Sometimes male workers, not male employers, may want to keep women out. Sometimes, customers may not trust a woman, say, to fix their cars. Since the standard economic argument describes only a tendency, perhaps we had better see what the other side has to say.

The case for comparable worth

The case for comparable worth rests on two propositions. The first is that despite the standard economic argument, supply and demand does not work to eliminate discrimination in the job market. The second is that there is a better, fairer way than supply and demand to set pay scales. Both of these propositions must hold to establish a case for comparable worth. It would not be enough to say that supply and demand did not work perfectly unless an alternative worked better.

Labor market institutions Comparable worth advocates often point out that institutions, as well as markets, play a role in setting wages. Although the supply-and-demand model implies that everyone doing the same job should get the same pay, the world doesn't work that way. One institution that gets in the way is seniority. Most employers pay workers more the longer they remain on the job.

To a degree, this reflects the fact that more experienced workers tend to be more productive. But even in simple jobs where experience doesn't count for much, and jobs where young people with new ideas outperform older people with more experience, seniority tends to be reflected in higher pay. Why is this the case? Simply because both employers and workers see the seniority principle as fair.

Labor unions are another institution that gets in the way of supply and demand. Simple supply-and-demand theory cannot explain why workers in unionized steel and auto plants are paid half again as much, or sometimes even twice as much, as people doing comparable work in nonunionized plants.

Imperfect information also interferes with the operation of supply and demand. Several observers have suggested that imperfect information helps explain low pay for women. Employers perceive women as less strongly attached to the job market than men, and in fact, on the average, they are. Women tend to work fewer years of their adult lives than men and are more likely to leave the job market for a period in mid-career. Thus, employers may be reluctant to hire women for jobs that require extensive training, where frequent turnover would be expensive. Instead, they hire women mostly for lower-paying jobs for which training and job stability are less important.

Although it may be true that women on the average have a weaker attachment to the job market than men, the argument continues, these generalizations are not true of all women. Many women do want stable, long-term employment. But employers lack a good way of predicting which women applicants are which, so they lessen their risk by discriminating against women as a group. Doing so may be rational for employers, but it is unfair to women with strong career attachments.

In short, proponents of comparable worth portray the job market as a place in which the law of supply and demand is only one among many factors influencing pay and job choices. Since the operation of supply and demand has so many exceptions, why not make still another one?

Job evaluation In place of market wages, or at least as a way of adjusting such wages, advocates of comparable worth propose the use of job evaluation—a technique used by many large firms and government agencies—to help determine the relative pay of various jobs in the organization.

There are many job-evaluation techniques, but they have certain principles in common. They begin by identifying a number of traits thought to be relevant to pay-"initiative and ingenuity," "physical demand," "responsibility for equipment," "extent of supervision of others," and so on. Each job is then rated on a numerical scale according to each trait, and total points are evaluated according to a chosen formula. Thus, although the jobs might score very differently on individual traits, the composite ratings for, say, nurse and sign painter could come out about the same.

When each job has been rated, the scores can be displayed on a chart like that shown in Figure 10-4. The chart shows, as we would expect, that higher-rated jobs tend to receive higher pay. The positively sloped line shows the average relationship

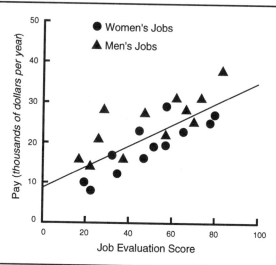

Figure 10-4 Hypothetical Job Evaluation Study

between rating and pay for all jobs. Everyone agrees that the tendency for higher-rated jobs to draw higher pay is fair. But comparable-worth advocates see it as unfair that jobs held predominantly by women (triangles) tend to fall below the line of those held predominantly by men (squares). Although the data shown in our figure are hypothetical, many actual job-evaluation studies show a similar pattern. The solution, say comparable-worth advocates, is to raise the pay of women's jobs by a sufficient percentage so that men's and women's jobs will be equally centered on the "fairness line."

Problems with job evaluation Critics of comparable worth, while acknowledging that job-evaluation studies can be a useful management tool, question the practicability of pressing such studies into service as a legal remedy for the pay gap. They see two problems.

First, job-evaluation studies have an inevitable element of subjectivity. The subjectivity arises partly from the decision of which job traits to include. For example, the Midwest Industrial Management Association's job-evaluation plan uses eleven traits. The federal government uses nine. Some widely used schemes use as few as four; others, twelve or more.

Second, there is a degree of subjectivity in scoring each job for any given trait. The less similar the jobs being rated, the greater the problem. For example, suppose one is rating a word processor operating compared with a data entry worker. Both workers sit at a keyboard all day, but perhaps the word processing operator, who deals with a wider variety of documents, might deserve a 4 on the "initiative and ingenuity" scale, whereas the data entry worker deserves only a 3. But how is the initiative and ingenuity required of a word processing operator to be compared to that required of a fork lift operator? It is easy to understand that two equally fair-minded observers might come up with different rankings.

Third, at the end, the scores for different characteristics need to be plugged into a formula to determine a composite score. The choice of formula is also somewhat subjective. Should the score be linear? Nonlinear? Should it have equal weights? Unequal weights? Evaluators differ in their answers. For example, analyst Richard Burr compared job-evaluation studies done by four state governments for three occupations: data entry, laundry work, and secretary.[2] Iowa ranked these occupations 3-2-1, Minnesota ranked them 1-2-3, Vermont ranked them 2-1-3, and Washington ranked them 2-3-1.

Managers of private firms, when confronted with such studies, can use their own intuition and apply such studies while taking other factors into account as well. But if the law were to require rigorous adherence to job evaluations, as some comparable-worth advocates believe it should, the results could be quite capricious.

There is also a second, quite separate problem with the job-evaluation technique: Job evaluation does not take supply and demand into account. To use one analyst's example, suppose we do a job-evaluation study of French-English translators and Spanish-English translators. Surely the job-evaluation scores for the two jobs would be identical. But would we expect the relative wages of the two translators to be the same in Miami as in Montreal? There is no reason we should; both the supply of and the demand for the two types of translators would differ widely in the two cities.

The problem is not just hypothetical. During the oil boom, one oil company commissioned a study that assigned identical ratings to accountants, attorneys, and petroleum engineers, considering complexity of the work, education required, and so on. It found, however, that it could get all the accountants and attorneys it wanted for $22,000 a year, but could not touch a petroleum engineer for less than $32,000. A few years later, when the oil slump hit, thousands of petroleum engineers were out of work. The company would then, perhaps, have been able to hire engineers for less than accountants.

In short, although job evaluation may often be a good management tool, as a supplement to other techniques, it is not clear that it would make good law. Critics foresee endless lawsuits about which consultant's job rankings are valid and when departures from job evaluation results are justified by supply and demand. Anecdotal evidence from attempts to implement comparable-worth policy suggests that job evaluations are far from objective, but in fact, are formed in an atmosphere of ideological pressure, union bargaining, and political influence. There appears to be no objective way to resolve such problems.

---

2 "Rank Injustice," *Policy Review* 73 (1986), cited in Ellen Frankel Paul, *Equity and Gender: The Comparable Worth Debate*, (New Brunswick, N.J.: Transaction Publishers, 1989), p. 55.

An evaluation

All things considered, how would a national comparable-worth policy rate in terms of efficiency, equality, and liberty? The question is an important one because Congress, the courts, state and local governments, and private firms all face comparable-worth issues.

First, efficiency. A good case can be made that discrimination lowers efficiency. Members of the groups discriminated against are discouraged from entering occupations where they could best use their skills. Instead, they work where they are less productive or leave the job market altogether. For a given working-age population, output suffers.

However, it is not clear that comparable worth is the kind of antidiscrimination policy that would improve efficiency. In particular, critics worry about situations where there are long lines of applicants for some jobs while others cannot be filled. Such a situation could lead to a less efficient job market.

In some cases, as we have pointed out, we accept policies that are inefficient if they promote fairness and equality. Is comparable worth such a policy? At first glance, it appears to be. Pushing up the salary levels of all the people who fall below the "fairness" line in Figure 10-4 (and possibly pushing down the salaries of those above the line) would clearly promote equality—or would it?

To answer this question we must, as always, look at the unintended as well as the intended effects of a comparable-worth policy. Comparable worth would promote equality if it had no indirect effects on the number of jobs or the choice of people to hold those jobs. But the unintended effects of a comparable-worth policy could well be substantial.

First, a policy of raising the relative pay of low-paid jobs held predominantly by women would tend to reduce the number of such jobs offered by employers. Take the case of nurses. With nurses' pay higher, other things being equal, hospitals would have less incentive to substitute nurses' work for doctors. At the same time, they would have more incentive to substitute the work of nurse's aides and orderlies for that of nurses. They would also buy more automatic equipment to allow each nurse to handle more patients. Fewer nurses would be hired, and some already on the job might be laid off. Presumably, those who kept their jobs would tend to be those from the best nursing schools or perhaps those with the most experience. Thus, a comparable-worth policy would be most helpful to those who least need the help.

A second effect of comparable-worth policy might be to attract men into occupations such as nurse and secretary that are now dominated by women. In one way, this would be welcome. Changing attitudes and equal opportunity legislation have already encouraged many women to enter careers such as law and pharmacy in which they were previously underrepresented. To generate a movement of men into traditional women's jobs would extend this process in a way that opponents of obsolete gender stereotypes would approve. But a comparable-worth policy would bring men into these occupations at the same time that the total number of jobs in them was shrinking. Under the new, more competitive conditions, some women would prosper. These would be the women with the best educations, the strongest job skills, and the fewest family commitments. The women helped most by comparable worth, in other words, would be those who are already making successful inroads in occupations traditionally dominated by men.

Finally, as comparable worth raised pay in women's occupations and attracted men into them, the characteristics of those occupations that attracted women to them in the first place would change. Sociologist Brigitte Berger cites data indicating that many American women work to help their families, their chief concern. This motive steers women into work with such features as easy entry and exit, and availability of flexible hours and part-time work. But if such jobs as nurse or secretary paid more, employers would have less incentive to tailor jobs to suit the needs of such women. They would begin to insist on stronger job attachment, just as they have in occupations dominated by men. Experience and training would count for more. With fewer positions open and more people of both sexes applying for the jobs, employers would be more likely to pass over women who wanted to work just to help their families.

In short, the impact of comparable worth on equality would be mixed. The most educated and most experienced women, and those most strongly attached to the labor force, would very likely be helped. They would keep their jobs and be paid more for them. Less educated and less experienced women, and those who work to help their families, but not necessarily full-time or for their whole careers, would fare less well. They would find jobs increasingly harder to get, in just those occupations that traditionally have been most open to them. Increasingly, their best work opportunities would be in low-paid occupations such as sales worker, counter clerk, and assembly worker. Since these jobs have traditionally attracted men and women in about equal numbers, they would presumably not be affected by a comparable-worth policy, except to the extent that a greater supply of applicants for such jobs would depress their level of pay.

Finally, we should consider the case for a comparable-worth policy in terms of the standard of liberty. Policies that fight discrimination can be defended on the grounds that they increase personal freedom. Although there are many disputes over how far such policies should go regarding affirmative action and quotas, people are no doubt freer today than they were when women and minorities were legally barred from many occupations, or when employers routinely fired women as soon as they got married.

It is not clear that comparable worth would be a useful extension of this trend toward greater personal freedom. The rights of women who want to move into men's occupations are already legally protected. Comparable worth would affect mainly those who have this freedom but choose not to exercise it. At the same time, a serious comparable-worth policy would constrain the freedom of employers to choose personnel practices best suited to their businesses.

All in all, the effects of a comparable-worth policy on efficiency, equality, and liberty would be mixed, at best. This does not mean that there is no place for comparable worth, but it does suggest that overzealous application of the principle could create more problems than it solved.

It is possible to identify certain applications where the promise of gains is relatively great and the dangers are relatively small.

First, equal pay for jobs of comparable worth, aided by job-evaluation studies, although not necessarily following them rigidly, is already seen as good human resource policy by many large firms. Eliminating overt and implicit discrimination within the organization can improve labor force morale and help the firm use each employee most productively.

Second, the principle of equal pay for work of comparable worth is a valid subject for labor-management negotiation. The collective bargaining process leaves room for exceptions where rigid applications of job-evaluation formulas would lead to clear inefficiencies or inequities.

Third, legislation or court action to promote comparable-worth policy may be more valid for government agencies than for the private sector. Government agencies are not as strongly exposed to the market forces that tend to align pay with productivity. It is not surprising that many of the best-known court cases have been brought against state and local governments, nor is it surprising that other state and local governments have taken the lead in voluntary application of the principle.

What most worries critics of comparable-worth policy is the prospect of blanket legislation that would force rigid adherence to job-evaluation formulas in the private sector, with no allowances for market influences. Many comparable-worth advocates tell the critics not to worry; such rigid application of the principle is not their intent. But intent is not always a good guide to the effects of a policy. Drug prohibition did not intend to increase deaths from impure drugs and dirty needles. Farm policy did not intend to evolve from a safety net for poor farmers into welfare for the rich. In the area of comparable worth, as elsewhere, the law of unintended consequences needs to be kept firmly in view.

Questions for thought and discussion

1. Proponents of comparable worth stress policies that would raise the pay of women whose jobs fall below the "fair pay" line on a chart such as that in Figure 10-4. Why not instead cut the pay of men whose jobs fall above the line? What problems would each alternative create in terms of supply and demand? Compare the two alternatives in terms of efficiency, equality, and liberty.

2. The current debate over comparable-worth policy focuses exclusively on women who work in low-paid occupations traditionally dominated by women. Why should such women get special attention from public policy, compared with women in low-paying jobs not traditionally dominated by women, such as sales clerks and

assembly workers? What about low-paying jobs traditionally dominated by men, such as certain types of farm labor? Would the comparable-worth approach be applicable there too? In short, why not apply comparable worth across the board, so that pay for all jobs would be set according to job-evaluation principles rather than supply and demand? Discuss.

3. Opponents of comparable worth often say that if secretaries or nurses want higher pay, they should seek jobs as electricians, truck drivers, or sign painters. Some labor unions and some employers have, in fact, tried actively to recruit women for such "men's" jobs, but they have not always gotten as many women to apply as they had hoped. Why, do you think, do more women not apply for such relatively well-paid jobs? Is it prejudice, discrimination, or stereotypes? Is it something about those jobs that most women just don't like? Discuss.

Selected references

Aaron, Henry J., and Cameran M. Lougy. *The Comparable Worth Controversy.* Washington, D.C.: Brookings, 1986. *A study of the possible impact of a comparable worth policy.*

Brown, Clair, and Joseph A. Pechman, eds. *Gender in the Workplace.* Washington, D.C.: Brookings, 1987. *Discusses a number of issues of gender in the workplace, including comparable worth.*

Goldin, Claudia Dale. *Understanding the Gender Gap: An Economic History of American Women.* New York: Oxford University Press, 1990. *Uses the tools of economic history to place gender gap issues in perspective.*

Paul, Ellen Frankel. *Equity and Gender: The Comparable Worth Debate.* New Brunswick, N.J.: Transaction Publishers, 1989. *This study, which tends to be critical of comparable worth policies, gives extensive attention to legal and legislative aspects of the debate.*

Treiman, Donald J., and Heidi I. Hartmann, eds. *Women, Work, and Wages: Equal Pay for Jobs of Equal Value.* Washington, D.C.: National Academy of Sciences, 1982. *These authors tend to be skeptical of the standard economics of gender in the labor market and sympathetic (with some reservations) toward comparable worth remedies.*

Key terms

Cohort. A group of individuals born or entering a market during a given time period.

Derived demand. The situation where demand for a certain type of labor (or other productive input) reflects demand for the good produced by that input.

Human capital. Investment in education or training, including on-the-job training, that increases a worker's productive potential.

11

Social Security: Third Rail of American Politics

The Social Security system is known as "the third rail of American politics." Like the electrified third rail of the New York subway, it is said that if you touch it, you're dead. But a few bold (or reckless) politicians have had the courage to tell the truth: The Social Security system, as has existed since the Great Depression, just can't go on. Senators Bob Kerry (Democrat from Nebraska) and John Danforth (Republican from Missouri) are two of them. As co-chairmen of a special Bipartisan Commission on Entitlement and Tax Reform, they implored their fellow legislators to fix the system now. If they did not, they warned, Social Security and related entitlement programs would swallow up the entire federal budget by 2030, bankrupting the government, forcing a doubling of taxes, or requiring the elimination of virtually all other federal activities.

It is easy to understand why Social Security is so well liked. Born of the Great Depression, when bank failures and bankruptcies wiped out the savings of many retirees, Social Security has been the major source of retirement income for millions of our senior citizens. Partly because of Social Security, people over 65, for the first time in the nation's history, have incomes higher than the average for the whole population. What's more, the value of benefits that most retirees have received has exceeded the value of taxes paid.

Consider the case of Ida Fuller. From the time she became the first Social Security retiree in January 1941 to the time she died in January 1975, this former legal secretary drew some $21,000 in retirement benefits from the system, having paid in a total of only $22.54 in payroll taxes.

Not everyone covered by Social Security has done as well as Ida Fuller, of course, but most people retiring today will end up getting more out of Social Security than they would have gotten by investing their payroll taxes privately in the stock market or in corporate bonds.

If you are under 35 years of age, however, things look pretty bleak. Chances are you will be a loser, and your losses could be substantial. The taxes you will pay in over your working life will substantially exceed the value of the benefits you can reasonably expect. Compared with the alternative of investing in a private retirement account, Social Security is simply a terrible financial deal for young people today.

Just why will this long-running gravy train, which has faithfully delivered the goods to your parents' and grandparents' generations, run out of steam before it gets to your station? To see why many economists think it will, and why, as a result, America needs a new agreement between its generations, we need to understand just how the Social Security system works.

How the system works and how it doesn't work

One of the strange things about Social Security is that the people who like it so well rarely understand how it actually works. The most common mistake is to think that Social Security works like a private insurance program or a private pension fund. One source of this mistaken view is the Social Security Administration itself.

For example, the booklet, *Your Social Security*, widely circulated by the Social Security Administration, begins:

> The basic idea of social security is a simple one: during working years employees, their employers, and self-employed people pay social security contributions which are pooled in special trust funds. When earnings stop or are reduced because the worker retires, dies, or becomes disabled, monthly cash benefits are paid to replace part of the earnings the family has lost.

The booklet goes on:

> Nine out of ten working people in the United States are now building protection for themselves and their families under the Social Security program.

Let's look at some of the ways in which these claims are misleading.

There are no trust funds All dollars paid into the Social Security system are immediately paid out—the very day, the very hour, the very minute. There are no dollars being stashed away in bank vaults for future use. Therefore, there are no special trust funds, at least not in any meaningful sense. In its early years, when the system ran a surplus, the extra tax dollars collected were spent on other federal programs. Then for many years, when the system ran a deficit, the extra dollars spent came from general tax revenues. Today, the system is again running a surplus. But surplus or deficit, in reality the system is strictly on a pay-as-you-go basis: All dollars received from Social Security taxes will be spent on Social Security benefits as they are received.

What about mysterious "trust funds"? To see exactly how they work, let's try a simple thought experiment. Suppose you decide to set up a fund for the future purchase of a car. You take an empty pickle jar and paste a label on it that says, "Car Fund." Each month you promise to put $50 into the car fund, and each month you faithfully keep this promise. But, as time passes, other needs become more pressing, and you find yourself short of cash.

So what can you do? You could borrow money from a bank or run up your credit card balances, but the interest rate would be high. So why not try an easier way? Why not borrow the money from the car fund? After all, if you don't trust yourself to pay your own money back, how can you ask some other lender to trust you?

So you borrow money from your car fund, and you write an IOU to yourself, promising to pay it back. Just to keep things honest, you even promise to pay interest to your car fund on the money borrowed. And things work out pretty well. In fact, they work out so well that you proceed to borrow all of the money in the car fund. Each month, instead of putting $50 in the fund, you simply write an IOU to the fund—a promise to pay it $50 plus interest, sometime. Then you spend the $50 cash on something else.

Is this one big charade? An attempt at self-delusion? Not necessarily. All of the elaborate bookkeeping may have psychological effects; it may strengthen your resolve to buy a car eventually. But don't overlook the down-to-earth realities: (1) You are operating on a pay-as-you-go standard. All of the money you earn is being spent as you earn it. (2) When the day comes to buy the car you promised yourself, you can't buy it with your own IOUs. You will have to make the sacrifices then that you are not making today.

Exactly the same is true of the Social Security trust fund. The government "invests" the Social Security taxes it collects in its federal government bonds. These are—in the most literal sense—nothing but IOUs that the government has written to itself. In return for the IOUs, the Treasury takes your Social Security tax dollars and pays them out as benefits to people who are now retired. If there is anything left, the Treasury writes more IOUs and uses the proceeds for federal workers' salaries, war planes, farm subsidies, and so on. All of the funds collected in the past have already been spent; the only way that benefits can be paid today and in the future is by collecting taxes today and in the future. The existence of the trust fund may make people feel better (people who don't understand how it works), but if it were abolished tomorrow, the only real effect would be to relieve government accountants of some extra bookkeeping.

This is one reason why the statements of the Social Security Administration are so misleading. Social Security taxes paid by today's workers do not finance their own future benefits, but someone else's current benefits or some other form of federal spending. When today's workers retire, their benefits will have to be financed by taxes imposed on future generations of workers.

It is instructive to compare the Social Security system with two other financial arrangements—a fully funded private pension plan and a type of confidence racket called a Ponzi scheme.

A *fully funded* private pension plan differs from Social Security because, as premiums are paid in, the company must accumulate a fund large enough at each moment to finance all promised future benefits. The fund must be invested in assets other than the firm's own bonds or stocks. Such a plan does not rely on future contributions to pay benefits. Even if the plan were suddenly unable to attract new participants, it would still be able to pay existing participants out of the money it had already accumulated.

A *Ponzi scheme* is superficially similar to a private pension plan in that participants pay money into the scheme in return for a promise to get their money back, with interest, in the future. Unlike a pension plan, however, a Ponzi scheme does not accumulate assets to meet its promises. Instead, it relies on recruiting new participants when its promises come due and using their premiums to pay the initial participants. Because it does not have to tie up resources in long-term assets, a Ponzi scheme can offer its initial participants much more attractive rates of return than an actuarially sound fund—say 50 or 100 percent per annum.

The only trouble is that in order to meet its obligations, it must recruit more and more new members each year. Sooner or later the scheme is doomed to collapse, and when it does so, the last round of new participants is left holding the bag. If the organizers are as smart as the original Boston con artist who gave his name to the idea, they usually run off with all of the funds just before the scheme is due to die of natural causes.

Of the two—a fully funded private pension plan and a Ponzi scheme—the Social Security system more closely resembles the latter. There are two important differences, though. First, Social Security is legal, and Ponzi schemes are not. And second, the Social Security system need not collapse; it can rely on the power of taxation to recruit new members to pay old claims, whether those new members want to be recruited or not. But even this requires the consent of future voters. That brings us to our next point.

Social Security benefits are not guaranteed When the Social Security Act was being debated in Congress in 1935, its framers wanted to assure members of the public that their financial stake in the program would be absolutely secure. No one, they reasoned, should feel that he or she was taking a chance by "investing" with the government.

"We can't ask support for a plan not at least as good as any American could buy from a private insurance company," said the report of the House Finance Subcommittee. "The very least a citizen should expect is to get his money back upon retirement."

To guarantee this, two important provisions were included in the original act. First, Congress decided that if, at the retirement age of 65 a taxpayer had paid into the system without having qualified for benefits for some reason, all the taxes he or she had paid would be refunded. Second, if a fully qualified taxpayer died before reaching 65, a sum equal to the amount he or she had paid in taxes was to be given to that taxpayer's estate.

It took Congress all of four years to take back these promises. In 1939, with applications for refunds piling up, it became apparent that the financial integrity of the system was threatened. So the original act was amended, and those waiting for refund checks received a form letter instead, telling how the amendment would make the system stronger.

As time passed, the worker's assurance of benefits became even less secure. Workers entering the system today must pay at least 10 years' worth of taxes for the right to any retirement benefits. If a male worker dies before reaching 65, his wife is entitled to collect a monthly death benefit only if she is "caring for his dependent children." If the couple's children are grown or if they never had any children, the wife is entitled only to a nominal burial fee.

Several Supreme Court rulings have further eroded the notion that workers in some sense "own" the money they pay in taxes. The court has ruled that money collected in Social Security taxes need not be paid to Social Security beneficiaries. The fact that a worker has paid taxes does not necessarily obligate the government to pay that worker any benefits, and promises made by one Congress may be rescinded by a later Congress.

These rulings are regularly ignored by the public information staff of the Social Security Administration. Instead, we have been told that payroll deductions "are strictly accounted for and kept separate from the general funds in the U.S. Treasury" and that your Social Security card is "proof of your insurance policy with the government."

The crucial difference between such claims made on behalf of a government agency and similar statements made by a private insurance company is that private companies are legally obligated to abide by the terms of their contracts. The government, by and large, is under no such obligation. Whether today's youth will be able to collect retirement benefits in the future depends solely upon the willingness of future voters to shoulder increasing tax burdens. For example, if young voters in the year 2030 are not willing to pay taxes at double today's rates, benefits for people born in the 1970s and later will have to be cut. In short, future benefits are simply not guaranteed.

Benefits are largely unrelated to taxes paid Under private insurance policies or pension plans, a direct relationship exists between contributions and expected benefits. In general, the higher the premium paid, the higher the benefit. Although the Social Security Administration implies that under Social Security the benefits received are related to the taxes paid, the relationship is very weak.

In practice, people who pay vastly different Social Security taxes over their working lives may receive the same benefits upon retirement. At the same time, people who pay the same amount in taxes may receive very different benefit payments. And people who continue working after the age of 65 are required to pay additional taxes, often without receiving any benefits while they continue to work.

Moreover, millions of people who pay taxes will never receive any benefits because they will not have paid taxes long enough to qualify. Many others will lose their own benefits because of their spouse's eligibility. A retired wife 65 or older is entitled to 50 percent of her husband's benefit. A widow who is 62 or older gets 82.5 percent of her husband's benefit. But a wife or a widow cannot receive both the benefit based on her earnings and the benefit she is entitled to as a wife or widow. For many wives and widows, her share of the husband's benefit is larger than her own, so she never collects a cent on the taxes she pays into the system.

In short, considerations other than the amount paid into the program determine the benefits received. As a consequence, the program bears only a scant resemblance to the ordinary concept of insurance.

Business does not pay taxes From its very inception, the Social Security Administration has continued to propagate the idea that only part of a worker's Social Security tax is paid by the workers. The remainder, it is claimed, is paid by the business firm that employs the worker.

Economic theory says otherwise. A business firm is nothing but a legal relationship between workers, managers, stockholders, creditors, consumers, and many others. Although governments often tax legal relationships, relationships never bear the ultimate burden of those taxes. Only people do.

Economists generally agree that the full burden of payroll taxes ultimately falls on the workers themselves. Under current practice, a worker receiving $100 a week in wages will have $7.65 deducted from his or her paycheck for Social Security and related Medicare taxes, thus receiving net pay of $93.35 (not taking income taxes into account). The employer will chip in another $7.65, making the total payroll tax equal to $15.30. To the employer the extra $7.65 is just another labor cost, whether it goes to the government or to the worker, so the total cost of hiring this employee is $107.65 per week.

Economists believe that in the absence of the Social Security payroll tax, the employer would have been willing to pay and the worker would have received a wage of $107.65 for exactly the same work. In other words, the entire $15.30 (or 15.3 percent of the gross wage) is actually paid by the worker. It is likely, however, that many workers do not realize that they are paying over 15 percent of their wages to finance Social Security. This is partly because they do not read the fine print on their pay statement, or because they don't realize that the item usually labeled "FICA" (Federal Insurance Contributions Act) refers to Social Security and Medicare. They also do not realize how much Social Security tax they are paying because they don't realize the FICA deduction is matched (at the worker's expense) by the employer.

The problem of future financing Once we strip the concept of Social Security of false and improper analogies to private insurance, the idea of Social Security is a simple one. Money is transferred from workers to nonworkers. In 1994, for example, about $460 billion was collected from taxpayers, of which about $320 billion was paid out in Social Security benefits and the rest spent on Medicare benefits and other federal programs.

The basic problem of Social Security is also simple—where to find the additional taxes to finance the increasing benefits Congress has promised to current and future retirees. The math is inescapable: Future workers must bear heavier and heavier tax burdens, or future retirees must accept lower benefits, or some combination of the two.

The source of our Social Security problem dates back to the day the program first began paying benefits to retired workers. In 1940, hundreds of thousands began collecting benefits after paying Social Security taxes for only 36 months. In 1950, when Congress extended coverage to ten million self-employed individuals, many were old enough to draw benefits after paying Social Security for as brief a period as 18 months. A self-employed businessperson who had paid only $121.50 could retire on $80.00 a month in 1952. Any such person who lived another 30 years (and some did) would have collected total benefits of over $43,000 in return for $121.50 in taxes.

This example is illustrates a pattern that has characterized Social Security from the beginning: Higher benefits require higher taxes to finance them. As late as 1949, the total Social Security payroll tax was only 4 percent of the first $3,000 of income. That means that the maximum annual tax was only $60.00. Since then, Congress has raised the maximum tax many times. In 1994, it was 15.3 percent of the first $60,600 of earnings, or $9,271.80.

What's more, if present demographic trends continue, higher and higher taxes will be needed just to maintain today's benefit levels, because the ratio of taxpayers to beneficiaries has been falling. In the early years, there were about seven taxpayers for each beneficiary. Today the ratio is close to 3 to 1. In the next century, when today's youth reach retirement age, the ratio is expected to be 2 to 1.

In fact, for today's youth to retire at benefit levels currently written into law, future workers will have to pay 20 to 40 percent of their salaries in Social Security taxes! That's in addition to the other taxes these workers will have to pay to finance all other government programs. Such an enormous burden raises the prospect of a taxpayer revolt, under which the government would welsh on its remaining Social Security obligations—just as it welshed on its refund promises in the 1930s.

The social security surplus The long-term financial threat to the Social Security system is obscured by the fact that the system is currently running a huge surplus. As of 1994, Social Security taxes exceeded Social Security benefits by some $125 billion. The rate of accumulation is projected to increase to a high of about $500 billion a year at its peak in 2015. The enormous surpluses would seem to lay to rest all retirement fears of today's youth, but they do not.

Part of the reason is demographic. Today's retirees are the relatively small generations born in the first three decades of the century. Today's work force, on the other hand, includes the huge "baby boom" generation born in the first decade after World War II. The baby boomers' payroll taxes generate the surplus. But beginning in the second decade of the twenty-first century, the baby boomers will begin to retire. And at that time, the prime-age work force will consist of the small "birth dearth" generation born in the 1960s to 1980s.

This would be no problem if there were a real Social Security trust fund that was invested in real assets, as private pension funds are. But remember: The so-called trust fund is just a pickle jar full of IOUs. The government can make good on the IOUs for the benefit of retiring baby-boomers only by taxing the pants off those poor birth-dearthers. And that means you, dear reader.

It might be thought that even though the IOUs piling up in Social Security's pickle jar are worthless, they are at least harmless. But many economists disagree. They see two dangers in the Social Security surplus.

First, the surplus in the Social Security fund disguises the size of the federal government's operating deficit. Says Senator Donald W. Riegle of Michigan, "We're engaged in an accounting trick." Riegle and others fear that the apparent shrinking of the deficit as the Social Security surplus grows will create a temptation for Congress to reach deeper and deeper into the pickle jar to finance new spending programs. Once those new programs are on the books-mass transit aid, a space station, whatever—Congress won't be able to turn them off when the Social Security surplus starts to shrink after 2015.

Second, some economists think that the sheer size of the Social Security surplus will discourage today's workers from saving as much as they otherwise would. They see all those IOUs in the pickle jar, and they say, "Ah, I'm well taken care of. Why not buy that new BMW?" Thus, to the extent people falsely perceive their Social Security payments as a form of saving, there will be less real saving. Less real saving means less accumulation of capital in real assets like factories, computers, and research facilities. Less capital, in turn, means a weaker, less productive economy in the twenty-first century, just when a strong economy is needed to make good on all those IOUs.

How to fix the system

Can the system be fixed? Many economists have thought long and hard about it. A number of improvements have been suggested, any one of which would be an improvement over the present system.

Create a real trust fund One proposal, put forward by former Budget Director James C. Miller among others, is to invest the Social Security surplus in genuine assets. He proposes that the trust fund buy a broad range of corporate stocks, bonds, mortgage-based securities, and the like, just as private pension funds do. This proposal would help in two ways.

First, it would encourage capital accumulation. With the Social Security system in the market to buy $40 billion, $100 billion, and eventually $500 billion worth of stocks and bonds each year, corporations would find it easier to issue securities to finance new investment projects. Those new factories, computers, and research parks we need to strengthen the economy in the next century would become a reality.[1]

Second, it would force the federal government to finance its operating deficit through income taxes or real borrowing from the public. The true size of the operating deficit would become apparent. Without the option of dipping into the pickle jar, Congress might discover the self-discipline it needs to get its spending priorities in order.

However, this plan has the disadvantage that even though funds would be better invested, government would retain full control over the system. Many people are made uneasy by the fact that government would become a shareholder and creditor of private industry on a massive scale. As a result, Miller's proposal has not achieved wide support.

Cut benefits Another way to save the Social Security system would be to cut benefits. Never mind that promises have been made—as we have seen, those promises are not legally binding.

One way to cut benefits would be to raise the retirement age. In the past, retirees acquired right to full benefits at age 65. They could opt to receive limited benefits at age 62. Legislation passed in 1983 called for the retirement age to creep up gradually, so that those born after 1950 will have to wait to age 67 to receive full benefits. A proposal discussed by the 1994 Bipartisan Committee on Entitlements and Tax Reforms was to increase the retirement age to age 70.

---

1 There is one hitch in this reasoning. People might (correctly) perceive that investing the Social Security trust fund in private securities would make it a more meaningful guarantee of their future retirement benefits. With their minds at rest, they might then channel less of their income into the nation's saving stream through banks and other household savings instruments. That would offset the hoped-for boost to investment.

Some argue that such an increase would simply recognize changing reality. In 1940, a 65-year-old man could expect to live another 12 years. Today, the life expectancy of a man at age 65 is 15 years, and, in the next century, it could well rise another couple of years.

Another way to cut benefits would be to make Social Security into a means-tested, safety net program. Social Security is now a system that transfers income from workers to elderly nonworkers regardless of their incomes. Without their Social Security checks, some of these elderly nonworkers would be poor, although a majority have sufficient private assets to escape poverty even without those checks. Many recipients of Social Security benefits are, in fact, very wealthy.

Some argue, that the only component of Social Security that makes sense is the part that acts as a safety net for the elderly who, for whatever reason, have not accumulated enough wealth or private pension benefits to live comfortably. In 1983, the government did take a small step in this direction. Since that time, retired people with total incomes above a certain limit have had to pay income tax on a portion of their Social Security benefits. Another proposal put before the 1994 Bipartisan Commission was to raise this percentage to further concentrate Social Security on the needy elderly.

The trouble with these proposals is that they step squarely on that fatal third rail. Despite the urgings of the bold (or reckless) Senators Kerry and Danforth, other members of the 1994 Bipartisan Commission would not go on record as advocates of benefit cuts. That is simple, political reality.

The privatization solution There is a possible solution to the Social Security crisis, however, that would result, over time, in a fully funded system but would not welch on promised benefits to anyone. This solution, which Peter J. Ferrara calls "a new compact between the generations," is to privatize the system in a way that is completely voluntary.[2] Older workers, or anyone else who likes the current system, could stay in it. Younger workers, for whom the current system is a very unattractive financial proposition, could opt out.

Ferrara's new compact goes back to one of the original motives behind Social Security, which was to force people to provide for their own retirement. If people were left free to make their own decisions about the future, some might choose to make no provision for retirement. Upon reaching old age, these people would present the rest of society with an unfortunate choice: Support them or watch them starve. Social Security, it was argued, eliminates this difficulty.

In fact, Social Security, as we have seen, does not actually force people to provide for their own retirement. It forces them to provide for someone else's retirement. However, there is a way to accomplish the original objective and solve

---

2 "Social Security: A New Compact Between the Generations," in Edward H. Crane and David Boaz, eds., *An American Vision* (Washington, D.C.: Cato Institute, 1989), Ch. 13.

some long-term problems at the same time. We could insist that individuals either participate in Social Security or invest in an approved retirement plan, much as we insist that automobile drivers carry liability insurance. The choice of retirement program, like the choice of liability insurance, could largely be left up to the individual.

Many ways implementing such a new compact can be imagined. Ferrara's suggestion is to give workers the option of contributing up to 15 percent of their salaries to a qualified pension fund, similar to today's IRAs, Keough plans, and 401(k) plans. The workers would continue to pay Social Security taxes to support elderly retirees, but they would not "pay twice" for their own benefits. Instead, their contributions to their private plans would be fully offset by credits against their income taxes. People who chose this option would receive proportionately smaller Social Security benefits when they retired, or none at all if they opted for the private plan for their entire working careers. But even without Social Security, their total retirement income would be higher, because their private plans would earn a greater rate of return than the rate implicit in the current Social Security scheme.

As time went on, the amount of Social Security benefits paid out would decrease. As it did so, the rate at which Social Security taxes needed to be paid would also fall. During the transition, however, government revenues as a whole would fall because of the income tax credit for private pension contributions. But, as Ferrara points out, there is no real increase in government deficit. His plan would simply unmask the accounting trick on which the current system is based by forcing the government to issue real securities to the public instead of the phony IOUs that now go into the trust funds. Doing so would only make explicit the implicit debt the government already owes future retirees under the current system.

Although Ferrara's proposal is tailored to fit the specifics of the American situation, similar plans have been implemented abroad. For example, a few years ago Britain began to allow companies with approved private pension plans to opt their workers out of the government's second-tier Social Security scheme. (All workers are required to be in the first-tier plan.) Workers who are opted out forego the right to receive second-tier Social Security benefits. In return, they receive a reduction in their payroll tax of 7 percent of taxable earnings.

The British system does not solve any short-run problems. Today's retired workers have to be paid the promised benefits. And the government has to raise the taxes to pay these benefits. But since 1978, more than half of all British workers have taken the option of opting out. That means that Britain's long-run Social Security obligations have been greatly reduced. Chile, Singapore, and Japan are among the other countries allowing workers to opt out of their Social Security systems.

An evaluation

Our analysis has made it clear why Social Security has been so popular in the past: The first generations to enter the system were big winners, so they have voted enthusiastically to sustain it. But now a different reality faces today's young workers. It is time to ask whether Social Security was a good idea in the first place, and whether it should continue or be replaced. Let's consider these questions in terms of our usual three standards.

Liberty Social Security clearly violates the standard of liberty—in this case, the liberty of the worker-taxpayer. Taking a percentage of people's incomes without their consent violates the Lockean principle that people are entitled to the product of their labor. The only benefit that workers receive in return is the promise that upon their retirement, government will take from others and give to them. The workers' rights to dispose of their own incomes as they see fit—including the right to provide for their own retirement as they choose—are clearly violated. Opt-out systems like those of Britain, Chile, and other countries are one way of addressing this concern.

Equality The effects of Social Security on the distribution of income are less clear. Social Security taxes are paid only up to a certain level of income ($60,600 as of 1994), so that low- and middle-income workers pay a higher percentage of their total incomes to Social Security than do high-income professionals. On the tax side, then, inequality is increased. On the other hand, low-income retirees receive a higher percentage of preretirement wages than do high-income retirees. On the benefit side, then, inequality is reduced.

What about the degree of inequality between taxpayers and beneficiaries? Since Social Security transfers income from workers to nonworkers, and since most of the nonworkers are retired, it would seem that such transfers must reduce inequality of income and wealth between the two groups. This conclusion may be false, however.

For one thing, when Social Security benefits are included, people over age 65 have higher incomes on average than persons under 65. In addition, retired people frequently have more assets. Seventy percent of the elderly own their own homes and thus avoid the burden of rents or high-cost mortgages. And every state offers some property tax relief to the elderly. Many also derive income from unreported jobs and receive financial help from their children. Medicare picks up a large number of medical bills.

But even after we account for the value of wealth and other sources of assistance, some tough questions need to be answered. Suppose we want to compare a young couple with two children to a retired couple. What would equality mean here? Should the first family have twice as much income as the second? That is, should we perform a mere head count? Or should we make some allowance for the fact that people in different circumstances may have different needs?

Another tough question involves the value of leisure time. Suppose a male worker has the option to continue working at a salary of $20,000 a year. Instead, he chooses to retire. His choice reveals that he places a higher value on retirement (leisure time) than on the $20,000. Many economists would argue that the worker's extra leisure time is worth at least $20,000. Accordingly, they would argue that the worker's real income has not been reduced at all—he has simply substituted one kind of income (leisure time) for another kind of income (money). If we agree with this argument, then many aged persons are much better off than their money income and wealth would indicate.

There is yet a further difficulty. When we ask what difference Social Security makes, we have to imagine what would happen if Social Security did not exist; that is, what would the financial position of the aged be? To perform this mental experiment, we have to recognize that in the absence of Social Security, many retirees would qualify for welfare assistance such as food stamps. In addition, many would receive more financial help from their children. In the days before Social Security, most of the aged relied on their children as their primary means of support. In the modern world, children might not be as charitable, but few would be completely indifferent. So a great many Social Security dollars simply replace other income transfers that would occur in the absence of Social Security.

Whether Social Security creates more equality, then, probably hinges on our answers to some tough questions: What should be done about the value of leisure time? Should we make allowances for differences in needs? How much income would the elderly receive without their Social Security checks? Unfortunately, very different answers to these questions are perfectly defensible.

Many economists feel uncomfortable comparing the well being of a 19-year-old worker with a 70-year-old retiree. The differences in circumstances are so great, they say, that such comparisons are meaningless. So they propose a different way of looking at the equality question. They ask, What happens to the same generation over time? The question is a reasonable one. But so far, no one has come up with an answer.

During their working years, low-income workers pay a higher percentage of their incomes in Social Security taxes than do high-income workers. The low-income workers will also pay taxes for more years, since they typically do not remain in school as long.

At the receiving end, low-income workers can expect to receive a higher percentage of their preretirement income in the form of benefits. Two factors work against them, however. First, people with low incomes have a shorter life expectancy, so they cannot expect to collect benefits for as many years. Second, Social Security benefits are reduced if the retiree continues to work at another job and receive wage income. By contrast, people who have assets such as stocks and bonds are not penalized for the income they receive from these assets.

Differences in the demographics of the black and white populations of the United States further complicate the issue of equality. In general, blacks do not get as good a deal from Social Security as whites. Blacks have a lower life expectancy than whites. And the black population as a whole is younger than the white population. A black man aged 35 can expect to receive just two years, eight months of Social Security checks if he retires at 65. Yet he pays exactly the same rate of Social Security taxes as his white counterpart, who can expect to receive seven years, six months of benefits. A white woman aged 35 can expect to receive 44 percent more in benefits than a black woman of the same age.

The 1983 reforms of Social Security were devastating to the expectations of black participants. A study by the National Center for Policy Analysis found that a black man aged 25 lost more than 80 percent of his expected benefits as a result of the reforms, chiefly because of the scheduled increase in the retirement age. By comparison, a white man aged 25 lost just 22 percent of his expected benefits. Before the reforms, the white 25-year-old could expect to receive about four times as much in total benefits as a black of the same age. After the reforms, the white man could expect to receive fifteen times the black man's benefits.

Because of all of these considerations, economists are uncertain about how Social Security affects inequality-whether it causes inequality for society as a whole at a certain point in time, or whether it causes inequality within a single generation over time. If Social Security does reduce inequality, there is no reason to believe that it reduces it very much.

Efficiency Effects on economic efficiency are more straightforward. Like any other tax, the Social Security payroll tax distorts the work-leisure trade-off that workers face. It discourages productive work and encourages other activities. In 1940, when the Social Security tax was only 2 percent each on employees and employers, and income taxes were also relatively low, this distortive effect was probably mild; today, with the combined Social Security tax rate over to 15 percent, things are quite different.

Economists have always known that income and payroll taxes discourage production: They tend to push society inside its production-possibility frontier. From the point of view of efficiency, this loss must be balanced by a corresponding gain, such as an additional road or a bridge that enhances productivity. Unfortunately, Social Security offers few corresponding gains. Even if workers want to make some provision for the poverty-stricken elderly, most benefits do not go to people who are poor. In the main, Social Security simply transfers income from one group to another. Society as a whole has fewer goods and services as a result.

The way benefits are paid also discourages productivity. As a retired person's earned income rises, benefits are reduced. Beyond a certain level of income, taxes must be paid on the remaining benefits. For retirees of certain ages and incomes in certain states, the combined tax and benefit reduction may be so great that it does not pay to work at all. The productive contribution of vigorous and energetic elderly people—and there are more of these with each elderly generation—are thus lost to the economy.

Finally, as we have seen, some economists also believe that Social Security reduces private savings and thereby lowers the long-term growth rate for the economy as a whole. People who know they can count on Social Security benefits, it is argued, will be less inclined to save for their retirement. Whereas private savings provide a source of funds for business investment, Social Security taxes are simply paid out to beneficiaries.

All in all, then, Social Security threatens to weaken the economy just when it will need great strength to meet the demographic challenges of the next century. Perhaps the time has come, after all, to grasp that notorious third rail of American politics, and to conclude a new compact between generations.

Questions for thought and discussion

1. Prior to 1940, there were virtually no government programs to systematically supplement retirement incomes for the elderly. What methods and institutions do you think society relied upon to deal with the problem of retirement? Could the same methods and institutions be used today? If not, why?

2. Statistical evidence suggests that women workers are far more likely to be discouraged from working by high payroll and income taxes than men. Can you think of any reasons to explain this phenomenon? What implications do these results have for future production in this country?

3. Calculating the value Social Security has for you yourself is difficult because of two special problems. As an advanced exercise, outline a method for making such a calculation that deals with each of them.
   a. Taxes are paid and benefits are received in different time periods, yet most people place a higher weight on a dollar today than on the promise of a dollar 40 years from now.
   b. The benefits you can expect to receive depend upon how long you live. There is some probability that you will die this year and some probability that you will live to be 90.

Selected references

Ferrara, Peter J. "Social Security: A New Compact Between the Generations," in Edward H. Crane and David Boaz, eds., *An American Vision*. Washington, D.C.: Cato Institute, 1989. *A good, short presentation of Ferrara's proposals for reform.*

——, ed. *Social Security: Prospects for Real Reform*. Washington, D.C.: Cato Institute, 1985. *A collection of papers by many experts on the Social Security system.*

——. *Social Security: The Inherent Contradiction*. Washington, D.C.: Cato Institute, 1980. *A detailed critique of the origins and operation of Social Security.*

Goodman, John C. *Social Security in the United Kingdom: Contracting Out of the System.* Washington, D.C.: American Enterprise Institute, 1981. *Goodman believes that some elements of the British system could be used to improve Social Security in America.*

National Center for Policy Analysis. *The Effect of Social Security Reforms on Black Americans.* Dallas, Texas: NCPA, 1983. *African-Americans were severely disadvantaged by the 1983 reforms of Social Security.*

Key terms

Fully funded. A characteristic of a private pension plan under which contributions are invested in marketable assets that can later be sold to pay pension benefits.

Ponzi scheme. Also known as a pyramid scheme. A type of fraud in which participants are asked to make contributions which will be "invested" to earn high benefits. However, contributions are not invested and later contributions are used to pay benefits to early contributors until at some point the scheme is liquidated, with the organizers pocketing all contributions that remain in the fund.

12

Give Me Your Young, Your Energetic: The Economics of Immigration

Give me your tired, your poor,
Your huddled masses yearning to be free
        -Inscription at the base of the
        Statue of Liberty

These words reflect one attitude toward immigration held by many Americans: that this country should be, and is, a safe haven for the world's oppressed and a land of opportunity for those denied opportunity in their countries of origin. Others, however, hold the opposite view, one that might be expressed as "Give me your young, your energetic, your hardest workers yearning to get ahead." This view suggests that the country can benefit by selectively opening its doors to people with skills and abilities that will enable them to support themselves and benefit their host country in the process. Each view reflects the historical reality of American immigration to some degree, and each view plays a role in the current debate on immigration.

When California voters went to the polls in November 1994 to vote on the state's Proposition 187, they expressed a still different view: "Young or old, repressed or free, just stay home!" On its face, that ballot initiative was aimed at combating illegal immigration, principally by cutting illegal immigrants off from most public services, including schools and welfare services. However, the debate surrounding it, and the majority that it received on election day, showed that many people fear the effects of legal and illegal immigration alike.

The eventual fate of Proposition 187 itself was unknown at the time this chapter was written. Voters had approved it, but courts blocked implementation of many of its provisions, and a long legal battle lay ahead. Nonetheless, the larger issues raised by Proposition 187 are worth looking at because they are sure to remain on the nation's political and economic agenda for some time. In particular, we need to ask:

- Who are the immigrants to the United States, and how much do they contribute to the economy?
- Who gains and who loses from immigration?
- What kind of immigration policy should the country have?

In this chapter we will try to bring basic economic reasoning to bear on these questions, even if we cannot provide definitive answers to all of them.

Who are the immigrants?

A short history of immigration The United States is, as everyone knows, a nation of immigrants. From its inception until the 1920s, immigration was virtually unrestricted. As Figure 12-1 shows, the greatest wave of immigration of all time came in the first decade of the twentieth century. At that time, immigration accounted for over half of the entire increase in population, and the percentage of the population that was foreign-born approached 15 percent.[1]

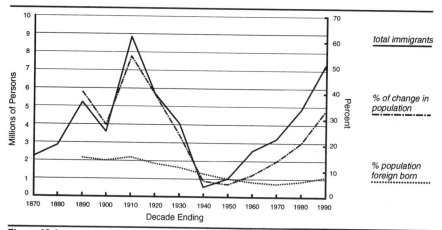

Figure 12-1

---

[1] Figure 12-1 shows legal immigration only. The U.S. General Accounting Office has estimated that illegal immigrants total between 1 and 2 percent of the U.S. population as of the early 1990s, and that the net increase in illegal immigrants is 200,000-300,000 per year. The number of illegal entries per year is much larger, probably on the order of 1.5 to 2.5 million, but this includes many who shuttle back and forth across the border for short stays.

The first comprehensive legislation controlling immigration was passed in the 1920s. The aim of this legislation was both to restrict the total number of immigrants and to introduce a quota system based on the ethnic composition of the U.S. population as of 1920. In practice, this meant awarding some 60 percent of available visas to immigrants from Germany and the United Kingdom.

During the Great Depression of the 1930s, immigration fell off sharply as unemployment in the United States soared to a quarter of the labor force. In some years, more people left the country than came to it. During and after World War II, immigration began to climb again. A further round of legislation in 1965 increased the total number of available immigrant visas and abolished the nationality-based quota system. As the chart shows, immigration is once again approaching the peak levels of early in the century, in absolute numbers if not as a percentage of the population.

The 1965 legislation replaced the old quotas with a new set of criteria that emphasize family ties to U.S. residents, and it also offered some preference to professionals of exceptional ability and workers in categories of short labor supply. These changes, together with changing political and economic conditions in source countries, led to sharp changes in the ethnic makeup of immigrants. As shown in Figure 12-2a, the bulk of immigrants in the 1950s originated in Europe and Canada, whereas by the 1980s, as shown in Figure 12-2b, the majority came from Asia and Latin America, with Mexico by far the largest single source.

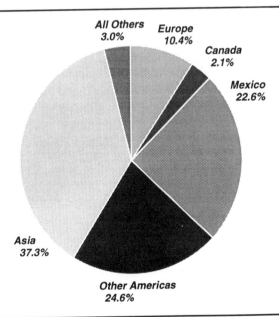

Figure 12-2a Immigration by Region of Origin. 1951-1960

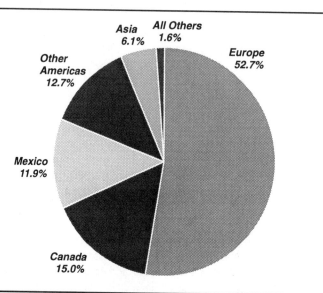

Figure 12-2b Immigration by Region of Origin, 1981-1990

Demographic characteristics of immigrants The most stricking characteristic of immigrants is their relative youth. Among immigrants, 26 percent are in the age group 25-34 years compared with 16 percent of natives. About 60 percent are aged

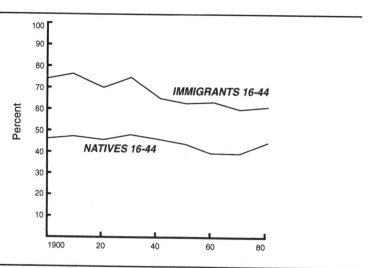

Figure 12-3 Percentages of U.S. Immigrants and Natives Between the Ages of 16 and 44, and the Percentage of Natives Over 65 (with Projections Through to the Year 2050)

16-44, compared with 45 percent of natives. As figure 12-3 shows, the relative youth of immigrants is a phenomenon that has persisted for all of this century.[2]

Although the gap in average age between immigrants and natives has narrowed somewhat in recent years, this is not true of all categories of immigrants. The percentage of young people among those admitted under the occupational preference category of visa is considerably higher than the average, whereas the family preference and refugee categories attract many older immigrants. Today, immigrants are nearly balanced between men and women, a change from early in the century, when two-thirds of immigrants were men.

The preceding data refer to legal immigrants only. Data on illegal immigrants are, for obvious reasons, fragmentary, being based on small surveys of the illegal immigrant population or on official actions such as border apprehensions and deportations. Nevertheless, it appears that the population of illegal immigrants differs from that of legal immigrants in important ways. First, there is a strong preponderance of men, up to 90 percent, according to some sources. Second, illegal immigrants are even more heavily concentrated than legal immigrants in the young working-age group. Border apprehensions of young children are reported to be relatively rare. Third, illegal immigrants are much more likely to return to their host country. Their average stay appears to be only 6 to 12 months, and total returns in any one year are perhaps 80 percent of total arrivals. By contrast, only about a third of legal immigrants eventually return to their countries of origin.

Education If you spend much of your time on a typical American college campus, you are certain to encounter immigrants frequently. One of the first to come to mind is that math professor from India who teaches your calculus course and brings honor to your university with distinguished publications in the best journals. Then there is the Latin American immigrant who empties the wastebaskets in your dormitory.

Of course, these are stereotypes—but many stereotypes contain an element of truth. The truth here is that the educational distribution of immigrants is concentrated in both low- and high-education brackets, that is to say, it is strongly **bimodal**. The average number of years of schooling of immigrants differs little from native U.S. citizens, but there are more in both the highest and lowest categories of educational attainment. According to data collected by the U.S. Bureau of the Census, 12.8 percent of immigrants had fewer than 5 years of elementary education, compared with just 2.9 percent of native U.S. citizens. But 12.5 percent had five or more years of university education, compared with just 7.5 percent of natives.[3]

---

2 Extensive data on characteristics of immigrants can be found in Julian Simon, *The Economic Consequences of Immigration* (Cambridge, Mass.: Basil Blackwell, 1989), especially Ch. 3.

3 1980 Census of Population, data for those immigrating in the 1970s, cited by Simon, Table 3.1.

Your college's math professor and janitorial worker are included in those data. People in the middle range of the educational spectrum—say, the purchasing manager who orders furniture for the math professor's office or the maintenance supervisor who keeps the trash compactor operating—are more likely to be U.S.-born.

Do immigrants help or hurt the U.S. economy?

The political debates inspired by California's Proposition 187 included many conflicting claims as to whether immigrants in general, and illegal immigrants in particular, help or hurt the U.S. economy. The geographical, demographic, and educational characteristics of immigrants influence their impact in complex ways. In this section, we will explore three aspects of the economic impact of immigration: First, does immigration have a favorable impact on the prosperity of the economy as a whole, as measured by the average level of real income? Second, do immigrants take jobs from native workers and/or force down their wages? And third, do immigrants pay their way in terms of taxes and government benefits, or are they a net burden on native taxpayers?

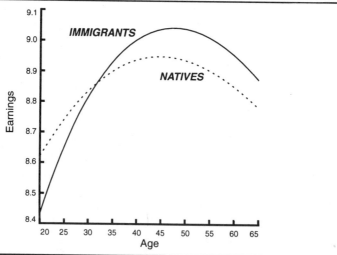

Figure 12-4 The Cross-Section of Age-Earning Profiles of Immigrants and Natives in the United States, 1970

Impact on average real income Do immigrants help or hurt the U.S. economy? One way to interpret this question is to ask whether their arrival raises or lowers average *real income*. This question is of interest from two rather different points of view. Some people, who are inclined to view the country as a collective entity, see a payoff to higher average real income in terms of the country's prestige and influence in world affairs. Others, more interested in the well-being of individuals, recognize that an increasing average level of prosperity has spillover effects on all citizens in terms of improved job opportunities, a better selection of consumer goods, a stronger tax base to support public services, and so on.

The traditional answer to this question has been that immigration does add to American prosperity, if not immediately then at least with only a short lag. This answer is based on the contrasting age-income profiles of immigrants and natives shown in Figure 12-4. That chart indicates that young immigrants initially have lower incomes than native citizens, but that by the time they reach their mid-30s, their incomes exceed those of natives.

One interpretation of these data is based on the idea that income is jointly determined by human capital and work effort. Human capital, as we saw in Chapter 10, means productivity-enhancing education and skills. When immigrants arrive, their average level of formal education is about the same as natives (although differently distributed, as we have seen). However, they lag in "language capital" and other specific cultural traits that affect their economic success. As their language skills improve and they become more integrated into the community, the gap in human capital disappears and their incomes rise.

Moreover, many people believe that immigrants are, on average, more energetic and hard working than individuals chosen at random from either the country of origin or the host country. In part, this belief is based on the plausible (although not quantifiable) notion that only people with above-average energy and initiative make the necessary effort to move to a new country in the first place. Some data support this notion. Historically, immigrants and children of immigrants have had higher labor force participation rates than U.S. natives, although this difference appears to have narrowed as labor force participation has risen for the native U.S. population. Another indicator of energy and initiative is the tendency to become self-employed or to start one's own business, areas where immigrants appear to surpass native-born citizens. This tendency seems to be especially pronounced among some groups, including Asians and Cubans.[4]

However, recent studies have cast some doubt on the traditional interpretation of the pattern shown in Figure 12-4. The problem is that the figure is based on *cross-sectional data*—a snapshot at a moment in time of all immigrants currently living in the country. Because of the typical age profile of immigrants, the 20-year-olds in such a snapshot represent a newer cohort of immigrants than do the 40-year-olds. It could be that the steep, early section of the cross-sectional, age-income curve represents not success over time by an unchanged "typical" immigrant, but rather, a decline over time in the average performance of immigrants

---

4 See Simon, Ch. 4.

in successive cohorts. Available data are not entirely conclusive in this regard, but they do suggest that the cross-sectional data exaggerate the pattern of success. The changing ethnic pattern of immigration, the increased emphasis on family ties, and the increase in refugees does appear to have lowered the average human capital that recent immigrant cohorts have brought. It is far from certain, then, that today's new arrivals will reach or exceed income parity with natives as they grow older.[5]

Impact on jobs and wages   Of all the charges brought by opponents of immigration, none has more impact than the claim that immigrants take jobs from American workers. Public opinion polls indicate that two-thirds of U.S. citizens questioned believe this to be true. Yet there is little or no evidence to support the claim.

Consider one of the most dramatic immigration "experiments" of all time: the 1980 Mariel boat lift. In this episode, Cuban leader Fidel Castro suddenly allowed 125,000 Cubans, mostly unskilled workers, to leave for the United States. Most of them headed for Miami. Almost overnight, the city's labor force jumped an astonishing 7 percent. Yet there was no measurable effect on either wages or the unemployment rate in the city. Broader studies confirm this experience. To the extent the effect of immigrants on wages and employment is measurable at all, it is tiny. Statistical studies suggest that adding 10 percent immigrants to a city's labor force (an even greater addition than in the Mariel episode) would depress wages by

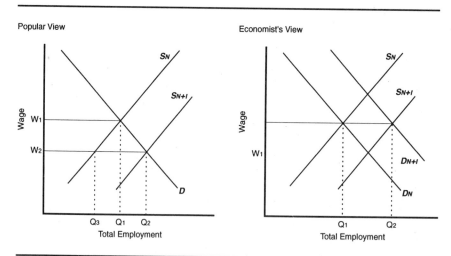

Figure 12-5

5 For a thorough and rather technical discussion of this issue, see George J. Borjas, "The Economics of
   Immigration," *Journal of Economic Literature*, December 1994, pp. 1671-80.

only two-tenths of one percent, and would have a similarly small effect on the unemployment rate.[6]

These results are exactly what the theory of supply and demand lead us to expect. The problem with the popular view that immigrants take jobs from natives is that it considers only the direct impact of immigrants as a supply of new labor, while ignoring their indirect impact as a source of demand. Figure 12-5 shows the reasoning involved. Part (a) shows the popular view. The arrival of a wave of immigrants shifts the supply curve from S_N to S_{N+I}. This depresses wages from W_I to W_2. Total employment is increased from Q_1 to Q_2, but employment of native workers decreases from Q_1 to Q_3, as those workers move down and to the left along the native labor supply curve, S_N. In the popular view, these displaced native workers are forced to turn to welfare or unemployment benefits to feed their families.

But the popular view is largely false. It neglects the fact that immigrants enter the economy not just as workers but also as consumers and savers. Like those already in the country, they spend the great bulk of their earnings on food, housing, transportation, and so on. Labor is needed in the food, housing, and transportation industries to produce those goods and services, so jobs are created there, either for native workers or other immigrant workers. Immigrants, like natives, also save some of their income. The banks where they deposit their savings make loans to factories for equipment purchases and builders for housing construction, creating still more jobs. The sum of immigrants' saving and consumption equals their earnings, so the increase in demand matches the increase in supply. As shown in Part (b) of Figure 12-5, the demand curve shifts from D_N to D_{N+I} at the same time the supply curve shifts, leaving the wage unchanged at W_I and employment opportunities for natives unchanged at Q_1.[7]

Popular perceptions tend to differ from economic analysis here because the supply effects in the labor market are more visible than the demand effects. If you walk into a shop or factory, you can see in a moment which of the employment positions are *occupied* by immigrants—they look different, talk with foreign accents, perhaps even dress differently. But, unless the whole workplace is immigrant-owned and operated, it is not obvious which employment positions are *created* by immigrants. You cannot say, "there, that worker is putting the tire on a

---

6 Both the Mariel episode and the statistical studies are discussed in Borjas, pp. 1695-1700.

7 What if the immigrants send part of their pay to relatives still living abroad, as many do? The chain of transactions is then longer, but the conclusion is unchanged. Either the dollars they sent abroad return to the United States, or they do not. If they come back to pay for purchases of U.S. goods, they add to demand for workers producing those goods. If they come back as investments in U.S. financial markets, they create jobs in investment-oriented sectors of the economy, just as do the savings of U.S. workers. If the dollars never come back—say, if the foreign relatives of immigrants stuff their mattresses with U.S. twenty-dollar bills—U.S. natives are then the biggest winners of all: They get to divide up the goods produced by the immigrant workers without having to share the goods they themselves produce with anyone.

car that will be bought by an immigrant," or "that bank clerk is entering account data of an immigrant."

This generally positive assessment of the wage and employment impact of immigration does deserve one important qualification, however. Figure 12-5 assumes that there is just one homogeneous labor market for the whole country. In fact, there are separate markets for skills and professions of many different kinds. The situation shown in the diagram would hold for each of these markets if the mix of skills and professions among immigrants were the same as for the native-born labor force, but as we have seen, that is not the case. Instead, immigrants are over-represented at both the high-skill and low-skill ends of the scale.

Consider the labor market for stone masons. Immigrants are represented more strongly than average in this occupation, so the supply curve for masons is shifted to the right more than average. However, the immigrant masons do not spend a correspondingly large percentage of their incomes buying stone houses or having stone decks installed next to their swimming pools. That means that they shift the demand curve for masons to the right by only an average amount. The result is thus intermediate between the cases shown in Parts (a) and (b) of Figure 12-5. There is some downward pressure on masons' wages and some reduction in employment among native-born workers in this particular occupation.

The impact of immigration on skilled trades like stone masonry, and on professions like medicine and engineering, is not a major public policy issue. But the impact on the low end of the labor market does cause concern. A rising immigration rate over the past two decades has coincided with other labor market changes, such as increased computerization of blue-collar jobs, that have reduced the demand for low-skill workers of all kinds. On the whole, the wage of high-school dropouts relative to high-school graduates in the United States fell by about 10 percent between 1980 and 1990. Some studies suggest that as much of a third of the decline may be attributable to competition from immigrants, among whom the percentage of high-school dropouts is higher than for the native population.[8]

It has also been suggested that immigration tends to lower the wage rate in the host country by raising the ratio of labor to capital, and hence depressing labor productivity. To construct a somewhat exaggerated example, a construction contractor might decide to use ten immigrant laborers with wheelbarrows to build a road rather than one native worker with a bulldozer. This capital dilution effect probably does act to depress wages slightly, at least in the short run. However, over time, we must remember that immigrants are savers as well as consumers. Their savings make it possible to equip all ten workers with bulldozers. Furthermore, some observers, including immigration specialist Julian Simon, think the negative productivity effect of capital dilution is offset by a favorable effect of immigration on innovation and entrepreneurship. On balance, after at most a short

---

8 See Borjas, p. 1699.

lag, he thinks immigration raises, rather than lowers, productivity in the host country.

Welfare, public services, and taxes One of the most controversial issues in the economics of immigration is the impact of immigrants on the public sector, as taxpayers and users of public services. If one were to base one's research solely on call-in talk shows, one might think that the entire immigrant population consisted of women with six children apiece, who live on welfare and park their kids in the public schools while spending their days pestering the doctors at city-run clinics.

What do economists have to say about immigration, welfare, and taxes? Not enough to completely resolve the issue, it turns out.

The analysis begins with one big factor in the immigrant's favor: their age. The argument is simple. If you are born in the United States, you draw on government services in your childhood as a student in a public school, you become a net payer of taxes during your working years, and you then draw again on the government budget as a retired recipient of Social Security benefits. If you are an immigrant, you go to school in your home country, arrive in time to begin a long career as a taxpayer, and receive Social Security only decades later. If immigrants were in all other respects the same as natives, this life-cycle effect would make them net payers of taxes over their lifetimes.

There are qualifications, however. One is that not all immigrants work. A certain percentage live on welfare or other forms of public assistance from the time of their arrival. The percentage receiving welfare (more precisely, Aid to Families with Dependent Children, Supplemental Social Security, and other means-tested assistance programs) is a little higher for immigrants (9.1 percent) than for natives (7.4 percent).

This percentage varies strongly from one immigrant group to another. Welfare rates are especially high for political refugees. On the other hand, they are lower than average for illegal immigrants. One reason is that even without measures like Proposition 187, illegals don't qualify for many public benefits (although their U.S.-born children may). Second, illegal immigrants are predominantly young men, the least likely category to receive benefits. Finally, although millions of illegal immigrants enter the country each year, most return home after a relatively short stay. The percentage of illegal immigrants who stay to retirement age is smaller than for legal immigrants, and even those who do stay may face deportation if they put in a claim for their Social Security benefits.

Anti-immigrant forces often point out that even if the newcomers are net taxpayers on average, this does not necessarily help the communities where they are concentrated. Californians in particular complain that immigrants use schools, hospitals, and welfare benefits that come from the state budget while paying taxes mostly to the federal government. Clearly, there is some validity to this view, and some understandable anger at federal government mandates that require states to provide services to illegals and their children. But this issue does not bear on the broader question of whether immigrants are a burden to the economy as a whole.

Why not resolve this issue once and for all by looking at the numbers on taxes and benefits? the reader might ask. There have been many attempts to do so, but the issue is far from resolved. One problem is that of measuring the amount of public services "used" by immigrants. Studies that look just at means-tested benefits tend to conclude that immigrants more than pay their way. But immigrants presumably use all public services. They send their children to school, they call the local fire department when their houses catch on fire, and they depend on the U.S. military to protect them from foreign threats. How is one to measure the cost of protecting an added immigrant from attack by foreign terrorists? If it is assumed that each resident "uses" an equal share of the government budget in this and all other respects, and if, in addition, pessimistic assumptions are made about job displacement and unemployment, immigrants begin to look like a net burden. These and other issues lie behind such disparate studies as one by Donald Huddle, who concludes that immigrants are a $42 billion net burden, and one by Jeffrey Passel and Rebecca Clark, who conclude that they generate a $27 billion net surplus.[9]

An evaluation
of policy options

Because immigration is such a diverse phenomenon, the extreme policy options of closing or opening the borders altogether are not really on the political agenda. Rather, policy debates center on less radical options.

One option, clearly, is to keep matters as they are—accept immigrants at rates approaching the historic peak, with about the same mix of skilled workers, family members, and refugees.

A second option is to restrict the total flow of immigrants without greatly changing the composition of the flow. This option would include special efforts to reduce the flow of illegal immigrants.

A third option is to focus on improving the average "quality" of those immigrants. In principle, this could be done without changing the total number of immigrants, but people who think that immigration should be liberalized often also favor policies that would attract especially beneficial immigrants. There are several variants on this approach, depending on what one has in mind by quality. Educational achievement would be one obvious measure. Another would be willingness to start a business, or to bring in a substantial amount of financial capital. Preference for people of young working age would be another variant. And some people, who

---

9 Donald Huddle, "The Costs of Immigration," Rice University, July 1993; and Jeffrey S. Passel and Rebecca L. Clark, "How Much Do Immigrants Really Cost?," Urban Institute, February 1994. Both studies are cited and discussed in Borjas.

consider ethnic homogeneity a valued characteristic of a country, might want to return to a system of quotas by country of origin in proportion to the country of origin of the existing population. Various measures of quality could be combined in some sort of point system, as used in some countries today. It should be kept in mind that U.S. policy already offers some quality-related preferences, so this option also would be a change in degree, not in kind.

The remainder of this section will look at these various policy options in terms of our standards of efficiency, equality, and liberty.

Immigration and efficiency   In a market economy, there is a very strong presumption that international migration is efficiency-enhancing, just as there is the same presumption for trade in goods and services. Political refugees aside, most immigrants change their countries of residence in the belief that they can use their skills more productively elsewhere. To find work with existing employers in their host country, they must convince the employer that they will contribute more, relative to the wage they demand, than does the next-most-attractive native worker. If they become self-employed, they must convince their customers that their services are a better value for the price than those offered by the next-most-attractive native producer. In short, successful immigration benefits both the immigrant and the employers and consumers of the host country.

But what about native workers who are displaced or whose wages are lowered by immigrants? Displacement, to the extent it does occur (which, as we have seen, is much less than popularly thought) comes into the balance under the heading of equality, not efficiency. Efficiency is a matter of producing the greatest volume of goods with given resources, or a given quantity of goods at least cost. In the labor market, this means putting the most productive worker into a given job, assuming the same wage, or using the worker whose opportunity costs are lowest, as measured by the lowest wage that will be accepted, assuming equal productivity. From the point of view of the standard of efficiency, the workers' country of origin has no relevance whatsoever. For a Mexican immigrant to replace a less productive U.S.-born worker has just as beneficial an impact on efficiency than for a worker from New York to displace a less productive one from Iowa.

This is not to say that some individuals would not prefer to see the immigrants stay home even at the cost of a less efficient economy. Every market economy operates through a balance of competition and cooperation among individuals that creates winners and losers in specific situations. The situation can be compared to that of a college band, where, let us imagine, you play the clarinet. On the day of the competition for first chair in the clarinet section, you might wish that your closest competitor, a person who plays just a little better than you do, would catch a cold or bruise a finger. If the competitor played less well that day, you would move up in the sectional ranking. But you would not wish the same of any other member of the band—neither of the drummer, nor of the clarinetists who are below your level in the sectional ranking. You want all of them to play as well as possible, because you get a greater reward out of playing in a band that is as good as possible overall.

By the same token, workers might wish that certain individual immigrants—their close competitors—would go home. But those same people nevertheless benefit from participation in an economy that is more efficient and productive overall because of immigration.

For completeness, it should be said that immigration could reduce efficiency if it is motivated by considerations other than opportunity cost or productivity. For example, immigration motivated solely by the desire to receive higher welfare benefits in the host country than are available at home cannot be presumed to be efficient. Similarly, immigration by political refugees or close family relations does not carry as strong a presumption of benefit as strictly "economic" immigration does. A case could be made, on efficiency grounds, for altering immigration standards accordingly. It is not clear, however, that a crackdown on illegal immigrants would enhance efficiency. It could even be argued that illegal immigrants are more likely than average to be motivated by narrowly economic considerations, and hence to benefit efficiency.

Immigration and equality Two separate questions arise under the heading of equality. One is, How does immigration affect equality worldwide? Since immigration is overwhelmingly from poor countries to more prosperous ones, this question answers itself. A real believer in equality of all people, worldwide, must be pro-immigration.

Furthermore, worldwide equality is more likely to be enhanced by immigration of low-skill workers than of high-skill workers. Thus, the perspective of worldwide equality would weigh against immigration criteria that gave an advantage to individuals with above-average skills or education.

A concern with worldwide equality also best fits the traditional American attitude reflected in the lines, "Give me your tired, your poor." It argues for a strong element of compassion in immigration. We should accept political refugees, it would say, even though we know that this category of immigrant places an above-average burden on public services. It would allow legal, foreign-born residents to bring along their elderly relatives, no matter if they contribute nothing to U.S. gross domestic product or tax revenues.

Of course, one can also ask, How does immigration affect equality among the native-born population, leaving the immigrant's own welfare out of the picture entirely? The discussion surrounding Figure 12-5 suggests an answer to this question. High-skill immigrants will tend to depress the wages of professions that are initially higher paid, thus making the distribution of income among natives more equal. Low-skill immigrants tend to do the opposite. This point of view would, thus, tend to favor a system like Canada's which awards would-be immigrants extra points for education and professional skills.

Immigration and liberty Today, most people take it as part of the natural order of things that a nation can and should "control its borders." A century ago, however, the predominant view was that free international movement was the norm. Most countries did not then even issue passports. The few that did try to control international travel and migration, such as Russia, were looked on as not-quite-full members in the community of civilized nations.[10]

In part, the issue of liberty and immigration parallels that of equality. Do we believe that the notion "All people are created equal" applies to *all*, regardless of citizenship or birth, or only to all holders of valid U.S. passports and immigrant "green cards"? This aspect of the immigration question sometimes divides moderate classical liberals from radical libertarians. Many moderate classical liberals view control of immigration as a legitimate function of government, a part of maintaining the conditions for an orderly market economy, along with other functions like providing a court system and police protection. Some radical libertarians insist not only that those born abroad have equal rights, but that native U.S. citizens have the right to enter into whatever contracts they want with foreign citizens, even employment contracts. This line of reasoning leads logically to an open-border policy that would exclude only criminals. Of course, these libertarians would also disapprove of immigration solely to qualify for U.S. government handouts. But their solution would be to end the handouts, not close the borders.

Questions for review and discussion

1. Would finding a cure for AIDS cause unemployment and depress wages? This might seem an odd question, but consider that a person re-entering the labor force after recovery from a disabling disease is in somewhat the same position as an immigrant. Use the ideas discussed in this chapter to address the effects on supply and demand for labor of a cure for AIDS. Are their differences between this case and the case of immigration? If so, what differences?

2. Julian Simon, Gary Becker, and Barry Chiswick, among other economists, have suggested that immigrant visas could be sold at auction. Foreign citizens would bid on the right to immigrate, and the proceeds of the auction would be additional revenue for the U.S. government. How would you evaluate such an auction system in terms of efficiency, equality, and liberty?

3. Education is a big export for the United States. It is relatively easy to get a visa to enter the country as a student. However, studying does not automatically qualify one to remain as an immigrant after graduation. Evaluate a policy that would make

---

10During the Cold War, anti-Communist propagandists made much of the "inhuman" policy of the "slave states" that not only restricted emigration, but denied even temporary foreign travel to many citizens. During that period, Western countries accepted refugees from communism with open arms. Numerous observers have seen it as ironic that these same Western countries hastily erected barriers to immigration from these countries as soon as they began to permit free emigration.

it easier for foreign graduates of U.S. universities to remain as immigrants, applying the usual standards of efficiency, equality, and liberty. Under the heading of equality, consider both the worldwide perspective, and the perspective of equality within the United States.

4. During the Haitian refugee crisis of the early 1990s, and earlier during the civil war in El Salvador, immigration authorities struggled to distinguish "political" from "economic" refugees. They were much more willing to admit a person who had been threatened by political thugs or tortured by the secret police than to admit someone who just wanted a chance to earn a decent living. Do you think the bias against "economic" refugees was sound policy? Discuss in terms of efficiency, equality, and liberty.

Selected references

Borjas, George. "The Economics of Immigration." *Journal of Economic Literature*, December 1994, pp. 1667-1717. *A thorough review of the technical economic literature, with an extensive bibliography.*

Greenwood, Michael J., and John M. McDowell. "U.S. Immigration Reform: Policy Issues and Economic Analysis." *Contemporary Policy Issues*, Spring 1985, pp. *This article, written in the context of legislative debates of the mid-1980s, gives particular attention to illegal immigration.*

Simon, Julian L. *The Economic Consequences of Immigration.* Cambridge, Mass.: Basil Blackwell, 1989. *Simon reaches strongly proimmigration conclusions, but stops short of advocating an open-border policy.*

Key terms

Bimodal distribution. A distribution in which observations cluster in two distinct peaks.

Real income. Income measured in a way that corrects for the effects of inflation.

Cross-sectional data. Data drawn from different groups (e.g., immigrants and natives, young and old) at a single point in time.

13

Russia the Lawless

In the summer, Moscow residents like nothing better than to escape the city's heat and dirt to spend long, northern evenings at a suburban *dacha,* or summer house. In the days of Soviet communism, only the elite-government officials, ballerinas, hockey stars-had access to a decent dacha, with a kitchen and plumbing. Mere mortals counted themselves lucky to have a tarpaper shack and a few square meters to plant potatoes.

Today, things are changing. The beginnings of a middle class are emerging. An honest person with energy and a good education can earn enough money to aspire to some of the good things in life. That is the position in which "Tatiana" (not her real name) found herself in the summer of 1993.

Tatiana, a skilled interpreter, had earned enough money that she and her husband could consider building a new dacha, with modern conveniences, to replace a shack her husband had inherited from his parents. They answered a contractor's ad in their local newspaper. The contractor seemed honest and knowledgeable. He gave them a bid of $20,000, with half of the sum payable in advance, in cash. They signed the contract and paid.

Months went by and nothing happened. The contractor was working on a bigger project nearby. Tatiana and her husband complained, they demanded their money back. Finally, when winter was already beginning, the builders dug a crude hole in the ground, laid some bricks, dumped a pile of lumber, and disappeared again. They demanded an additional $25,000 to continue working.

When spring came and the ground thawed, the work on the basement turned out to be almost worthless. Tatiana and her husband hired another builder to erect the frame of the dacha and went to court to sue the original contractor. The contractor did not show up for the first court hearing. At a second court hearing, the judge again postponed a decision, this time to allow a technical inspection of the work done. The next day the half-finished dacha burned to the ground. Police determined that the cause was arson.

Friends told Tatiana to heed the warning and drop her case, but she refused to do so. A few nights later her phone rang. "I heard you had some problems with your dacha," a voice said. "You're bringing too many problems on respected people. You don't have two heads to lose. I hope I'm calling for the first and the last time."

Friends now told Tatiana to take her family and leave the country. But if she had survived the years of communism, why leave now? She installed a steel door on her apartment and took a tape of the phone call to the police. They were sympathetic, but said there was little they could do. Now Tatiana worries every time she reads in the paper about people who have disappeared, every time her son is late coming home from school. "We are like a mouse in the corner," she says. "We can't hide. We just wait to see what will happen."[1]

Tatiana's story is a story of life in a country without law. Law is a key element of what William Niskanen calls the "soft infrastructure" of a market economy.[2] The economy's hard infrastructure, made up of highways, bridges, and powerlines, provides physical links between buyers and sellers. Its soft infrastructure, which consists of legal relationships, accounting rules, and cultural attitudes, is no less essential. Without these institutions, a market economy is as seriously crippled as it would be if a hurricane blew down every telephone pole and flooded every power plant.

Russia's emerging market economy has inherited a shabby but intact hard infrastructure from the Communist era. Unfortunately, its soft infrastructure is in much worse shape. Tatiana's story provides an illustration of the vast gaps in the country's legal system, the soft infrastructure's most critical element. In this chapter, as we examine the operation of an economy where law barely exists, we will achieve a better understanding of the importance of legal institutions to our own economy, in which they are too often taken for granted.

---

1 Based on Margaret Shapiro, "Swindle, Arson, Threats Leave Middle-Class Family Shaken, in Despair," *Washington Post*, November 22, 1994, p. A1.

2 "The Soft Infrastructure of a Market Economy," *Cato Journal*, Fall 1991, pp. 233-38.

The market for protection services:
Libertarian theory

A market economy is based on voluntary, mutually beneficial exchange. Exchange, in turn, is based on the notions of property and contract. Without **property rights**-that is, without some set of rules to establish that this apple is mine and that pen is yours-it is meaningless to talk of exchanging my apple for your pen. And, except where exchanges are instantaneous (and really, even then), there must be some notion of enforceable agreements, or **contracts**. Contracts permit us to reach an agreement on Monday that I will give you an apple on Tuesday in exchange for a pen that you will deliver on Wednesday, and to be reasonable certain that each step will be carried out on schedule.

If you have lived all your life in the United States or another developed market economy, you no doubt take it for granted that responsibility for enforcing property rights and contracts lies with a government-run system of courts and police. But what if the government fails to provide these services? What if you end up in Tatiana's position, where the police are sympathetic, but underpaid, overworked, and admittedly incapable of helping you to protect your property? Where the courts cannot enforce your contracts, not only because they, too, are overworked, but also because they are uncertain how to apply old rules in changing circumstances that they were not designed to fit? What if you find that the police and courts are not only overworked and ill-equipped, but corrupted by the very people from whom you need protection? Do you have any alternative?

Maybe. You may be able to hire private guards to protect your property and a private arbitration service to settle contract disputes. Every day in the United States, people use private protection and arbitration services as a supplement to the government's police and courts. Some libertarian theorists think that it would be possible to privatize the police and courts altogether, so that the government would not have to get involved in law enforcement at all. Their writings suggest that private institutions might emerge spontaneously to provide law and order in a country like Russia, where the government police and court systems have all but collapsed. In this section, we will look at the theory of privatized protection services compare the theory with the situation in Russia.

Arbitration of disputes in a market economy Many writers have discussed the possibility of a system in which police and dispute resolution services are privately provided, but no one in more detail than Morris and Linda Tannehill in their libertarian classic, *The Market for Liberty*.[3] Their vision of protection of property

---

3 Privately published by the authors in Lansing, Michigan, in 1970 and reprinted in 1993 by Fox and Wilkes, San Francisco. See especially Chs 8-11. This summary necessarily leaves out many details, we hope without distorting the essentials.

and enforcement of contracts in a society without government can be summarized as follows:

The basic mechanism for resolving disputes in such a society is **arbitration**. This approach is especially applicable in the case of contract disputes, because the parties to a contract can agree in advance, as an integral part of the contract, to take all disputes to a designated arbitration service. There is nothing at all radical about this idea. Millions of contracts in the United States today contain clauses that specify that disputes will be heard by an arbitrator, and, in fact, a far greater number of disputes are resolved by private arbitration than by the government courts. Arbitration agencies depend on a reputation for impartiality to attract customers. Competition keeps them honest; no one would knowingly enter into a contract that called for arbitration by a dishonest agent.

Of course, many disputes arise between individuals who are not bound by contracts. In the American legal system, such disputes are classified as torts and crimes. Torts, as discussed in Chapter 7, are cases where one person harms another either accidentally (as when a brick falling from a building injures a pedestrian) or intentionally (as when a bartender strikes a customer during an argument or a merchant knowingly sells a defective product to a consumer). Crimes are cases in which a private individual causes harm to the government (for example, by cheating on taxes) or causes a harm to another individual (such as murder) that is so serious as to be considered damaging to the social order as a whole.

Along with the distinction between torts and crimes goes a difference in the way wrongs are put right. The remedy for a tort is usually one of *restitution*-return of stolen property or payment of monetary compensation to the injured party by the party causing the harm. The remedy for crime is usually *retribution*-a jail term or a fine paid to the government by the guilty party. Economists tend to prefer restitution as the more marketlike approach. It can be viewed as an attempt to restore, or at least approximate, the situation that would have been produced if aggression had not been committed. Retribution, in contrast, is aimed at punishing the aggressor rather than compensating the victim. It may have a value as a deterrent, but it does not attempt to set the market back to the position it was in before the aggression was committed.

In the American legal system, the categories of crimes and torts overlap. For example, if a person steals your car and wrecks it, you can take advantage of tort law to sue the person and collect money damages, and at the same time the government can prosecute the thief and impose a jail sentence. In a society without government, the legal category of crime (by definition, an offense against government) would cease to exist, but tort law would remain. You could still sue the car thief and obtain monetary compensation for your loss, and the heirs of a murder victim could sue the murderer for a large sum as compensation. (This can be done under American law today, by the way.) The only difference is that the dispute would be heard by a private arbitration agency instead of a government court.

Potential problems with voluntary arbitration   At this point in the argument, a number of objections arise about the adequacy of depending entirely on private dispute resolution. The Tannehills proceed to deal with each of them in turn.

First, there is the obvious problem that you don't want to wait until your store is robbed and then sue the robber; instead, you would rather protect your store from robbery in the first place. You have an inherent right to protect your own life and property under the doctrine of self-defense, but defending yourself might take up too much of your time. The solution, in a society without government, is to hire a private protection agency. After all, in the United States today many businesses and some individuals use private guard services, and many competing agencies offer their services in the yellow pages. In fact, the government police offer actual protection against anticipated crime only in rare cases. Usually they are called in after a crime is committed.

The second problem arises if a thief or other aggressor[4] slips past your protection service and runs off with your TV set. How do you catch him (or her-but men steal more TV sets) in order to make a claim? Self-defense gives you the right to track him down yourself and grab your property back. You even have a right to use stealth, trickery, or force (but not excessive force) to do so. If you don't want to do the job yourself, you hire a private detective.

A third possible problem is that dealing with private guards and detectives might itself be too expensive or time-consuming for the average individual. In this case, you can buy insurance, and rely on the insurance company to track down the thief or protect your property. Again, this is only an extension of what happens today.

A fourth problem concerns disputes that can arise when the identity of the aggressor is in doubt, for example, when the suspect claims mistaken identity when your detective agency catches up with him, or when there is a disagreement over how much compensation should be paid in the case of a painful personal injury. Such disputes obviously require arbitration, but unlike the case of contract disputes, there has been no agreement in advance as to who will serve as arbitrator.

The Tannehills argue that it would be in the self-interest of the accused aggressor to cooperate with the victim's agents in naming an arbitrator. Most people would carry insurance against the possibility of such an accusation, just as people carry automobile liability insurance today. They would not want their reputations in the community damaged by appearing to be uncooperative. If there were real difficulty in agreeing on an arbitrator, the victim and accused aggressor could each choose their own, and the two arbitrators could choose a third to form a three-judge panel.

What if the accused aggressor really is guilty and simply refuses to cooperate, or tries to run away? In that case, the rule of self-defense gives the victim (or his

---

4 We can't technically call this person a *criminal* in a society where there is no government against which to commit crimes, and the legal term *tortfeasor* is too awkward.

guard service) the right to hold the aggressor by force and assess an appropriate penalty. (They would have to be cautious, though-if the person were innocent after all, or if excessive force were used, the accused aggressor could turn the tables and sue the victim for damages.

Warring defense agencies and organized aggression Up to this point, all arguments point to an equilibrium in which, with relatively rare exceptions, self-interest will cause everyone to cooperate in the market-based system of private dispute resolution. However, there remains one final objection to be dealt with: Is it not possible that some ruthless aggressor could assemble a gang of thugs strong enough to defy any private protection service, or alternatively, that one or more of the protection services themselves might turn to aggression as a means of enrichment? If this happened, social order could collapse into a state of open warfare between armed gangs.

Recognizing the potential seriousness of this objection, the Tannehills devote an entire chapter to refuting it. They offer three arguments.

First, they argue that it would be unprofitable for any protection agency to develop a reputation as an aggressor. Customers would not want to use an agency that had a reputation for using excessive force, because they could themselves be held liable for damages caused by their out-of-control agents. Employees would hesitate to work for such a company because they might be injured in the line of duty by people exercising the right of self-defense. Insurance companies would not do business with an aggressor agency because of excessive risk.

Second, the Tannehills point out that today, organized criminal gangs depend heavily for their incomes on the distorted markets for illegal goods and services—drugs, prostitution, gambling, and so on. In a libertarian society, all of those markets would be dominated by legitimate businesses, leaving no extraordinary profit opportunities for outlaws.

Finally, the authors of *The Market for Liberty* believe that it would simply be too expensive to maintain the armed force that such a gang would require. In their view, an aggressive gang would need a near monopoly to avoid the threat that legitimate protection services would unite to crush it. Such a monopoly would be almost impossible to achieve, in their view. They argue that, unlike government tax authorities, such a gang could not force people to pay tribute. "A market relationship is a free relationship, and if a customer doesn't like a company's service or mistrusts its goals, he is free to take his business elsewhere, or to start his own competitive company, or to do without the service altogether and just provide for himself."

In short, they contend that a peaceful citizen of a libertarian society would have less to fear from gangs of aggressors than a citizen of the United States today has to fear from overzealous members of the government police force.

The market for protection services: Russian reality[5]

The near-collapse of the normal government police and court systems in Russia today provides a laboratory in which some aspects of the libertarian theory of private protection can be tested. Some aspects of the theory are confirmed, although not always in the expected form. But in many if not most respects, Russian reality is considerable less stable and benign than the libertarian utopia sketched by the Tannehills. Let's consider some details.

Confirmed: Protection can be privatized On the most basic level, the Russian experience confirms that it is possible for the market to provide protection services on a private basis, largely without the backup of government courts and police. Hundreds of protection services exist today in Moscow alone. Virtually every business subscribes to such a service. Many protection services depend on "word-of-mouth" to publicize their activities, but others openly advertise their availability. One popular advertising medium in Moscow is to arrange to have a city bus or trolley car painted with your company's name and message. Along with buses advertising cigarettes and candy bars, one can see some bearing distinctive military-style camouflage paint, and the message "League of Afghan War Veterans: All Kinds of Protection Services," along with a telephone and fax number.

In Russian slang, your protection service is called your *krysha*, or roof. You would also be understood if you simply referred to them as "my guys." Many of the services offered by your *krysha* bear a recognizable resemblance to the services described in libertarian writings like the Tannehills'.

First of all, "your guys" can provide armed or unarmed guards (your choice) to protect your business premises. Such guards can be seen in almost any store, restaurant, or bank. They are considered reasonably effective in protecting your place of business from the casual shoplifter or bank robber who might be foolish enough to try to operate on a freelance basis.

Second, your *krysha* offers detective services. If someone does slip past or overpower the guard on duty and run off with the contents of your cash register, "your guys" will try to find out who it was. A good protection agency will be well plugged in to underworld information channels, and will often be able to track down the culprit faster than a standard government police force could. If the aggressor is an individual operator, or a group with significantly less firepower than your own protection agency, he will probably be brought to account—if you are lucky, with the loot still in his possession. (We will return shortly to the possibility that the aggressor might be a large, well-armed group.)

---

5 This section is based, in part, on first-hand information provided to author Edwin Dolan by students at the American Institute of Business and Economics in Moscow, where he teaches.

Third, your *krysha* can, under certain circumstances, provide for the arbitration of disputes. Suppose, for example, that you operate a pizza restaurant on the north side of Moscow and I run a similar restaurant on the south side. You begin looking for a location to open a branch in my neighborhood, and I object to the additional competition. We do not have to meet in the middle of the street and fight this issue out with bare knuckles, as in an old Western. Instead, with a simple telephone call, we can arrange for "my guys" to meet "your guys" and negotiate a solution.

An outsider might think that such a "negotiation" would quickly become a shootout. This does occasionally happen, but it needs to be remembered that both protection agencies are in business for the money, not for the fun of shooting guns. Shootouts are expensive and counterproductive. Instead, certain standardized rituals and conventions are used to avoid violence. For example, each side will reveal how big a stake it places in the dispute by the way they arrive at the negotiating site. If my guys show up in a Russian-made Volga and yours show up in a Mercedes 300, that is a sign that your terms will probably be accepted as the basis of the bargain. If my guys show up with three 600 model Mercedes, each filled with armed guards, that is a signal that you should offer better terms.

These rituals are much like those that can be observed in the animal kingdom. When two peacocks compete to see which will get to mate with the most beautiful peahen in their flock, they do not slash away at each other with claws and beaks. Instead, the two peacocks strut and fan out their tail feathers. The one with the best feathers wins, and no blood is shed. Compared with a violent solution, this behavior increases the probability that the whole flock will survive.

Sometimes Russian protection services show a better appreciation of property rights and efficiency than do government police services. For example, in most American cities, a band that wants to play music on the streets has to get a permit from the police. Usually there is a standard fee (say $25) that gives the right to play anywhere in the city. Specific street corners are allocated on a first-come, first-serve basis.

In Moscow, the system for street bands works somewhat differently. Each region of the city is considered the territory of one or another protection agency. Bands pay the agency a share of the money that pedestrians toss in their guitar cases. Even though a guitar case may contain a hundred dollars or more in cash, no thief in his right mind will try to grab it, because he knows the protector is somewhere in the crowd. Because the protectors work on a percentage basis, they have an incentive to allocate the best locations—say, the busiest metro stations—to the bands that play the best music. In contrast to the inefficient American first-come, first-serve system, placing the best bands on the busiest corners is mutually beneficial to the bands, the public, and, of course, the protectors.

Shortcomings of the Russian system The traits of contemporary Russian reality just outlined show that the idea of a competitive market in protection services is not an empty fantasy. As the Russian police system has declined in effectiveness, private agencies have taken on much of the load. But in many ways, the protection industry in Russia falls short of the peaceful and orderly system envisioned by theorists like the Tannehills.

First, the division of labor is different. Theoretical models subdivide legal services into several specialties—guard services, detective services, arbitration services, and punishment services being some of the most important. Starting from the current American system, the Tannehills envision insurance companies as being the main coordinators of these separate activities. In the Russian case, insurance plays hardly any role. Instead, the guard services are the basic units, performing other functions—such as detection, punishment, arbitration-as necessary. Particularly significant is the absence of independent, impartial arbitration agencies. Instead, if disputes are settled without violence, it is by direct negotiation between the parties' *kryshas*.

The weak development of insurance in Russia is particularly unfortunate for individuals like Tatiana in the story at the beginning of this chapter. A business firm, like a bank or restaurant, has constant need for protection services and can establish a regular relationship with an appropriate agency. An individual cannot do so practically. In an ideal world, Tatiana and her husband would be able to purchase insurance against the trouble they found themselves in. The insurance company would not only compensate them for their loss on the arson incident, but would investigate the episode, and, if necessary, even provide guard services in response to the threats the couple received. In practice, however, no such coverage is available, so Tatiana and her husband have little recourse.

Second, the importance of business reputation plays out quite differently in Russian reality than in the Tannehill model. In the model, agents that overstep the bounds of legitimate use of force in self-defense find their reputations threatened. Everyone prefers to deal with agents that play strictly by the rules. In Russian reality, reputation is also critically important-but what counts is a reputation for toughness, for making a credible show of force, and for carrying through on threats when necessary. True, there is a point beyond which reckless use of violence is counterproductive. But occasionally making the error of going too far in pursuit of a client's interest is far less damaging to reputation than to back off too often in the face of a show of force that may, in part, be bluff. As a result, the protection game in Russia is more a contact sport, like rugby, than one of finesse, like billiards.

The element of reputation in business dealings operates defectively in another way, as well. To the extent that the system of justice operates imperfectly, the risk of dealing with someone who turns out to be a cheat is greater than it otherwise would be. That means it is more dangerous to deal with strangers. If you want a house built, it is not really prudent to answer an ad in the paper, or several ads, to get competing bids. To play it safe, you are better to give the contract to Uncle Vanya. He may not give you a very good price, but at least you know he won't cheat you too badly because he is, after all, your mother's brother. However, as a result of dealing only with people you know, the economy as a whole operates less efficiently because there is less of a chance that the best match of partners will be found for each particular deal.

Third, the process of dispute resolution in the Russian protection industry does not observe high standards of due process. When "your guys" confront "my guys" to settle some issue, there are no clear rules of evidence, right to cross-examination, observation of legal precedent, rights of appeal, or any of the other procedural rules that are so important to ensuring that justice is done. The practical result is that innocent parties are too often punished, guilty parties too often go free, and remedies are too often poorly matched to actual harms.

Fourth, in comparison with the theoretical model of libertarian justice, the Russian system depends too much on retribution as a remedy for wrongs and not enough on restitution. Suppose, for example, that Tatiana's story had involved renovating a restaurant for Petya's Pizza, and that Petya, as a savvy businessman, had a good protection agency. Ideally, Petya's "guys" would meet with the contractor's "guys" and work out a monetary settlement. But, in practice, it is just as likely that Petya's "guys" will track down the contractor and break his thumbs (or worse). As in the criminal justice system of a normal economy, this action has some value as a deterrent, but it does not really correct the wrong from the victim's point of view.

Extortion Perhaps more serious than any of these shortcomings of private justice, Russian style, is one additional departure from the libertarian ideal. A basic tenet of the Tannehill model is that the contract between the protection agency and its client is a voluntary one. If, instead, the protection agency comes to the client and demands a fee for "protection" against a harm that the agency itself threatens to commit, the protector is guilty of **extortion**. To put it more simply, if I offer to protect you against the risk that some stranger will throw a rock through your window, I am offering a legitimate service. If I offer to protect you against the risk that *I myself* will throw a rock through your window, I am an extortionist.

A fundamental flaw of the current Russian system of private justice is that there is no sharp line between legitimate protection and extortion. Many, if not most, Russian protection agencies are in both businesses at once. Let's take the case of Petya's Pizza. When Petya decides to open his restaurant, he often (although not always) has a real choice, at the outset, of selecting among two or more agencies to act as his *krysha*. What he does not have is the option of doing without a *krysha* altogether. If he opens for business without protection, he is fair game for the first thug who walks through the door with a revolver in his pocket and demands protection money. If he turns down the offered "protection," he will get his windows smashed that very night, and be due for worse the following week.

The exact procedure for matching protectors with clients is fairly complicated. Some industries are controlled by specialized gangs. For example, one gang may establish the right to protect all the casinos in a city and another all of the automobile dealerships. In some cases there are territorial monopolies. Street vendors are likely to be in this situation. In other cases, a bank, for example, may have a choice of agencies when it first sets up shop, but after that, it may not be free to terminate the relationship and hire a competing *krysha* that offers a lower fee.

Complicated as they are, the rules of the extortion racket are not entirely devoid of economic rationality. One basic principle is that each client should only have to pay off one extortionist. That extortionist then has an interest in seeing the client prosper, so he can extract as much loot as possible. The situation is similar to that of raising dairy cows. A farmer who owns a cow has the assurance that no one else gets to milk her. The farmer then has every interest in feeding the cow well, keeping the wolves away, calling the vet when the cow gets sick, and so on. If all farmers in town had the right to milk any cow they could catch, the cows would soon be milked dry and no one would find it worthwhile protecting any particular cow against wolves.

In the end, then, the Russian system reaches a market equilibrium, of a sort. It is possible, one way or another, to carry on a business. Houses get built, restaurants open, banks make loans, cars get repaired. But business life is much less certain than most American entrepreneurs would find acceptable. The costs of protection eat up a bigger portion of a firm's total operating costs. (As just one indication, many banks have more guards than operating staff on their payrolls.) And the prudent businessperson avoids making important deals with strangers, playing it safe, but also passing up many opportunities.

Taxation, bureaucracy and corruption

The preceding section focused on ways in which the reality of the private protection market in Russia falls short of the hopes of theorists like the Tannehills. In fairness, however, it must be pointed out that Russia is not a perfect test of libertarian doctrine. The theorists envision a system in which government does not exist at all. In Russia, government plays a very important role. The problem is that instead of playing the role of protector, its role is all too often that of another competing extortionist.

To put it in terms of our dairy farming example, government officials act as a whole horde of competing farmers who try to milk the poor cow every time she pokes her nose out of the barn. Consider the following very typical example:

When Ukraine and Georgia went their own ways after the breakup of the Soviet Union, Russia was left with just one major port on the Black Sea: Novorossiisk. This change brought something of a boom to the city. The shops are full of imported goods now—sweaters, cigarettes, canned beer, you name it. Oddly, however, there are few big importers in the city.

Instead, most of the imported goods are brought in by people like "Lena" and "Natasha", who work as *chelnoki*, or shuttles. Every few weeks they board a ship to make the 32-hour journey across the Black Sea to Istanbul, in Turkey. There, they fill suitcases with leather jackets, Reebok sports shoes, and other consumer goods, which they bring home for sale in Novorossiisk. "We make a little money, we get out of the house, it's better than sitting around all day," says Lena, a self-described housewife.

Most of the goods Lena and Natasha bring home are subject to high import duties, 150 percent or more. But as "tourists," the *chelnoki* can bring home $2,000 worth of goods once a month for "personal use." They show false receipts to customs officials to fit their suitcase-loads within the $2,000 limit, and often add a bribe to get their documents stamped. There are other business expenses, too. Gangs of extortionists control the Novorossiisk docks, taking a cut of the proceeds as protection fees. In the end, the shuttles clear only about 5 percent profit on their trip.

Some wholesale traders have tried to make the operation more efficient by bringing in goods by the container-load, but it doesn't work well. "As soon as you make it a big business, you become a target of the mafia and the tax officials," says the director of one local shipping company. As a result, the shuttle business is flourishing. A few kilometers down the coast from Novorossiisk, the Gelendzhik oceanographic institute has refitted its research ships to haul *chelnoki* back and forth to Istanbul. "You have to adapt," says Sergei, the skipper of the ship Professor Zubow, once the pride of the Soviet research fleet.[6]

Let's consider some of the economic implications òf the situation in which the Novorossiisk *chelnoki* find themselves.

Taxation Every government relies on taxation to cover its expenses. Taxation always introduces distortions in a market economy. However, there are some well-established principles that permit the distortions to be minimized. The following are three such principles:

- Taxes should be imposed on the broadest base possible at the lowest rates needed to raise a required amount of revenue.

- Once taxes are imposed, as much as possible of the taxes due should be collected.

- Tax rules should not be changed more often than necessary, and the process of collection should be open and predictable.

In the United States, efforts are made to observe these principles, although the system is far from perfect. For example, in the 1980s, the maximum rate on the personal income tax was reduced from 50 percent to 30 percent, and, at the same time, the tax base was broadened by eliminating many loopholes and exemptions

---

6 Based on David Filipov, "The 'Suitcase Route' to Istanbul," *Moscow Times*, International Weekly Edition, December 4, 1994, 29.

that allowed some classes of income to escape taxation. The system of withholding income and payroll taxes before wages are paid helps collection of a high percentage of these taxes, although some cash transactions escape government notice. And tax laws are published and available for inspection, even though the complaint is often made that they are so complex only lawyers and accountants can fully understand them.

Russia's system, on the other hand, violates these and other principles of sound taxation in the most flagrant ways. Tax rates are very high. The 150 percent import duties in Novorossiisk are an example; import duties in the United States rarely exceed 10 percent. Payroll taxes for health and pensions in Russia are imposed at a 38 percent rate, compared to 15 percent for U.S. Social Security taxes. Yet, despite these very high tax rates, very little tax revenue is actually collected. The Russian government manages to collect only about 11 percent of gross domestic product in taxes, compared with about 30 percent in the United States. Furthermore, the Russian tax system is constantly changing. Rules are not published. Even tax lawyers and accountants cannot obtain consistent interpretations. Worst of all, local tax and customs officials often ignore the central government's rules and interpret tax law any way they see fit.

A bad tax system provides incentives for entrepreneurs to do business in ways that minimize taxes rather than maximizing efficiency. The import business in Novorossiisk is typical. It would be much cheaper to ship Reeboks to Russia in containers, ten thousand pairs at a time, than to carry them across the sea in suitcases, ten pairs at a time. But ten pairs can get by the customs officials where ten thousand cannot. This pattern of behavior is repeated all over the country millions of times every day. It is a further manifestation of the fundamental lawlessness of the economic system.

Bureaucratic corruption   Burdensome, rapidly changing, and conflicting regulations and tax laws create a climate in which official corruption flourishes. Even the simplest activities of everyday life, like getting an annual safety inspection for your car, require bribes. Traffic police stand on Moscow streets all day long, shaking down motorists for minor infractions, even a dirty windshield. Everyone knows to pay the fine in cash, without a receipt, at half the officially stated rate. Military officers accept bribes to sell their troops' winter boots and even their tanks. Cabinet ministers accept bribes of millions of dollars to issue permits to export oil or prospect for gold. Some university professors routinely require bribes to issue any grade higher than a "4," the equivalent of a B. If you give them the bribe, they will issue your "5" without even reading your exam paper.

It might seem that if a country's laws are bad, it is better to pay a bribe to evade them than to have them enforced efficiently. But to think that confuses cause and effect. To a very considerable extent, the laws are bad *because* bad laws encourage bribes. For example, the Moscow city government has consistently lagged behind the rest of the country in liberalizing rules on real estate ownership. There are lots of private stores and offices, but all of them occupy space that is leased from the city government. Almost every day, the health inspector, the electric inspector, or the gas inspector drops by for a visit. If he doesn't leave with a pocket full of cash, your lease may be canceled. If you owned the property, it would be far more difficult to extort bribes.

With so many farmers milking each cow, the poor cows are not nearly as productive as they should be. As explained in the preceding section, the bosses of the protection rackets try to enforce the economically rational rule that each victim has to deal with only one extortionist. But the demands of tax inspectors and corrupt officials come from many directions at once, destroying even the weak link of common interest in business success that unites a private extortionist and his victim. How can the beleaguered retailer or banker to escape this trap? One solution is to call on one's *krysha* to help put some order into the demands of corrupt officials. The "mafia" then becomes a clearinghouse for official corruption, leading to a situation in which the government and the criminal underworld become one great interconnected web that defies rational analysis.

"Why is it that the majority of Russians do not even make an effort to be law-abiding citizens?" asks Konstantin Zuyev, a senior researcher at the Institute of Philosophy of the Russian Academy of Sciences. "The most important thing, it seems to me, is that if some authority feels free not to live up to its obligations to me and if it is not interested in my rights and interests and if it is capable of changing the rules of the game without any warning or explanation then I-an ordinary citizen who in principle would like to be law abiding-will do everything I can to get around the authorities and avoid their rules and taxes. Moreover, I will not even be ashamed that I am being dishonest. On the contrary, I will feel a distinct moral satisfaction that I was able to repay them in the same coin they gave me."[7]

An evaluation

The rule of law Fifty years ago Friedrich von Hayek, in his classic book *The Road to Serfdom*, wrote that "Nothing distinguishes more clearly conditions in a free country from those in a country under arbitrary government than the observance in the former of the great principles known as the Rule of Law. Stripped of all technicalities, this means that government in all its actions is bound by rules fixed and announced beforehand—rules which make it possible to foresee with fair certainty how the authority will use its coercive powers in given circumstances and to plan one's individual affairs on the basis of this knowledge. . . . While every law restricts individual freedom to some extent by altering the means which people may use in the pursuit of their aims, under the Rule of Law . . . the individual is free to

---

7 "You're the Boss and I'm a Fool," *Moscow Times*, International Weekly Edition, Dec. 4, 1994, p. 39.

pursue his personal ends and desires, certain that the powers of government will not be used deliberately to frustrate his efforts."[8]

In evaluating the importance of the Rule of Law to the operation of a market economy, it is not easy to divide the discussion into categories of efficiency, liberty, and equality. At this most basic level of public policy, the three standards come together. An efficient economy is one that permits the greatest possible realization of voluntary, mutually beneficial transactions. Crime, oppressive taxation, and official corruption all work on the opposite principle from voluntary mutual benefit. As entrepreneurs are forced to devote a greater part of their effort to avoiding the theft of the wealth they have created, they have less time and energy to devote to creating wealth, and the whole society becomes poorer.

In the absence of the Rule of Law, equality suffers just as much as liberty and efficiency. A new hierarchy of wealth emerges, with gangsters and corrupt officials at the top. Below them, there are opportunities to earn a good income in banking, commerce, or some other line of productive business, but these opportunities, too, are shaped by the general environment of lawlessness. One of the first things to suffer is healthy business competition. In a free market economy, competition tends to push prices and profits down to the level of opportunity costs. Underworld thugs and government looters don't like that; they want fat profits to plunder. They prefer a market that is dominated, as much as possible, by monopolies in each sphere of business.

Take our imaginary firm, Petya's Pizza, for example. In a free market, if Petya's store earns a good profit, Sasha's Subs will probably open a branch right across the street. But that is harder to do in the Russian context. The corrupt tax inspectors, health inspectors, and protection gangs who are all taking a cut of Petya's profits will unite to make trouble for Sasha. Even farmers who elbow one another for the right to be the first to milk a cow can see that it makes sense to limit the number of cows allowed in the pasture.

Meanwhile, ordinary teachers and doctors and engineers find it harder than they should to work their way into the middle class. The three great symbols of a middle class life in Russia are an apartment that one owns rather than rents, a car, and a dacha. All three are special targets of crime and corruption. Tatiana's burnt-out dacha is fairly tame compared with some stories that appear in the Russian press. A racketeer, posing as a real estate agent, tricks a pensioner into signing away title to a downtown apartment in exchange for a cash payment plus a new apartment in the suburbs. The pensioner "disappears" on the way to the new apartment. The racketeer then sells the apartment to a young couple in exchange for their life's savings. A month later a corrupt official, working in partnership with the racketeer, sends the couple an eviction notice because some paperwork is not in order. A huge bribe must be paid to fix things up. Such domino chains of corrupt and criminal

---

8 Chicago: University of Chicago Press, 1944: pp. 72-73 (Ch. 6).

behavior are constantly at work to keep Russian society stratified between haves and have-nots.

Lessons for Russia When Hayek wrote *The Road to Serfdom* before the end of World War II, he saw the communist and fascist models of centralized totalitarianism as the chief enemies of the Rule of Law. The sobering lesson for Russia is that bringing the old totalitarian system to an end was not enough to guarantee stability and prosperity. A free and prosperous market economy cannot be expected to emerge until the Rule of Law is established, in a country where it has never really taken root—not under the Tsars, not under the communists, and not now.

The makeshift system of quasicriminal private protection services that has sprung up to fill the vacuum caused by collapse of the Soviet police state is not enough. A hopeful sign is the recent approval of a new civil code that gives legal definition to basic concepts of contract and property—but the new code will remain empty paper without a more honest and efficient court system to enforce it. The inescapable fact is that building the "soft infrastructure" of a market economy will require a huge investment for which the necessary resources will be hard to find. If they are not found, drift, stagnation, and chaos are the best the country can expect.

Lessons for America There are lessons for America in the Russian experience, as well. Americans can, of course, be thankful that the U.S. police and legal systems work far better than those of Russia, but they do not in all respects live up to the strictest standards of the Rule of Law. In several earlier chapters we have been critical of areas of government regulation in which bureaucrats can arbitrarily impose their decisions to override those of the market. Chapters 3 and 4 explored the choice between bureaucratic and market-oriented solutions to problems of the health care system. Chapter 5 showed the degree to which drug prohibition has led to a breakdown of law and order in an entire sector of the economy. The war on drugs has produced living conditions for millions of inner city Americans that bear a disturbing resemblance to the situation in Russia—warring gangs, corrupt police, and the destruction of the law-abiding middle class. America, too, needs to invest in improvements to its soft infrastructure.

Looking at many of the problem areas outlined in this book, we can see good reason to heed Thomas Jefferson's dictum that the government governs best that governs least. That sentiment is one of the driving forces behind the movement toward deregulation and privatization that has achieved significant successes in the United States and other countries since the beginning of the 1980s.

It is possible to sympathize with radical libertarians like the Tannehills, who want to privatize everything, even judges in their chambers and police on the beat. If we were to take Russia's experience as a valid laboratory test of private justice, it would be tempting to dismiss the radical libertarian view out of hand. However, in fairness, it should be pointed out that the Russian experiment has taken place in almost the least favorable conditions imaginable. What the Tannehills had in mind was privatization of an existing system of justice that already (although not perfectly) embodies Hayek's concept of the Rule of Law. Russia, in contrast, is heir to Soviet totalitarianism, which succeeded in suppressing crime in the street only at the cost of abolishing the Rule of Law altogether in favor of one-party dictatorship. A fair test of the Tannehill model will require the appearance of a better laboratory.

Questions for review and discussion

1. We have noted that individual Russian citizens like Tatiana and her husband are not able to buy insurance that will protect them from the type of fraud to which they fell victim. Review the concepts of adverse selection and moral hazard that were introduced in Chapter 4. Do you think these are significant factors inhibiting emergence of this type of insurance?

2. Look through your personal papers (or ask to see those of your parents or some friends) to find some contracts, for example, a credit card agreement, a student loan agreement, an insurance policy, or an apartment rental contract. Do any of these contracts contain clauses about how disputes are to be settled? If so, is a private arbitration agency to be involved?

3. The argument is sometimes heard that corruption of government officials itself is a step toward a market system, even a form of privatization. Do you think this is ever true? For each of the following examples, comment on the effects of official corruption in terms of efficiency, equality, and liberty:

   a. In a Western state where groundwater is in short supply, the State Bureau of Water is required by law to issue a well permit to any farmer on payment of a nominal $10 permit fee. Instead, corrupt officials will issue permits only after payment of a bribe of several thousand dollars.

   b. Corrupt customs officials accept bribes from cocaine importers to allow drug shipments into the country. As a result, the street price of cocaine falls significantly.

   c. Judges are supposed to follow strict sentencing guidelines, including longer sentences for repeat offenders. Instead, a powerful criminal gang that extorts money from retail shopkeepers is able, by bribery, to get reduced sentences for its members no matter how often they are caught by the police.

4. This chapter has discussed freedom, the market, and the Rule of Law without ever mentioning democracy. Do you think that democracy is a necessary condition for implementing the Rule of Law, as defined by Hayek? A sufficient condition? Discuss.

Selected references

Hayek, F.A. *The Road to Serfdom*. Chicago: University of Chicago Press, 1944. *The classic statement of the importance of the Rule of Law for a free society.*

The Moscow Times. This English-language daily newspaper, published in Moscow, is the best general source on the always-changing political and economic situation in Russia. An international weekly digest of the newspaper is available from Russian Information Services, Montpelier, Vermont.

Tannehill, Morris and Linda Tannehill. *The Market for Liberty*. Ann Arbor, Michigan: Morris and Linda Tannehill, 1970. (Reprinted in 1993 by Fox and Wilkes, San Francisco.) *One of the most detailed statements of the radical libertarian vision of a free-market society without a government.*

Key terms

Property rights. A system of rules establishing who is entitled to possession and use of land, tangible items, and ideas.

Contract. A legally enforceable agreement.

Arbitration. Settlement of a dispute by an impartial third party, subject to advance agreement that the settlement will be accepted.

Extortion. An offense that consists in demanding payment in return for the promise not to carry out a threat to harm the payer.

Glossary

Adverse selection. The tendency of people most likely to suffer a loss to be most likely to seek insurance.

Agent. A person who acts on behalf of another, known as the *principal*.

Arbitration. Settlement of a dispute by an impartial third party, subject to advance agreement that the settlement will be accepted.

Bimodal distribution. A distribution in which observations cluster in two distinct peaks.

Cartel. An association of firms who cooperate to restrict output and raise prices of the product they sell.

Classical liberal (libertarian). One who shares the views of such political thinkers as John Locke and Thomas Jefferson, to the effect that there is a broad area within which each individual has a right to act in accordance with private choice, free from force, threat, or coercion by others.

Cohort. A group of individuals born or entering a market during a given time period.

Contestable market. One that competitors can enter and leave quickly and with little cost.

Contract. A legally enforceable agreement.

Copayment rate. Under the terms of an insurance policy, the percentage of a given loss that the policyholder must pay out of pocket.

Cross-sectional data. Data drawn from different groups (e.g., immigrants and natives, young and old) at a single point in time.

Cross-subsidization. In a regulated industry, a policy of purposely charging one group of customers a price higher than cost in order to sell to another group at a price below cost.

Deductible clause. A clause in an insurance policy that specifies a limit below which the policyholder must pay the entire cost of a loss.

Deficiency payment. A payment the government makes to farmers reflecting the difference between the market equilibrium price, at which a commodity is actually sold, and a higher *target price*.

Derived demand. The situation where demand for a certain type of labor (or other productive input) reflects demand for the good produced by that input.

Dread risk. A risk having an ability to inspire apprehension and discomfort that is large in relation to the actual mathematical expected value of loss.

Efficiency. Acting in a way that best achieves goals given the circumstances or that achieves given goals with a minimum of expense, waste, and effort.

Elastic demand. A situation in which a one percent increase in price results in more than a one percent decrease in quantity demanded, so that total revenue decreases.

Elasticity of demand (price elasticity of demand). The percentage by which the quantity of a good demanded changes in response to a one percent change in the good's price, other things being equal.

Entrepreneurship. The process of looking for ways to break through constraints by inventing new techniques, developing new products, devising new methods of organization, and experimenting with new ways of achieving goals.

Expected value. The value of a loss (or gain) multiplied by the probability that it will occur.

Externality (external effect). A situation in which the activities of a producer, seller, or buyer of a good have effects on other people who are not parties to the activities in question.

Extortion. An offense that consists of demanding payment in return for the promise not to carry out a threat to harm the payer.

Fixed cost. An element of cost (e.g., rent on the company's headquarters building) that does not change in response to short-run changes in volume of output or number of customers served.

Franchised monopoly. A private firm whose monopoly status in a given market is protected by laws or government regulations that prevent the entry of competitors.

Fully funded. A characteristic of a private pension plan under which contributions are invested in marketable assets that can later be sold to pay pension benefits.

Gross domestic product (GDP). The most commonly used measure of the nation's total annual output of goods and services.

Herfindahl index. A measure of concentration, equal to the sum of squared market shares of firms in a market, having a value of 1 for pure monopoly and approaching 0 as the number of firms becomes large and their market shares small.

Human capital. Investment in education or training, including on-the-job training, that increases a worker's productive potential.

Inelastic demand. A situation in which a one percent increase in price results in less than a one percent decrease in quantity demanded, so that total revenue increases.

Inferior good. A good on which people tend to spend less as their incomes rise.

Information asymmetry. A situation in which one party to a contract (such as the holder of an insurance policy) has information not available to the other party (the company issuing the policy).

Insurable risk. A risk that fits certain characteristics: It should be fortuitous, many similar units should be exposed to it, the loss should be measurable, the loss should strike at random, and the probability of loss should be small.

Libertarian. See Classical Liberal.

Marginal cost. The cost of serving one additional customer or increasing output by one unit.

Maximizing. Doing the best one can to achieve one's goals, given the constraints imposed by circumstances.

Merit good. A good of which it is thought that everyone deserves a fair share, regardless of ability to pay.

Monitoring. The process of observing and evaluating the performance of an agent or subordinate.

Moral hazard. A situation in which an insured party, knowing that a loss will be covered, takes fewer precautions to avoid loss.

Negligence. In tort law, the failure to take reasonable, cost-effective precautions to avoid harm to another.

Normal good. A good that people want more of as their incomes increase.

Normal good. A good on which people are willing to spend more as their incomes rise.

Normative economics. Ethical or philosophical evaluation of an economic situation or policy as good or bad.

Opportunity costs. The costs of obtaining one benefit stated in terms of the foregone opportunity to obtain another benefit instead.

Ponzi scheme. Also known as a pyramid scheme. A type of fraud in which participants are asked to make contributions which will be "invested" to earn high benefits. However, contributions are <u>not</u> invested and later contributions are used to pay benefits to early contributors until at some point the scheme is liquidated, with the organizers pocketing all contributions that remain in the fund.

Price discrimination. A situation in which a firm charges different prices to different customers for the same service, with the price difference not reflecting a difference in cost.

Principal. A person on whose behalf another person, known as an *agent,* acts.

Privatization. Turning over government production of goods and services to the private sector through contracting out or sale of government enterprises.

Production-possibility frontier. A graph showing the various combinations of two goods that can be obtained on the basis of available resources and technology; obtainable combinations are represented by points on or below the frontier.

Property rights. A system of rules establishing who is entitled to possession and use of land, tangible items, and ideas.

Psychometrics. An approach to risk assessments that attempts to measure people's subjective perceptions of risk.

Public choice theory. A branch of economics that focuses on the political system as a set of institutions through which people act in pursuit of their own private goals.

Real income. Income measured in a way that corrects for the effects of inflation.

Rent seeking. The efforts of business firms, households, labor unions and others to influence economic policy in ways that favor their own economic interests.

Rent. The difference between what one receives from the sale of a good or service, and what could have been earned by devoting the same time or resources to the next best use.

Risk pooling. A principle of insurance according to which risk is spread among a large pool of individuals facing similar risk of loss.

Target price. A policy under which farm commodities are sold at the market equilibrium price but farmers receive a *deficiency payment* equal to the difference between the market price and a higher target price.

Tort liability. A legal principle under which a person who causes a harm (tort) to another person, for example, by negligence or by selling an unsafe product, can be made to pay damages to the harmed party.

Total revenue. The quantity of a good sold multiplied by its price.

Underwriting. In insurance, the process of classifying risks into similar groups and calculating appropriate premiums.